Mapping the Language of Racism

Discourse and the legitimation of exploitation

Margaret Wetherell and Jonathan Potter

HARVESTER
WHEATSHEAF

New York · London · Toronto · Sydney · Tokyo · Singapore

First published 1992 by
Harvester Wheatsheaf
Campus 400, Maylands Avenue
Hemel Hempstead
Hertfordshire, HP2 7EZ
A division of
Simon & Schuster International Group

Typeset in 10/12 pt Times
by Photoprint, Torquay, Devon
Printed and bound in Great Britain
by Hartnolls, Bodmin, Cornwall

British Library Cataloguing in Publication Data

A catalogue record for this book is available
from the British Library

ISBN 0–7450–0621–3 (hbk)
ISBN 0–7450–1020–2 (pbk)

1 2 3 4 5   96 95 94 93 92

To Sam

Contents

Acknowledgements

There are a number of people we wish to thank. Our research was supported by a grant from the Economic and Social Research Council (No. G00232226). We owe a considerable debt to our transcribers – Bridget Rothwell, Hilda Stiven and Anne Perrett. Farrell Burnett, our editor at Harvester Wheatsheaf, encouraged us throughout, and we would like to thank Ian Parker for his useful comments on a draft of Chapter 1.

Margaret Wetherell would like to acknowledge her debt to her colleagues at the Open University, particularly Stuart Hall, Gregor McLennan, John Clarke and the D103 Course Team; their influence and scholarship can be perceived throughout this text. Conversations with Stephen Reicher over the last fourteen years have also left their mark. John Turner, too, must bear some responsibility, despite theoretical disagreements, providing a model of intellectual rigour, and through his powerful critiques of individualism in social psychology. We would both like to thank the members of the Loughborough Discourse and Rhetoric Group. This book has benefited greatly from joint research and conversations in other contexts with Derek Edwards. Our analyses also drew substantially on the ideas and research of Michael Billig, and we often felt that we reached some new understanding only to discover that Mick had been there before. In a different context, this book would not have been possible without the contribution of Julie Swift.

In New Zealand, we are particularly grateful for the help and support of Ray Nairn and Tim McCreanor and for many fruitful discussions over the last few years; Ray also commented on drafts of Part II. Graham Vaughan and the Psychology Department of the University of Auckland provided a base for our empirical work and library facilities while the Auckland Branch of the Race Relations Office was a source of useful information and background. Finally, although Sybil Wetherell, John and Christine Wetherell, David Wetherell and Tricia Jew, would no doubt want to argue with many of our conclusions, we want to thank them for sustaining our work in New Zealand over the years and for their companionship in the process.

Introduction

As social psychologists and members of white majority groups we began our research into racism with the assumption that we should be able to use social psychology as a tool for studying our own cultures. It should be possible to develop social psychological methods and theories which could cut a slice through the communities to which we belonged and in this way develop a critical analysis of the codes and practices which sustain racism in those places. Gramsci (1971) has argued that the starting point for any critical account must be the historical process in which identity and self-consciousness are constructed: 'the infinity of traces deposited without leaving an inventory'. We wanted to begin developing inventories of traces – in this case for British colonial culture as manifested in the discourse of a group both representative of British traditions but at one remove. Our empirical work was concerned with white middle-class New Zealand and its colonial history.

In defining our task as mapping the language of racism in New Zealand we had in mind the notion of charting themes and ideologies, exploring the heterogeneous and layered texture of practices, arguments and representations which make up the taken for granted in a particular society. These things define culture and society; they specify what political actions will be seen as legitimate and what will be seen as merely 'trouble-making'; they lay out what counts as social progress and how it can be impeded; and they provide a sense of what racism is and how it should be most appropriately countered. All these things are mediated through patterns of signification and representations of others. We wanted to make that discursive practice the object of our map.

The aim of a map is to find your way round a certain terrain. Maps mark the route from A to B, avoiding swamps, noting landmarks, not getting lost in forests. Language, racist or otherwise, is not normally considered, however, something which could be mapped in this manner. Discourse seems insubstantial and transitory compared with the people, objects and events which furnish our world. Yet the metaphor forces us to see racist language in a new way. It emphasizes that discourse does have substance, it is a material which can be explored and charted. Racist practices may not fit together into a neat whole. Yet they have an organization, and that organization can be discovered and recorded. It is important to stress, however, that cultural maps and inventories keep changing. We do not want to suggest that the objects we discover will remain static or that the discovery is uncontested. Like the guide to a fast-growing city, new routes are often introduced and decrepit areas regularly bulldozed.

A third thought behind the metaphor of 'mapping' was that we would need to actively develop some surveying instruments in order to engage in this process – that the technology found in the conventional social psychology of racism, the concepts of stereotypes and attitudes, prejudiced and tolerant personalities and concepts of motives and identity, were not adequate to this task. Our goals in this book are thus both empirical and theoretical. Part I takes up the theoretical and methodological questions posed by discourse analyses of racism, and looks at the ways in which some recent developments in literary theory, post-structuralism, semiotics and cultural studies might be applied to the social psychological study of racist practices; while Part II tries to exemplify our conclusions through our case-study of racist discourse in New Zealand.

We shall argue that the study of discourse is one area in which social psychology could make a distinctive and productive contribution to broader investigations of racism. Discourse analysis focuses, above all, on quintessentially psychological activities – activities of justification, rationalization, categorization, attribution, making sense, naming, blaming and identifying. Discourse studies link those activities with collective forms of social action, and thus have the potential to integrate psychological concerns with social analysis. We wanted to investigate in this book some of the ways in which a social field of discourse becomes marked out as personal, subjective and psychological – as owned by an individual – and thus possessed as one's own characteristic beliefs, attitudes, opinions, thoughts and expressions.

As we have noted, however, if the study of discourse is to become a central part of the social psychology of racism, then the goals, aims and methods of that social psychology must change. We try in the course of this book to develop an extensive critique of existing social psychological accounts of racism, whether based on theories of prejudice, social identity, social cognition or personality. Social psychology, we shall argue, has often played a double role – investigating racism but also sustaining some of the ideological practices of racist discourse. We want to demonstrate the considerable overlap between lay and social psychological accounts of racism and analyze some of the reasons for these parallels.

In focusing in this book primarily on discourse – on meanings, conversations, narratives, explanations, accounts and anecdotes – we do not want to suggest that the study of racism should be equated with the study of certain streams of talk and writing. We are not wanting to argue that racism is a simple matter of linguistic practice. Investigations of racism must also focus on institutional practices, on discriminatory actions and on social structures and social divisions. But the study of these things is intertwined with the study of discourse. Our emphasis will be on the ways in which a society gives voice to racism and how forms of discourse institute, solidify, change, create and reproduce social formations.

We shall also be critical of some strands in the sociology of racism which have focused on those aspects, and particularly some strands in studies of ideology. We want to locate the study of racist discourse within the study of ideology more generally; we thus want to extend and preserve the concept, and the critical edge of ideology studies. This focus is essential if academic investigations of racism are to connect with anti-racist practice. But there are many tensions in conceptualizations of ideology which we shall try to document along with the reasons for our particular theoretical choices. Studies of ideology must, in our view, also change, and this book joins in the debate about the forms these changes should take.

Our case-study in Part II focuses upon white New Zealanders' accounts of relations with Māori New Zealanders. White Europeans are the majority group in New Zealand, descendants of the mainly British settlers of the nineteenth century; while Māori people are the indigenous population of New Zealand (Aotearoa). Following local parlance, we refer to our white sample as 'Pākehā' New Zealanders throughout our account. One of us (M.W.) is a former member of this culture, and this membership not only explains our focus but was used as a central resource in our research.

Our investigation was based on an archive of interviews with eighty-one Pākehā New Zealanders, and on the analysis of a sample of Hansard parliamentary proceedings, newspaper and magazine stories and transcripts of television reports, collected off and on during the last eight years and particularly during two concentrated periods of research in New Zealand in 1984/5 and 1989/90 (see Appendix 1). Some of our analyses of this material have been written up elsewhere (Potter and Wetherell, 1987; 1988a; 1988b; 1989; Wetherell and Potter, 1986; 1988; 1989). We have not tried to include or review this complementary body of work here; rather, we have attempted to provide a new and more wide-ranging account of the central themes in the discourse of Pākehā New Zealand focusing specifically on ideological effects.

We hope, obviously, that this case-study will interest New Zealand (and Australian) readers but, by most criteria, New Zealand must seem marginal to modern British concerns and perhaps of marginal interest to British (as well as American and European) readers. For many British people New Zealand exists somewhere 'down under', not exactly a 'third world' nation, but not quite of the 'first world', seemingly neither European, Asian, Pacific nor American. Famous only for the butter, the sheep, the rugby players, the mountains and for cities which seem to be closed at weekends.

In contrast to this impression, we want to argue that the pattern of social relations in New Zealand was, and remains, an intensely British concern. This involvement has several dimensions, not just arising from New Zealand's history as a British colony populated, by and large, by British migrants. We want to show how the way in which modern Pākehā New Zealanders make sense of 'race relations' implicates British colonial history and works out the remnants of the broader discursive systems through which the Empire was made accountable. We also want to demonstrate how Pākehā New Zealanders have at their disposal, ready to be deployed in argument, traces of a great many of the general intellectual resources of the Western world.

To narrate racism in New Zealand is to narrate a discursive history found across diverse societies and recognizable in the West Midlands of the United Kingdom (Cashmore, 1987), in Amsterdam (van Dijk, 1984), Brussels (Seidel, 1988) and in 1940s California (Adorno *et al.*, 1950). The discursive resources racism plunders – political ideologies of conservatism, liberalism and social reformism, the lay psychological analyses through which identity is construed and narrated in 'post-modern' consumer cultures, popular biology and social theory, the moral principles and practical dilemmas of Western ethics, the categorization systems of 'race', culture and nation – should to a large extent be seen as global resources.

Before we proceed, however, with our analysis and with outlining the premises structuring our particular version of discourse analysis, there is one remaining task for this Introduction. We want to try and illustrate in a much more concrete fashion the subject-matter of Part I of this book. We want to both indicate and introduce the shape of the main theoretical and methodological issues which are raised by the discourse analysis of racism.

Issues for discourse analysis

Discourse analysis pre-eminently involves a practical engagement with texts and talk. To illustrate some of the terms of this engagement, it helps, therefore, to examine a piece of discourse. This examination will also usefully indicate the kind of material we will be concerned with in the chapters which follow. The extract below comes from an interview conducted in 1984 and was one of several conducted with New Zealand politicians. In this case the politician was a member of the New Zealand Party, a third party in New Zealand politics, with considerable influence in the early 1980s as a right-wing pressure group for *laissez-faire* economic strategies. (The New Zealand Party eventually disbanded when Labour governments, first elected in 1984, began to take up this economic agenda.)

Our interviewee was a central figure in this political grouping. He was an election candidate for a key parliamentary seat, a retired lawyer, and well known for his contribution in the 1970s to the drafting of various pieces of social policy legislation. As he has now given up active politics, and since our interview was conducted on the basis that he was not acting as a public spokesperson for the New Zealand Party, we will refer to him throughout by the pseudonym of 'Sargeant'. Here is the sequence which will be our main concern (a description of transcription procedures and a guide to symbols can be found in Appendix 2).

> Wetherell: I understand that the New Zealand Party has no spokesman on Māori Affairs or women's matters either because that's regarded as um divisive and perhaps discriminatory to have a separation of that sort, can you tell me more about the reasoning behind that?
>
> Sargeant: Er, I had no part in that policy formation (0.2) in those areas (0.3) there, so far as Māori Affairs is concerned (0.3). For many years we prided ourselves in New Zealand in having a very harmonious multiracial society and I believe strongly in that and the older generation do, we're very fond of the Māori race as a generalization, er, they're they were one of the most advanced indigenous races in the world and by and large we got on pretty well. The risk of that attitude as I looking back now see it was – that feeling that it was harmonious – was just paternalism (yes). Er, I don't think so, <u>but</u> in the recent, in the last twenty years (0.2) when we've had more aggressive minority movements, people have created a Māori racist issue or Māori racial issue I think and er that, very sadly, is starting to widen and now there are all sorts of groups er (0.4) challenging what the European has done in New Zealand to the Māori. Much of it we're very ashamed of but mostly it's past history now just as it's past history the atrocities that the colonists committed on American Indians.

Sargeant begins by distancing himself from New Zealand Party policy on Māori Affairs. (In brief, this policy regarded equal opportunity type initiatives as an unegalitarian and unfair form of favouritism which 'discriminated' against the majority.) His response then goes on to develop one partial account of some of the history of Māori/Pākehā relations in New Zealand. This account displays in a condensed form many of the prevalent themes in Pākehā New Zealanders' racism and this prevalence explains its selection here.

The moves Sargeant makes would be extremely familiar to Māori readers but are no less offensive for that reason. Māoris are categorized as a 'race' and placed within a 'racial' hierarchy. They are described as an 'advanced' group, which seems to allow for some pride at the quality of 'our' indigenous people. Some injustice is acknowledged but it is then justified in a fashion repeated many times in our interviews – Pākehā atrocities are past history and should be seen as part of the vicissitudes of development. Sargeant's ideal for intergroup relations is 'multiracial harmony' and, in another very familiar Pākehā move, he seems to attribute divisiveness and the collapse of this ideal to the actions of Māori and other groups contesting discriminatory practices. Some groups in this extract are presented as more 'developed' than others, and Pākehā New Zealanders are presumably the most developed of all since Sargeant seems to place them in the position of guiding and looking after Māori people.

We could say, therefore, that this account attempts a description and an explanation, which are woven together into a defensive mitigation of Pākehā actions and history. But how can we now move beyond this characterization to some form of explanation of this account? In essence, the task of explanation requires the location of discourse in some social and psychological context.

In fact, there are three kinds of location required. Crudely, these turn around questions of 'reality', 'society', and 'identity'. Let us take 'reality' first. Sargeant's account is partly descriptive. He tells us what Māori people are like as a group, he describes a historical process and he divines the true attitude of the Pākehā people, specifically 'the older generation'. But how should we treat these 'facts' and these descriptions? The answer to this question is crucial for further analysis. On this answer hangs the choice of a theory of knowledge and a theory of language which will guide future investigation. There are also important implications here for anti-racist practice, and implications, too, for the analyst's own claims to knowledge.

One way of undermining Sargeant's account would be to describe his statement as a distorted representation of reality as opposed to a summary of the real facts. Our way would then be open to challenge the authenticity of his version and to present an alternative picture of what really is the case. This contrasting of representation and reality is one of the main ways in which much social psychology and sociology of racism has worked. As a consequence, the analytic task has become structured in a particular way. Analysis has become dominated by questions of correspondence. Explanations of racism come to consist of explanations of misrepresentation. Why does Sargeant represent reality in this way? Does his account correspond with reality, and, if not, why is his representation false, partial, deluded or mistaken?

These are valid questions, and in Part I we will describe a range of approaches from social psychology and sociology which have taken this line, and worked from this starting point. The main advantages of what we will describe as representational analyses of discourse are usually taken to be the avoidance of relativism, the firm contestation of racism and the way in which they secure the factual status of anti-racist descriptions and accounts. Representational analyses rest on a strong distinction between true accounts and false accounts and tend to posit a clear dichotomy between scientific accounts of the facts and speculative, biased or interested lay descriptions.

Analysts often see themselves as unmasking the delusions of lay people from a stance guaranteed by the authority of science and scientific fact.

In the course of Part I of the book we will also try, however, to argue against this epistemological stance. We will try to show how the direction of analyses of racism has been influenced by these assumptions about the nature and operation of discourse, and how these assumptions have led to some predictable cul-de-sacs. We will try, too, to outline an alternative framing of discourse and will argue that abandoning representational assumptions does not undermine anti-racism. It is still possible to mount a critique of Sargeant's discourse even as we reject the use of 'reality' and 'the real facts' as a means for contesting racist accounts from the perspective of social science.

The second issue concerns the significance of Sargeant's social actions. How do we put his words into a social context? At one extreme we could see Sargeant as part of a conspiracy, or rather, as engaged with other Pākehā in a deliberately orchestrated attempt to oppress Māori people. His discourse could be seen as part of a self-conscious campaign to protect his interests. Whether we see Sargeant as intentionally or unintentionally campaigning, one way of placing his words in some social context would be to examine the extent to which his discourse should be seen as 'the ruling ideas of the ruling classes'.

It is impossible to analyze racist discourse without making a set of decisions about social theory and the social context of discourse. How do we, as social scientists, characterize the society to which Sargeant refers? What is the efficacy of Sargeant's discourse? What role does it play within his society? How is Sargeant's account shaped, determined or influenced by social, economic and material conditions? And, indeed, is the relationship between racist discourse and other social practices best described as one of 'determination'?

Aspects of these questions revolve around questions of agency. Social groups such as male professional Pākehā New Zealanders, the group to which Sargeant belongs, could be seen as actively engaged in making history and telling their story in a way which furthers their interests. Alternatively, we could see Sargeant and others, if not as dupes, certainly as the effect of history, controlled by rather than controlling its flow. The issue of how to place discourse in a social context, like the question of 'reality', will similarly run right through Part I of this book. Again we shall contrast various positions within sociology and social psychology with our own.

The final item in our list of issues was the question of 'identity'. The problem here is how to connect Sargeant's discourse with his personal being – with his character, temperament and motive systems, with his self. Some have argued that discourse can always be read as symptomatic. That is, we can see in the words the outline of the individual underneath. Some accounts of racism have thus focused on the particular characteristics and personalities of racists, seeing a pattern in their discourse. Is this our view, too? Should discourse be read for signs of subjectivity? Is it useful to think of Sargeant as the author of his discourse and to look to the author for an explanation of the form of his words?

These issues – 'reality', 'society' and 'identity' – and the questions they raise are, we suggest, the ones which immediately confront anyone seeking to analyze racist discourse. It is impossible to take a step in any direction without implicitly or explicitly taking a line on these topics. Each raises questions about the practices and the procedures of reading texts and talk. Indeed, analysis involves resolving each of these issues in one way or another; and they are interconnected. Answers to one suggest the likely organization of answers to the others.

These questions, of course, also form the substance of philosophy, the sociology of knowledge and social theory. At the risk of seeming disingenuous, our interest here will be primarily practical. That is, our aim is not to develop and contribute substantive new positions but to work out a 'take' on these issues as a preliminary which will enable us to proceed with analysis. This 'practical' stance has the advantage that it allows us not to close off these debates, or assume that we have reached a final position. We want to leave open the possibility that, given different analytic tasks, different 'takes' may turn out to be preferable. We develop the position that some of the tensions here are not only irresolvable but may actually prove to be productive for analysis. The ironing-out of all theoretical contradictions and inconsistencies often leads to accounts which, although elegant and beautifully argued, can seem irrelevant when placed against the incoherence of social life.

We try to develop our analytic frame through critical reviews of key positions within the social psychology and sociology of racism. Our engagement will be selective. We will focus on those approaches which exemplify the resolutions of 'reality', 'society', and 'identity' which most clearly mesh or conflict with our own interests. As a consequence, within sociology, we will concentrate on Marxist analyses and developments in studies of ideology, on the work, that is, of Robert Miles and his colleagues, and Stuart Hall and Paul Gilroy; we will also draw on the social theories of Althusser and Foucault. In social psychology, we will examine social cognitive research on stereotyping and social categorization, the much earlier authoritarian personality studies conducted by Adorno and his colleagues and the social identity analysis of intergroup relations developed by Henri Tajfel and John Turner and their co-workers.

Chapter 1 consists of a detailed description of the 'political economy analysis' developed by Robert Miles. We try to indicate the stance he develops on representation and reality and the nature of the social, and we will try to deduce some of the implications of his approach for studies of identity. Miles's work has a particular advantage from our perspective. He has relatively systematically applied his ideas, through his joint research with Paul Spoonley, to the origins and manifestations of racism in New Zealand.

We can thus see in a very concrete way how this resolution of epistemological, sociological and psychological problems sets a frame for the interpretation and location of Pākehā discourse.

Chapter 2 then turns to various social psychological resolutions of these issues of 'reality', 'society' and 'identity'. Again, our focus is the implicit and sometimes explicit theory of discourse found in social cognition research, social identity theory and research on the authoritarian personality. What prescriptions for the analysis of racist discourse, for the process of 'taking an inventory', emerge from these traditions? How is racist discourse explained in these accounts?

Chapter 3 then begins to unravel the network of concepts outlined in Chapters 1 and 2. We argue that there are some, perhaps unexpected, allegiances between the accounts of ideology reviewed in Chapter 1 and work within social psychology. Our analytic choices in Chapter 3 will endorse views of language and discourse which focus on the ways in which discourse actively constructs social reality, and it is at this point that we turn to alternative currents within Marxism and social theory. We shall favour accounts of the constitutive nature of discourse over reflective and representational models. We also want to endorse accounts of the social context which blur distinctions between discursive relations and material relations since we want to look at the ways in which economic interests, social classes and other groupings are rhetorically and ideologically constructed.

We thus attempt in Chapter 3 to qualify and rework functionalist accounts of ideology which see forms of discourse as the property of social groups and as simply reflective of the material interests of those groups (working as the agents of history). Finally, we want to depict subjectivity as fragmented and contradictory and less 'authored' than the classic neo-Freudian psychoanalysis of racism suggests; and we want to move away from the perceptualist and cognitivist emphases in social identity theory and social cognition research, and away, too, from simple ontologies of the individual versus the social.

The final chapter in Part I discusses the nuts and bolts of analysis. Let us return to Sargeant and his discourse for a moment. It is clear that it is not sufficient to possess a theory of how to read his words, we also need a method for that reading. We need a set of taxonomic concepts for structuring and organizing the patterns we wish to identify in discourse. The concepts we shall draw upon here are ones which we and others have developed in previous studies of discourse and rhetoric. We also need to discuss some of the nuts and bolts of interviewing, and address important questions concerning the interviewer's stance and power relations within the interview (Bhavnani, 1991). These questions raise the issue of collusion with racist interviewees and the problem of resistance in situations which are potentially troubling for interviewer and interviewee alike.

Although Part I of this book is concerned with theory and with setting up the methodological frame which will inform the empirical work in Part II, it will become clear that there is considerable overlap in the *topics* of Part I and Part II. Questions of 'reality', 'society', and 'identity' are central issues not just for social scientists but in everyday discourse. To make sense of social relations in New Zealand, as a member of Pākehā society, it is also necessary to come to conclusions about the nature of knowledge, about the ideal and actual form of the 'social', and about people's motives and reasons for actions.

Both social scientists and the Pākehā New Zealanders we study are members of similar social formations with similar intellectual histories. Pākehā New Zealanders, as we shall try to demonstrate, are also engaged in developing social and psychological theories which will explain their own and others' actions. Most importantly, the Pākehā New Zealanders we interviewed are also attempting to develop an ethics and a moral philosophy which will justify their present and past actions and colonial history. There are some surprising parallels with the conclusions reached by social scientists. Part I of this book looks at how some social scientists, including ourselves, have developed a rhetoric for theoretical practice. Part II examines how some of these debates about the nature of groups and the meaning of social relations are brought to life as part of ideological practice in discussions of the Pākehā and Māori situation. These studies are introduced in more detail and briefly overviewed in the preface to Part II.

PART I

Theory and method

1
Ideology and political economy

We have chosen to focus in this chapter on the work of Robert Miles and his colleagues (1982; 1984a; 1987; 1988; 1989; Miles and Phizacklea, 1984) for several reasons. First, because this approach forms one very influential strand in the sociology of racism. It is also, as we noted in the Introduction, an account which has been extensively applied to the New Zealand situation (Miles, 1984b; Miles and Spoonley, 1985; Spoonley, 1988; see also Bedggood, 1975; 1980; Steven, 1989). But more importantly in terms of our theoretical project, Miles's work provides a coherent and lucid illustration of one systematic line of argument within Marxist analyses of ideology. In this work it is possible to see all the argumentative paraphernalia which go with traditional assumptions of 'ruling ideas for the ruling classes'. Miles's approach, however, does not just rehearse conventional approaches; it is also sensitive to recent developments in Marxist theorizing. This line of work, therefore, can be used to indicate a swathe of debates which are crucial to the analysis of racist material from a discourse perspective.

Like other investigators of ideology, Miles's general concern is to examine the varied connections between forms of meaning, in this case racist significations, and forms of power; what Gregor McLennan (1991) has described as the links between 'ideas about power and the power of ideas'. Miles also, however, and these are the elements which mark out his approach, wants to make strong distinctions between true ideas and false ideas, real relations and superficial appearances. He develops clear distinctions between economic, political and ideological processes and wants to explore the patterns of determination between these levels. His main focus is the ways in which racist ideology distorts social reality, reflects economic and political structures, and also acts as a condition of existence shaping those structures.

In describing these moves, therefore, we will be trying to explicate one possible position on the issues of 'reality', 'society' and 'identity' raised in the Introduction and thus one possible analytic frame in which discourse might be placed. We will look, first, at the question of epistemology and at the relationship Miles posits between representation and reality and between truth and falsity. This will lead on to his account of the social and the relationship between the discursive, the economic and the political. Miles finds in this relationship the explanation for misrepresentation and for the partiality and falsity of ideology. Finally, we turn to questions of identity and representation and at this point the net must be thrown wider to introduce one distinctive Marxist account of the role of human subjects and their experiences in ideological processes.

We will not try to do justice in this review to either the complexity and nuance of the political economy perspective Miles develops, or to the various shifts in the work of Miles and his colleagues over time. We are not proposing to question the scope and power of Miles's economic, historical and political analyses of racism. Our concern, as social psychologists, is with questions of representation, ideology and discourse, and we wish to use this work as a stimulus for the eventual development of our own approach to discourse analysis of racism in Chapter 3. We want, at the conclusion of this chapter, to be in a position of sufficient familiarity with this work to be able to comment on the implications of this method of framing discourse and to be able to evaluate its power and range. This emphasis dictates the shape of our review.

The falsity of 'race'

As Miles (1982; 1989) has noted, categorizations of social groups, assumptions about natural divisions between people, the assignment of traits and theories of the origins of group differences are central to racist discourse. This kind of descriptive work was evident in the extract from Sargeant examined in the Introduction, and, as we noted there, it raises crucial issues for investigators and for anti-racist practice.

The extract below provides another example of racial accounting and a further indication of the kinds of distinctions and arguments which are central to Miles's concerns. This extract comes from an interview conducted with two young women. The woman we have called Benton was twenty-four years old and listed her main occupation as mother and farmer's wife and her former occupation as Karitane nurse (children's nurse). The woman referred to as Anna James was twenty-six years old and worked as a commercial screen printer. This extract follows a discussion of some aspects of Māori culture Benton and James valued and their identification of particular Māori attitudes to family and the elderly which they thought Pākehā people should emulate.

> Wetherell: So do you think in the future, say fifty years' time, you'll see, the
> elements of this will be creeping into the New Zealand style of life,

	then if we do sort of become one people or integrated in that way, that's the kind of aspects of Māori culture that will affect our personalities and social relations and so on?
Benton:	Well I hope so but I still (.) and I'm a South Islander as well, and I still believe that there's a big, big, big difference between the South Island and the North Island.
Wetherell:	Yeah.
James:	And there always will be.
Benton:	And a lot of it is because there's so very few Māoris down there
Wetherell:	Yeah.
James:	and they're different.
Benton:	You just don't have the problems, you don't even think about it.
James:	They're white Māoris down there.
Benton:	You don't even talk about it.
James:	You know they're completely integrated into the, into the white society down there.
Wetherell:	Right, yeah.
James:	I think that the only possibility, you see, OK you're talking about um (0.2) you're ignoring um genes, and alright we we have a lot a lot of intermarriage, I mean none of the Māoris are pure, and um they do have a racial trait, a characteristic that that I don't know whether it's going to be dominant or not, but they're basically a lazy people, um and OK with a bit more intermarriage maybe that will be lost to a a larger extent with a bit of the old Protestant work ethic thrown in, it might improve them, but it (.) their life style is fundamentally different in that if they lived the way they wanted to on their maraes and things, they wouldn't get a hell of a lot done, which is fine, but you know how is that going to interact and relate with our life style? Which is you know // everybody works their butt off.
Benton:	I don't know (.) I don't know that lazy is so much the word as the fact that they're (.) more into – that's a terrible word to use – pleasurable activities, more into enjoying life and and not so much // money conscious as I think white people are.
James:	Yeah. But their way of enjoying life is different from ours.
Benton:	Oh sure it is. But I don't think lazy is the right word, that's all I'm saying.
James:	Oh well, I couldn't think of another word but it is, it is, it's a fundamental laziness, they don't actually, if they didn't have to work they wouldn't, you know?

The conversation moves in this extract to the denigration of Māori people and Māori culture and to a debate between Benton and James about how to characterize supposed Māori attributes. At this point in the interview, it makes sense to describe the discourse as racist. There can be no doubt that the account from James in particular with its emphasis on genes and 'fundamental laziness' meets the criteria for racism Miles and other social scientists wish to propose. Miles argues that racism attributes

. . . meanings to certain phenotypical and/or genetic characteristics of human beings in such a way as to create a system of categorisation, and by attributing additional (negatively evaluated) characteristics to the people sorted into those categories. This process of signification is therefore the basis for the creation of a hierarchy of groups, and for establishing criteria by which to include and exclude groups of people in the process of allocating resources and services. (1989, p. 3)

Benton and James identify phenotypically distinct groups. James clearly attributes negatively valued characteristics to one group, links those characteristics to biology and then constructs a hierarchy of superior and inferior attitudes. Although in this extract she does not argue for the exclusion of Māori people from resources and services, her argument has obvious potential to move in this direction. Benton demurs. She criticizes James's descriptive terminology and her evaluation but seems to agree with the premise of group differentiation.

The ascription of racism, therefore, partly involves being able to read discourse as conforming to a specified pattern of argument; but there is more to it than this. To describe discourse as racist, at least from a critical social scientific perspective, usually also involves a moral and political judgement. It is crucial that we not only note the negative characterization of certain groups but also go on to oppose and resist this characterization and describe the ways in which it is offensive, oppressive and wrong-headed. How does Miles achieve this task and how would he want to position the claims Benton and James make?

Miles (1982) has argued that the kinds of descriptions of groups Benton and James offer should be exposed to two connected forms of investigation. Firstly, how does this lay account of human groupings compare with a scientific analysis of social groups? And, secondly, do racial accounts accurately describe the real processes and social relations at work in the society in question? Miles concludes that if a discursive statement mistakes surface appearances for the real relations, and is on weak ground scientifically, then the way is open to conclude that this discourse is ideological.

Miles (1982) suggests that popular and everyday notions of race, which give meaning and significance to certain superficial physical characteristics, such as skin colour and physiognomy, are erroneous and obscurantist in two senses. Racial descriptions are contradicted by developments in modern biology and genetics and they perpetrate a conceptual terminology which is not adequate to describing the real nature of group relations. Miles would be sceptical, therefore, of both the natural scientific and social scientific validity of James's claims.

Anna James's account above seems to rest on three assumptions and it is the combination of these assumptions which is usually taken as defining some of the salient features of an ideology of racism (Reeves, 1983). As noted, she seems to take it as self-evident that people can be divided into biologically distinct types. Second, James seems to assume that each 'race' not only shares physical characteristics but also shares psychological and cultural characteristics which are also biologically transmitted. Finally, she seems to assume that a hierarchy of 'races' can be identified from the more advanced or developed to the more under-developed. Some value, as we noted, is thus put on what are thought to be 'racial' or unchanging biological characteristics.

There are a number of points, according to Miles (1982), where these claims contradict the current consensus within biological science, specifically the consensus in population genetics. Against the popular image of fixed types, such as Māori and white European, with consistent characteristics which are determined genetically, the population biologist emphasizes the complex genetic and environmental origins of differences. Biologists stress the possible inconsistency between phenotypical characteristics (physical appearence) and underlying genetic traits, and point to the difficulty of neatly categorizing races or rigidly separating one from another in terms of clear-cut genetic similarities.

Population geneticists also argue that the genetic variation within any population is usually greater than the average difference between populations. Miles similarly notes that the links between genetic traits and psychological and behavioural characteristics such as intelligence or laziness, which are often assumed in racist discourse, are a matter of debate and contention within both biology and psychology.

From this standpoint, then, James's account is not only out of line with recent scientific discoveries and thus false, it also displays the other features which Miles assumes distinguish ideological from non-ideological thinking. Along with some other Marxist accounts of ideology, Miles argues that ideology works in the main by confusing the social with the natural, mistaking surface appearances, skin colour and other physical characteristics, the phenomenal forms of social relations, for the essential underlying causes. Thus James across her interview tends to attribute New Zealand's intergroup problems to natural racial differences, whereas Miles (1984b) would argue that the *real* causes of current conflicts lie in the economic and political organization of New Zealand society.

Racial descriptions are seen as a smokescreen in this framework, distracting attention away from the actual social divisions between New Zealanders. Miles (1982) notes how ideological thinking works on the basis of simple physical signs of difference and mistakenly draws a social theory from these. James's accounts might be wrong-headed in this way but, according to Miles, this is no reason for social science to make the same mistake.

He suggests the accounts of social science can be distinguished from the accounts of ideology to the extent that social science concepts and theories eschew the domain of misrepresentation and are based on the real relations of economic production. Miles (1982) argues forcefully that since the terminologies of 'race' and 'racial' are based on misapprehensions, these concepts should be given no explanatory or descriptive utility within social science. Their illusory status should be further signified by quotation marks whenever the terms are used. Miles accuses social scientists such as John Rex (1970; 1973) who do seem to build their theories on the descriptive foundation of 'race' and 'race relations' of confusing ideology and science, and thus muddling the everyday and the academic.

To summarize, this treatment of racist discourse, and this analysis of ideology, begin by defining ideological statements as inaccurate and misleading representations of reality. The possibility of an epistemological break between reality and appearance, truth and falsity or essential forms and phenomenal forms is thus raised. Ideological discourse becomes discourse which obscures and mystifies, conceals and covers over real states of affairs, and which can be appropriately described as forms of false or deluded consciousness. This judgement is reached through the comparison of the racial account with the forms of the real described in certain categories of scientific research. One class of discourse (the scientific) is thus privileged and its neutrality assumed in order to reveal the non-neutral and interested nature of other forms of discourse.

It also becomes clear that if racial accounts are to be disputed, the social scientist becomes responsible for generating alternative explanations for the phenomena and patterns which Benton and James seek to describe and explain. What is the truth about the New Zealand situation? What forms do 'real relations' take? What, for Miles, is the essence of the matter as opposed to the phenomenal appearance, and why do some Pākehā New Zealanders get it wrong?

The history of the 'racial' account

Miles, unlike some strands of social psychology which we will review in the next chapter, is not suggesting that the popular ideology of racial difference arises simply because skin colour is an obvious distinguishing marker and perceptually striking basis for group formation. He suggests concepts of race, and indeed the very noticing of skin colour, become collectively shared and disseminated as popular ideologies partly because of the long history within Western cultures of the elaboration, articulation and application of these ideas.

Miles is interested, therefore, in exploring not only the falsity of some accounts of race but also the history of this collective delusion. Furthermore, this weight of history will help explain why James and those like her see events in this way. The placing of ideas in a historical context is typical of all studies of ideology, not just Miles's account. To describe something as ideological is also, usually, to acknowledge its historicity (Hall, 1978). What distinguishes Miles's approach is the kind of history which is proposed and the connections which are drawn between the history of ideas and the history of social and economic relations.

Many historians and social scientists (Banton, 1977; 1987; Biddiss, 1979; Jordan, 1974; Stephan, 1982; Walvin, 1973) have attempted to establish the chronology of the biological and racial accounts of social groups found in science and popular culture. This work, which Miles draws upon, suggests that the type of account offered by James, equating race with type or biological species and positing a racial hierarchy, is a relatively modern notion, emerging most clearly in the early decades of the nineteenth century.

In fact, as Banton (1987) has argued, there is not one form of racial accounting but many. The particular assumptions underlying James's account formed an orthodoxy within nineteenth-century science which later became the orthodoxy of twentieth-century lay opinion. For nineteenth-century scientists this type of account replaced an earlier, and rather different, notion of race based on lineage.

The definition of race as a form of lineage rested on the concept of ancestry and tracing common origins back through related individuals and family lines. It was not assumed that all members of the same lineage would have the same fixed biological characteristics. Indeed, the concept of lineage seemed to have a religious rather than a biological reference point. It chimed with the dominant theology of monogenesis or the biblical claim that all humans were descended from common stock: from the original parents, Adam and Eve. If that was the case, humans must all be part of the same kind of group but could be seen as differing in their lineage or their ancestral paths back to Adam and Eve. Thus the descendants of Cain and Abel might be portrayed as different races, meaning they belonged to different lineages.

Race as lineage was the dominant conception from the sixteenth to the late eighteenth centuries, used to make sense of national history, for instance (Miles, 1989). A group like the English could be described as having a common lineage which justified their collective action. However, the theory was eventually criticized for its weakness in explaining obvious phenotypical differences such as skin colour. Why were people so apparently different despite their common stock? A common variant of the lineage position suggested that, although all humans were descended from the same parents, environmental factors (like the heat of the sun) were responsible for the fact that some members of this family were black in colour and others white. This idea foundered under the observation that white Europeans transposed to the tropics did not become black in colour just as Africans in Europe did not whiten (Miles, 1989).

The alternative explanation, which developed in nineteenth-century science and which eventually replaced theological accounts, was this model, which we have read into James's discourse, of separate human types and different species of races with inbuilt and distinguishable biological characteristics arranged in a hierarchy.

Miles (1989) describes how classification fever swept the natural sciences as scientists rushed to identify the types and species. Many of those recognized as the pioneers of psychology, Gall, Broca, Galton, for example, were gripped by the task of defining racial characteristics through skull measurements, facial angles, brain size and so on. There was debate in psychological circles about the advantages and disadvantages of different European races – the Irish, for example, versus the Nordic, versus the Mediterranean – and Kamin (1977) has demonstrated how psychologists became involved in controversies over the 'best' kind of migrants to encourage into America.

Miles also documents the struggle in twentieth-century science against this racial theory and the eventual successful recasting of what was once seen as fact into ideology. The transition here, he argues, was fuelled by the political use made of racial theories in Nazi Germany and by developments in modern biology which, as we noted, rendered the idea of fixed types increasingly implausible. Biology has now moved the discussion onto genetic populations while in social science race has become understood as 'class' or as 'status' (Banton, 1987).

This type of historical analysis of discourse reveals not only the transitions in scientific and theological opinion, but also demonstrates the unevenness in the dissemination of ideas of race from scientific analysis to lay talk. Popular conceptions of race change slowly and in a jumble as ideas from the past become linked with newer formulations producing an intellectual sediment of the conceptual old and the new. Gramsci, for example, develops this point in his distinctions between the 'arbitrary' ideologies initiated by philosophical, intellectual and scientific speculation, and the 'organic' ideology found in common sense.

> Common sense is not something rigid and immobile, but is continually
> transforming itself, enriching itself with scientific ideas and with philosophical
> options which have entered ordinary life. 'Common sense' is the folklore of
> philosophy, and is always half-way between folklore properly speaking and the
> philosophy, science, and economics of the specialists. (Gramsci, 1971, p. 326)

It is not really surprising from this perspective that Anna James in an interview conducted in the 1980s articulates a conception of race effectively abandoned by scientists generations before. Traces of the race as lineage conception similarly persisted in lay discourse long after eighteenth-century scientists had moved on elsewhere. Here, for example, is one instance of the use of race as lineage taken from the novelist Henry James, writing in the late nineteenth and early twentieth centuries, almost a hundred years after other important sectors of the British intelligentsia had begun to jettison this conception.

> Mrs Ambient was quite such a wife as I should have expected him to have; slim
> and fair, with a long neck and pretty eyes and an air of good breeding. She
> shone with a certain coldness and practiced in intercourse a certain bland
> detachment, but she was clothed in gentleness as in one of those vaporous

redundant scarves that muffle the heroines of Gainsborough and Romney. She had also a vague air of race, justified by my afterwards learning that she was 'connected with the aristocracy'. (James, 1986, p. 63)

Mrs Ambient's 'race' refers not to her membership of the English 'race', which might be contrasted, at the time, to Celtic 'races', but to her family background and her lineage as a member of the aristocracy. As the writings of Henry James demonstrate, ideas and theories rejected by scientists and other intellectuals can still continue to be highly persuasive in literary and lay discourse. Some popular concepts remain rhetorically and politically effective long after their architects have moved on.

Henry James' co-option of race as lineage and our interviewees' references to races as though they were clear-cut biological species are out of step with the received scientific wisdom of their times. This is not to imply, however, that ideological change is seen as a matter of the inevitable progress, development and substitution of terms, as scientists gain more and more detailed knowledge. Miles and his colleagues are not criticizing Henry James or modern Pākehā New Zealanders for not reading the latest scientific journals. Nor are they implying that once representational history 'catches up' with science all will be well.

What distinguishes the history of discourse Miles wishes to offer is the argument that patterns of knowledge production are intimately connected to social and material conditions. For a more complete analysis of racist discourse, it is not enough to trace its history; Miles argues we need to be able to go on and demonstrate how the shape of this type of sense-making is connected to contradictions and conflicts within a social formation more generally. Indeed, all the transitions in the history of popular concepts of race should be theorized in this way.

Miles (1982), for example, argues against what he describes as idealist histories of race which explain the emergence and effects of ideas in terms of preceding ideas, as though the reasons for change are contained merely within intellectual and scientific debate. In his view:

> The problem is, therefore, to deconstruct the idea of 'race' and to reconstruct, historically and with due regard to the limitations placed upon social processes by production relations, the way in which 'racial' categorisation has become a significant feature of not only political and ideological relations, but also economic relations. The process of analytical reconstruction must accord due significance to the fact that 'race' and 'race relations' are not the given realities that they now appear but, rather, are ideological forms which have been articulated and reproduced by persons within classes, with consequent determinant effects upon economic and political relations. (Miles, 1982, p. 94)

The aim is to note how concepts in both scientific and public discourse are contested; how race becomes a site of dispute and conflict. Some meanings and representations persist as effective systems of social justification, in flagrant contestation with newer alternative conceptions, long after discursive movement is possible. Modern biologists may have moved onto population genetics but, Miles would argue, race talk continues in the discourse of Pākehā New Zealanders because it serves important justificatory functions. Discourses become ideological in this view not simply because they have a history, or because they are incorrect – weather reports also have a history and are also sometimes faulty – ideology is distinguished by its social functions and effectivity, even if that effectivity is sometimes difficult to theorize.

The political and economic context

> Consider the curious fate
> of the English immigrant:
> his wages taken from him
> and exported to the colonies;
> sated with abstinence, gorged on deprivation,
> he followed them; to be confronted on arrival
> with the ghost of his back wages, a load of debt;
> the bond of kinship, the heritage of Empire.
>
> (Fairburn, 1966, in Orsman and Moore, 1988)

The forms Miles's investigations of racism in New Zealand are likely to take and his explanations of the social role of racist ideologies in that context are predictable from the general shape his studies of racism in Britain assume. These studies begin explicitly with the concepts of capitalism and social class (Miles, 1982; Miles and Phizacklea, 1984) and emphasize the ways in which global conditions of capitalism and colonialism structure patterns of migration and the reception given to migrants in Britain and Western Europe. The history of racism is in large part, Miles argues, intertwined with the history of colonization.

Capitalist imperatives and needs for expansion resulted, Miles argues, in British colonization in various areas of the world. British perceptions of colonized people were structured, however, by pre-existing racist ideologies. Miles claims that the presence of an ideology of black inferiority and white superiority aided and abetted the exploitation of these countries to further the economic development of Britain, through slavery for example. One modern outcome of colonization is migration from countries, under-developed because of their colonial role, to countries such as Britain who at certain times have been able to afford to summon migrant labour to meet needs for workers not met by the indigenous British population.

Miles notes that migrants arrive in Britain to find an ideological climate still structured by ideologies of white dominance. The perceptions of British working-class people, for example, who might under other circumstances be expected to feel some solidarity with migrant workers are similarly clouded by ideologies of racism. Racism allows employers to organize migrant labour in particular ways and reinforces the systematic creation of minority disadvantage but it also offers the white working class an obvious way of making sense of their own disadvantage. The decline of working-class areas and patterns of unemployment can be attributed by this group to the presence of migrants.

The account of racism in New Zealand Miles offers similarly revolves around the effects of colonization and its history. Migration is an important theme, too, applied to understand the racism directed at recent Pacific Island migrants to New Zealand (Miles, 1984b), but much less relevant to understanding the position of Māori people, since in the New Zealand context it is the colonizers who were the 'migrants', with Māori people as the indigenous group.

Miles and Spoonley (1985) argue that British colonization of New Zealand in the nineteenth century was directly stimulated by economic developments in the United Kingdom; in particular, by the crisis of capitalism experienced from 1830 to 1850. Conflict between rising capitalist industrialists and the land-owning classes over the basis for agricultural production gave rise to social unrest, a large surplus population and the over-accumulation of capital (Bedggood, 1980). The establishment of a new settler colony in New Zealand became part of the solution to a problem of surplus population in the United Kingdom in the early nineteenth century (Steven, 1989).

New Zealand, however, was already inhabited by Māori people who, according to Miles and Spoonley, were organized in a pre-capitalist 'lineage' mode of production. The society emerging in the early stages of colonization can be described as the outcome, or the articulation, of contrasting modes of economic production and the conflict between them (Miles, 1984b). Indigenous Māori society was organized around the common ownership of land and around collective labour within a hierarchical political system of chiefs, family groupings and tribes. The dominant Māori ideological or representational system stressed the spiritual status of the land, its links to collective groupings of people and the importance of its protection (Bedggood, 1980).

Miles and Spoonley note that this social organization was remarkably persistent and resistant to the emerging settler capitalist organization. Indeed, it was maintained in a reduced form into the twentieth century. The conflict, however, between a mode of social relations based on private property and a mode based on communal ownership was eventually won for capitalism after a series of wars against Māori groupings, once the Pākehā population had increased sufficiently through migration.

The central contradictions or tensions, then, in contemporary New Zealand society which structure ideological accounting reflect not just the domination, which Miles and his colleagues would argue is typical of capitalism, of one class, the working class, by another class to maintain profit, but the victory of one mode of social relations over the mode identified with the Māori people. Miles and Spoonley point out that, since 1945, most Māori have been incorporated into the capitalist mode, usually within the working class. They note that the 1950s and 1960s were characterized by the rapid migration of Māori people to urban areas as they were increasingly 'summoned by the needs of capital' to work in factories and other industrial sites.

Miles would argue, therefore, that from these contradictions between the interests of Māori people, located mainly as working class, and Pākehā, located in a variety of class positions, emerges a distinctive set of representations and sense-making. The discourse of Sargeant and Benton and James indicate the form and tone this sense-making takes. Their discourse can thus be described as ideological in the additional sense that not only is it false, not only does it have a history, but because it justifies and attempts to legitimate the ascendancy of one group in a colonial conflict over others.

The social functions of ideology

As Billig (1982) notes, within some Marxist traditions, ideology is thought to work by imposing, usually liberal, metaphysical abstractions which conceal and obscure the real exploitative basis of social relations. Abstractions give the impression that society is rationally, reasonably and harmoniously ordered. Ideology is the means by which the ruling class consolidates and reproduces its advantage through presenting its partial and sectional interests as the universal interests of the entire community. We have seen that for Miles *et al.* the discourse of Benton and James can be analyzed as a form of false consciousness in the sense that it perpetrates theories of race discredited by geneticists. Now we can see how it also becomes defined as the consciousness of the ruling or dominant group.

Exactly how does the discourse of Pākehā New Zealanders work to conceal contradictions through metaphysical abstractions? Miles *et al.* could argue that these accounts draw upon a classic liberal humanist ideology. This humanitarian face allows Pākehā New Zealanders to cover over the exploitative aspects of New Zealand society with bland platitudes. Their accounts present Pākehā New Zealanders as liberal, kind and caring in their attitude to Māori people. Pākehā become concerned with the protection and welfare of the Māori people who, because they are an 'advanced race', are seen as more worthy and responsive to Pākehā care. This kind of account, in Sargeant's case, as we noted in the Introduction, also proposes a commonplace 'practical' argument which suggests that since atrocities are a matter of past history, New Zealanders should forget them and forge onwards.

This might seem like merely a personal attack on someone like Anna James. A woman has been asked for her opinions and the analyst of ideology then proceeds to vilify what she has to say as pseudo-liberalism while accusing her of mouthing platitudes. This, of course, is to some extent what ideological critique must be about within the tradition Miles represents. It is the counterposing of false or interested accounts with other accounts based either on science or revolutionary practice.

Humanitarian glosses upon social relations have their own history in the New Zealand context; and, as we have seen, an important part of this treatment of discourse is the continual tracing of ideological and social history. Humanitarianism, for example, has been described as the dominant ideology of the British Colonial Office as it negotiated its way to the Treaty of Waitangi and the political deal with the Māori people which set up New Zealand as a settler colony. Sargeant's account presented in the Introduction indicates that it continues to survive in modern New Zealand.

Bedggood (1980) argues that this ideology of protectiveness and care for the best interests of the Māori people should be unmasked as an illusion. Humanitarian ideals and moral suasion directed towards the Māori people by the early settlers were the most expedient methods of obtaining political domination given the risks of alternative military methods.

> If we understand the function of ideology, then we can see the ideological
> purpose the humanitarian explanation has in obscuring exploitative class
> relations in New Zealand. It creates a mythology in which the colonial state acts
> in an economically 'neutral' way to establish the rule of law and prevent the
> settlers from plundering Māori land. Under the protection of the neutral state
> the Māori people are able to act as equals in persuing [sic] their 'economic'
> interests in the market-place. This mythology completely misrepresents the
> functions of the State in creating the conditions for capitalist production.
> (Bedggood, 1980, p. 23)

Bedggood, Miles and Spoonley are admirably clear about the ideological role discourse can play in New Zealand. Their analysis sets the accounts of Pākehā New Zealanders within a political and economic context, arguing that these accounts are misrepresentations of real social relations. Misrepresentation is necessary to preserve the colonial and capitalist status quo, conceal its actual interests and reproduce the relations of economic production which have been established in New Zealand. The actual interests of most Pākehā people do not, in fact, lie in the 'care' and 'protection' of Māori people but in controlling the political and economic agenda to retain a position of dominance.

What is less clear in these accounts is the possible ways ideology might articulate with and influence political and economic conditions. How effective is ideology? Do the representations of people such as Sargeant, Benton and James have any power which makes them worthy of study? Is ideology an epiphenomenon, a polluting but insubstantial cloud floating above the social relations of production, or does it have characteristic effects within a social formation?

The effectivity of ideology

In traditional Marxist accounts of ideology, the forms ideas take in what is seen as the superstructure are assumed to be determined by the economic base or infrastructure. A cause–effect type of relationship is proposed so that changes in the economic base, and in the social relations requiring legitimation and justification, automatically produce appropriate changes in manifestations and expressions of thought. Difficult questions immediately arise, however, about how this social determination works and what does the determining (Donald, 1986). Attempts to describe concrete chains of cause and effect have frequently proved banal, crude and over-simplistic (Hall, 1988a).

In common with other Marxist theorists, Miles has moved away from base–superstructure understandings of the power and role of ideology towards a looser framework of connections. Miles (1982) describes ideas, discourse and the kinds of accounts we have been analyzing as relatively autonomous. Ideas, he says, appear and are given social support in certain contexts. As James Donald (1986) notes, in these new Marxist perspectives social determination comes to mean not cause and effect, but the setting of limits and the exerting of pressures on patterns of ideas, so that in some social contexts some chains of thought become more persuasive and more prevalent than in others.

Miles (1989) describes, for example, how some aspects of the ideology of racism pre-date capitalism and he points out that racism is found in non-capitalist societies. As further evidence for the independence of ideology, he reports that racism often persists even when it interferes with the economic interests and well-being of the bourgeoisie. There is no straightforward relationship, therefore, between patterns of social organization and patterns of thought and talk.

In this model ideas reflect social circumstances even if they are not actually pre-determined by those circumstances; but what role does ideology actually play in a society? Is it possible that ideas might act back on the economic base and may there be some reciprocal influence between forms of discourse and social relations? Miles (1989) argues that ideology is a 'condition of existence' for capitalism, and particularly important in its reproduction. He notes with regard to racist ideology:

> Racism was not simply a legitimation of class exploitation (although it was that) but, more important, it constructed the social world in a way that identified a certain population as a labouring class. The problem that remained was to organise the social world in such a way that forced the population into its 'natural' class position: in other words, reality had to be brought into line with that representation in order to ensure the material objective of production.
> (1989, p. 105)

Miles is discussing here patterns of colonization in Kenya, but the same general point about the construction of conditions for exploitation can be made about New Zealand. Although Māori people were not, initially at least, defined as labourers by white settlers, racist ideology was crucial in the alienation of Māori land and the disregard of relevant legal procedures (Kelsey, 1990). Because white settlers in New Zealand could recognize and describe Māoris as an inferior 'race', they could establish (and continue to establish) the basis for capitalist forms of agricultural production in a way which would simply have been inconceivable if the rights of Māoris had been regarded as equivalent to the rights of white groups, particularly white men. Similarly, in contemporary New Zealand, Māori people make up an intensely disadvantaged group (Waldegrave and Coventry, 1987). Using the terminology of some Marxist analyses they could be described as a 'sub-proletariat'. That is, Māori suffer not simply from class disadvantage because of their typical position as unskilled wage labourers, but suffer also from additional exclusionary and discriminatory practices in housing, schools and employment which stem from the ideology of racism (New Zealand Race Relations Office, 1986; 1987; 1991).

Pākehā discourse, therefore, counts as more than 'just talk', and becomes powerful as a form of social action in its own right. The words of Pākehā New Zealanders such as Benton and James are part of the broader 'ideological field' which sustained colonization in the first place and which reproduces Māori disadvantage and exclusion on a daily basis. The point Miles is making, which is central to his definition of discourse as ideology, is that words have concrete effects. Indeed, they could even be said to have material effects to the extent that social and physical landscapes become shaped and reshaped as a result of the representation.

The image of society emerging in a broad sweep of recent Marxist theory (e.g. Althusser, 1971; 1977; Coward and Ellis, 1977; Hall, 1980) has tried to stress the intertwined, complex and even unfathomable nature of the connections between different levels of social organization, and thus between discourse and social processes. Societies have come to be understood in this work as 'social formations'. Any particular society is seen as a structured ensemble of social relations forming a distinctive and characteristic unity. A social formation unifies three distinctive levels: economics, politics and ideology. These three are distinctive elements because they are viewed as operating around different practices and objects (McLennan *et al.*, 1978).

To put it another way, the economic base, politics and ideology are thought to 'articulate' together, producing all the social forms which distinguish a particular society, such as New Zealand, at a particular moment in time (Coward and Ellis, 1977). The structure which results, this specific social formation, is always, according to Althusser (1971), structured in dominance; there is always some form of domination or power relation within the structure. Hall (1980) argues that this new concept of 'articulation' has considerable advantages over 'simple Marxism'. It allows for the changing particularity of a social formation to be adequately tackled, especially social formations structured by 'race', and helps explain the emergence of racism in different forms at different moments.

The notion of articulation is difficult to define and describe. To 'articulate' could mean to 'express' but, as Hall (1980) argues, this would commit Marxist analyses of ideology back to the reductionist formulation where ideology is an expression of, and determined by, modes of economic production. Hall claims that recent theorists, such as Althusser, intend articulation to be understood more in the anatomical sense of 'joining together'. If we apply this back then to the notion of a society as an articulation of three levels (the economic, the political and the ideological) what emerges is the impression of a society as a structural unity where each level has relative autonomy but is linked and connected to the other.

Althusser argues that ideology is constrained by the economic mode of production found in a society but only in the narrow sense that the economic determines what other kinds of practices will be dominant in the overall articulation; politics, for example, in ancient social formations (McLennan *et al.*, 1978). Any constraint can only be 'in the last instance' because, as we have seen with the example Miles developed of Kenyan colonization, ideology is also seen as a condition of existence for the economic; it helps reproduce the workers and the social conditions which allow a mode of production to flourish.

One important implication of the 'articulation' model is this point that ideology, and thus discourse in this formulation, become crucial and effective in their own right, a distinctive site for struggles for power.

> Ideology then governs people's activities within economic and political practices;
> so the idea of a social revolution that is not accompanied by a revolution in
> ideology is a recipe for disaster; a recipe for the return to the structures that
> have been overthrown, brought about by the way that people habitually and
> unconsciously act and relate. (Coward and Ellis, 1977, p. 72)

The argument that ideas, ideologies and representations are a material rather than an ineffable or spiritual force in society requires further elaboration. It seems, in fact, to mean several things. First, that ideology is forceful and effective; it has visible results, particularly for the objects of racist ideologies. Second, that ideology is found within institutions. It has a concrete life embodied in 'ideological state apparatuses', to use Althusser's terminology, such as schools, churches, the mass media, trade unions, in all the places where people are subjected and trained to recognize themselves in particular ways. Finally, ideology is material in that it constitutes particular individuals and fixes them into positions within hierarchies. People are produced as particular kinds of beings pre-disposed to certain kinds of activities. Representation is thus embedded in institutions and tied to action in everyday life. Ideology is not, therefore, just about ideas or beliefs but concerns practical conduct and the bodily existence of human beings. And, with this point, we turn to questions about identity, subjectivity and the status of the individual in this form of analysis of racist discourse as ideology.

Discursive representation, reality and individual experience

Various accounts of subjectivity from a materialist standpoint are available, including Althusser's complex structuralist version based on the 'imaginary' and the process of 'interpellation'. For Miles, questions concerning individual experience and the psychological processes which might sustain ideology are subordinate to a focus on social process. None the less, there are traces of an implicit psychology of individuals and the cognitive process operating in his work which, if anything, seem to owe more to the 'humanist' than the 'structuralist' strands in Marxist accounts of subjectivity (Molina, 1978).

One point which seems taken for granted is the materialist claim that people's knowledge of the real world reflects their experiences in that world. Pākehā New Zealanders' knowledge, images, theories, and their ideas about what is going on in New Zealand are assumed to reflect their differential experiences of social relations. We saw earlier that Miles treats racial accounts as representations of reality. This implies the treatment of ideologies as systems of attitudes, beliefs and opinions which have the status of internal representations of external forms.

However, if Anna James's account, for instance, is based on direct experience and perception, if her account reflects her internal perception of the external world as she sees it, why is it such a misrepresentation of real social relations? Why does James not see clearly? One answer to this question seems to be that she is deluded because experience is only partial, and events are sometimes not what they seem. We take our lessons, Miles might argue, from what immediately surrounds us, but sometimes this environment leads common sense astray and limits the range of our penetration, just as a stick half submerged in water can look broken from certain angles (Boudon, 1989).

Misrepresentation is possible, in this model, because people are enmeshed in the contradictions and conflicts which distinguish the particular mode of production in which they live and work. False consciousness or a distorted representation of the world is the result of the experience of distorted and contradictory circumstances. Our angle of vision and what is available for us to look at depends on our interests and social position.

Larrain (1979) argues that Marx developed, particularly in his early work, a subtle and complex notion of the reality which is represented in discourse and consciousness. The reality which grounds the representation should be understood as 'practice'. The term suggests the constructive role human agents play in building the frame for their history and for their interpretation of that history.

In psychology, the 'environment' is usually understood as a static and unchanging world of solid physical objects. In contrast to this, Marx saw reality as continually transformed, moulded and produced through human activity and labour. Practice includes not only labouring within a physical environment for survival but conscious intentional and purposeful activity which begins to develop social structures and the possibilities for the transformation and reproduction of these.

This general account provides the basis for a specific interpretation of our interviewees and their lives. Women and men, like Anna James and her fellow New Zealanders, work on the world, they act in concert with others, they produce food, families and an infrastructure. Their production, however, gains an objective form outside any particular individual's efforts. Structures and modes of production set in motion acquire a reproductive dynamic of their own. This objectively existing human production sets the limits for what can be usually and typically thought in any historical period, as this classic statement from Marx suggests:

> Men [*sic*] make their own history, but they do not make it just as they please; they do not make it under circumstances chosen by themselves, but under circumstances directly encountered, given and transmitted from the past. (Marx, cited in Larrain, 1979, p. 42)

From the perspective of many Marxist analysts, then, Sargeant, Benton and James live in a world constructed from the labour of their own and past generations. Their experience of that world is determined by their social position in it and their own current practice. Because of the shape that world has assumed through its characteristic mode of production – the conflict which has emerged, for example, between those, mostly Māori, who provide profit for others from their labour and those, mostly Pākehā, whose assets are based on the accumulation of this profit – James's perception is partial and one-sided and reflects her interests in this conflict.

When Benton and James look at Māori people, therefore, they would see a group disadvantaged and in a subordinate social position; they see the power of their own group and their historical 'victories' over Māori groups. This 'reality' becomes the basis of their representation, but Sargeant and Anna James in particular mistake the social and constructive processes which produced Māori disadvantage as natural events with biological causes.

As an addendum, it is worth noting that with this notion of 'practice', it becomes less apt to talk of ideology as 'false' consciousness, or rather the notion of false consciousness becomes more complex. In one sense, Miles and his colleagues are arguing that Pākehā New Zealanders do see clearly what is available for them to see, they are not mistaking the evidence of their own eyes; but they observe from one side in a conflict only, and their perception is structured by their interests. If Māori people, on the other hand, were to articulate the same ideology, then a double falseness would begin to apply.

This adoption would indicate adherence to the ruling group's already partial perspective at the expense of the alternative knowledge available to those embroiled in the other side of the conflict.

One reason, then, why racist ideologies are so powerful, enduring and difficult to shift is because they possess what Miles (1982) calls, following Sayer (1979), 'practical adequacy'. Persuasive ideological accounts are those which are 'practically adequate in the face of the knowing subject' (Sayer, 1979, p. 8). Racism, says Miles, is a false explanation and representation of social processes, yet it has sufficient appearance of explanatory validity, given the way the world is, to make it work and become acceptable as common sense.

This reading of Marx, and this social psychological theory (see also Leonard, 1984; Seve, 1975) accords individual men and woman, such as Anna James and her fellow Pākehā, a powerful role. Their ideas may be reflections of the distortions within their social situation but people are active participants here. They produce the knowledge, they think their thoughts, they reach conclusions. They are in an important sense the source of knowledge and create it through their ruminations on their, albeit partial and pre-structured, experience.

Ideology in perspective

We have tried in this chapter to review Miles's approach to ideology from a number of angles – from his comparisons with science and from the perspectives of social and economic history and epistemology. Our focus throughout, however, has been on the theory of discourse which Miles explicitly and implicitly proposes. The main elements of this theory are clear if somewhat difficult to reconcile. Racist discourse is analyzed as a representation of a reality, where reality is seen as both historically contingent and socially determined. Racist discourse is ideological because it is both false (unscientific) and a partial form of knowledge defending particular vested interests.

Miles in his analyses of representations admits two possibilities: either a given representation will accurately reflect, capture and describe real social conditions, presenting social reality as it actually is; or a representation will falsify that reality, distorting, obscuring and clouding real conditions. Dominant social groups have a particular interest in falsity, in covering over the exploitative nature of their relations with other groups, and in representing these relations as natural, enduring and in everyone's interests.

Miles argues that, although they are inaccurate and misleading, false ideas can be powerful to the extent they offer 'practically adequate' and sufficiently 'sensible' explanations of social experience. Ideas become powerful when they come to constitute the conditions of existence for economic and political relations. Some ideas, such as racism, allow some relations of production to happen, and make these relations seem reasonable, acceptable and quite normal.

In general, Miles can be seen as placing ideology within a 'negative' rather than a 'positive' frame (Donald, 1986). Ideology becomes understood as discourse which conceals or mystifies. Ideologies are assumed, directly or indirectly, to serve social functions and sustain oppressive power relations. In this tradition, to appeal to ideology is to be critical of the motives, interests and meanings of powerful or ruling groups. (In contrast, looser or 'positive' approaches to ideology tend to equate ideology with common sense in general or with a wide range of cultural forms which have become normative in a particular society and which cement it together.)

If we were to follow the line Miles develops, the analysis of racist discourse would become a process of identifying claims within discourse, testing their credibility, developing histories of these ideas, exploring their relationship to social interests and to the material and social practices of the groups involved. Our task would be to identify the ruling ideas which structure the discourse of Pākehā New Zealanders, to develop a critique of these ideas through comparison with the real facts, and to show how these ideas become powerful as they intertwine with political and material processes.

It has sometimes proved difficult to work out the details of Miles's analytic mode. This difficulty reflects the fact that his main interest is not in discourse but in racist social formations. Some of the difficulty also arises, however, from an ambiguous relation to other currents in Marxist thought. At times it is possible to read this work as a recapitulation and instantiation of the recent history of attempts to resolve the tensions between materialist premises and economic reductionism. Miles's work at moments can be treated as a concrete exemplar of Althusser's various reworkings of Marx, particularly when Miles moves to discuss the constitutive force of ideology, articulations between the ideological, the economic and the political, and questions of the reproductive role of ideology. At other moments, the account Miles offers can be read more easily as an exemplification of more traditional and 'classic' readings of Marx, particularly when Miles links ideology to falsity and talks of the way ideas obscure the real and essential causes of social patterns.

Without doubt, these emphases have generated a powerful theory and methodology, and indicate the power of Marxist analyses of ideology in general and racism in particular. The account Miles and similar Marxist social theorists offer of the process of representation is complex and interesting. The representations found in discourse are seen as representations of a social world actively constructed through practice and human action. None the less, as we will try to show in Chapter 3, there are also some major problems here, particularly in the contrasting of science and ideology, and there are also some major difficulties in the formulation of discourse as both reflective, a medium which simply expresses, and thus stands to one side of 'the already there', and ideology as in some way constitutive of social conditions.

The main advantage of the concept of ideology, as we see it, is the basic premise that knowledge, talk and texts are bound up with social and material processes and the emphasis on historical analysis. Ideology within the tradition Miles exemplifies also has the strongly critical edge necessary for anti-racist practice. To describe someone's opinions as ideological is to mount a critique of those opinions. This conception of ideology draws attention to processes of legitimation, rationalization and justification, and in this sense discourse is seen as a form of social action. We want to retain in our own analyses some of the power of 'negative' formulations of ideology, but we will argue that the distinctions Miles draws between economic, political and ideological processes are not as clear-cut as he suggests.

Our position on this work is thus mixed. On the one hand, we want to follow some of Miles's prescriptions for discourse analysis and we see ourselves, to a large extent, as building on this work. We also plan to use Miles's findings as a major resource in our own analyses of racist discourse. Our review has therefore tried to serve a double function: laying out a position so that it can be criticized but also putting in place some of the arguments and ideas which will structure our empirical work in Part II. The accounts of how discursive practices intertwine with other social practices in the New Zealand context will prove particularly useful; but we also want to place these insights within a quite different analytic frame. It seems to us that this perspective on ideology excludes too much and rules out of investigation some crucial topics for anti-racist practice. Chapter 3 will outline this argument, but first we turn, in Chapter 2, to social psychology and the treatment of racist discourse within the psychological field.

2
Cognition, identity and personality

Presented with racist discourse, the sociologist generally sees ideology and begins to search for the social functions of this form of talk. A few social psychologists also see ideology but most perceive a problem of 'negative attitudes towards social groups' (Ashmore and Del Boca, 1976; Stephan, 1985). While the sociology of racism looks outwards to political and economic relations to explain 'misrepresentation', social psychology tends to look inwards, or to some interstice between the 'individual' and the 'social'. The investigative trail in social psychology generally focuses on the psychological functions of 'negativity', and attends to distortions or flaws within individuals.

We will focus on three distinctive styles of social psychological research: a motivational or authoritarian personality account of racism associated with Adorno *et al.* (1950), a social cognitive account developed in recent years by a number of European and American researchers (see Stephan, 1985, for a review), and an account based on the concept of social identity worked out by Henri Tajfel and later John Turner (e.g. Hogg and Abrams, 1988; Tajfel, 1981; Turner and Giles, 1981; Turner *et al.*, 1987).

Reviews of socio-psychological research on racism and intergroup relations (Ashmore and Del Boca, 1976; 1981; Dovidio and Gaertner, 1986; Milner, 1981) stress the diversity of approaches available in social psychology. Cognitive analyses emphasizing the role of thought processes are contrasted with motivational studies exploring the emotional dynamics. Theories which stress individual or intrapersonal causes of racism are contrasted with theories emphasizing the societal, intergroup or interpersonal causes of conflict. The three we have chosen to review work across this range.

Social identity theory is a cognitive account at an intergroup level of analysis and has some motivational elements. Authoritarian personality research concentrates on the intertwining of psychological motivation andideology. Although often presented as an individualistic theory (e.g. Milner, 1981; Taylor and Moghaddam, 1987), in our view it is better described as straddling the individual/intergroup explanatory divide. The social cognition account, as the name suggests, focuses on cognitive processes and is more clearly individualistic in approach, locating the causes of racist stereotypes in irrational and biased judgement.

As before, our main concern will not be with the detail of each theory or the subtle differences between them. We will not try and review the empirical research each has generated. Our focus is on discourse and the standard moves each perspective makes as it works with the talk and texts of its subjects to generate an explanation of racism. We will try to build three descriptions which will clearly illustrate the conceptual frameworks and implicit discourse analyses employed.

It will become clear, as we move through these psychological narratives, that discourse becomes treated in these perspectives as symptomatic and, even, diagnostic. Conversations, accounts and social interaction, if examined at all, become scrutinized for traces of internally organized cognitions, motives, desires and psychopathologies. Analysis would come to involve turning over the discursive relics for clues to hidden subjective patterns. The contextualizing of discourse as false and partial ideology in Chapter 1 underlined some central debates for the discourse analysis of racism, the placing of discourse within a psychological framework picks up a different, but no less crucial, set of issues.

The conceptual dilemmas these diverse social psychological analyses share in common are two-fold. On the one hand, there is the familiar paradox of the 'individual' and the 'social' and this debate was presaged in the distinction mentioned above between individual, interpersonal and intergroup (social) levels of analysis. Each of the three socio-psychological perspectives we examine has a different answer, and privileges one or other term, the individual or the social, but all tend to agree that this is the 'master' (*sic*) problem of social psychology.

There is also the related problem of the idiosyncratic and the universal. To what extent should the social psychology of racism be based on individual differences and the eccentricities of the bigoted? Or, are phenomena such as group conflict shaped by psychological processes which we all share by virtue of being human? The approaches to discourse each style of research adopts, and the choices each makes, have been channelled by the prominence given to these general dilemmas. Part of our aim in Chapter 3 will be to question this general structuring of the socio-psychological field of enquiry. We begin first, however, with social cognition research and recent work on social categorization and stereotyping.

Reading cognitions

Like Miles and certain theorists of ideology, social cognition researchers structure their investigations of racism around a concern with error and the sources of misapprehension. Error in this perspective, however, is seen as indicating failures of individual rationality and not as a sign of contradictions in the social relations of economic production. Racist statements become equated with negative stereotypic statements about others. The problem of racism thus becomes reduced to a question of bias signalling deviation from an ideal of clear and unimpeded perception.

Social cognitive approaches suggest that analyses of racism should begin with explorations of some of the specific and localized cognitive strategies people employ to make sense of social and natural processes. This form of social psychology would want to investigate the intellectual work evident in our conversation with Wendy Benton and Anna James reproduced in Chapter 1, or evident in Sargeant's account of New Zealand's history reproduced in the Introduction. The focus of study would be the ways in which Sargeant, Benton and James order their perceptions, make distinctions, work out the causes of events, and arrange their memories into a set of anecdotes sustaining their argument. It is the cognitive events involved in thinking, remembering, judging and perceiving which are identified as a main focus for attempts to explain racism.

In this tradition of research it is assumed that people's social commentary will reveal typical biases and distortions which can generally be traced back to universally shared shortcomings in human cognition. Whereas Miles and Marxist theorists more generally are highly critical of racism and the social formation which generates this representation, social cognition researchers appear to be more philosophical and less ready to blame and castigate the racist, since they assume the potential for misjudgement is contained within us all. From a social cognitive perspective these shortcomings tend to be regarded as unfortunate but inevitable and seen as possibly adaptive products of human evolutionary history.

The social cognition approach to discourse will thus be more atomistic than the procedures theorists of ideology recommend. The focus is on relatively discrete moments of judgement, perception and acts of categorization. Racism becomes strategically reduced to categorical attitudinal statements and is no longer studied as a problem of broad ideological frameworks in which ethnocentrism and the denigration of minority groups become linked to other justificatory doctrines. 'Negativity' becomes equated with particular instances of faulty generalization and biased stereotypic judgement.

Social categorization and social stereotypes

Our review of some of this line of work and its typical theory of representational processes will focus on the cognitive processes thought to underlie social categorization and on the cognitive consequences of group division. We will follow the path laid out by Hamilton and Trolier (1986) in their account of the implications of social cognitive research for studies of prejudice, racism and discrimination (see Ashmore and Del Boca, 1981; Hamilton, 1981a; Hogg and Abrams, 1988; Stephan, 1985; Tajfel, 1981, for other reviews).

Hamilton and Trolier begin their account with a standard social cognitive point. Our social environment, they note, is rich and diverse yet humans are intellectually limited. We simply do not have the cognitive space for paying attention to all this richness, diversity and individual difference. According to Hamilton and Trolier, if we did try to perceive every individual we met as a unique individual, then, as with the hard disk on abused personal computers, the available processing capacity would become quickly over-loaded. Social interaction and the perception of others have to be organized, ordered and simplified, principally around a set of cognitive categories.

As Billig (1985) has noted, the dominant image in social cognition accounts is that of the bureaucrat and bureaucratic process. People are visualized as rather like tired and harassed clerks, running out of filing space in the office of their minds. The clerk is threatened with breakdown and disorganization if s/he does not impose some ordering system, however flawed, on the incoming information. Racism becomes indicative, in this model, not of generalized emotional, motivational and ideological failure, but of mundane limitations on rational mental organization.

The cognitive categorization of individuals into groups is thus one way of relieving the clerk through simplifying and ordering perception and judgement; and in this respect is thought to be necessary and advantageous. However, social cognition researchers argue that the process of categorization can also introduce certain misperceptions, akin to visual illusions, which may not be so advantageous.

Hamilton and Trolier review a large number of studies on these possible 'delusions'. Hamilton and Trolier would predict, for instance, that Pākehā New Zealanders such as Benton and James are likely to accentuate the similarity of those described as Māori, to see them as more like each other, as interchangeable, and more clearly differentiated from Pākehā New Zealanders. These kinds of mistakes would not happen if Māori and Pākehā were seen as individuals rather than as category members. Pākehā New Zealanders are also likely to imagine that all Māoris are homogeneous in their behaviour and traits, whereas their own group would be seen as more diverse and varied.

Hamilton and Trolier would expect that Benton and James, for example, might make more extreme judgements about the actions of those they have lumped together within a category. And, crucially, Benton and James will probably have a better memory for the negative actions of groups they see as outgroups, and, for the positive actions of their own group. There are other consequences attributed to categorization but these give a flavour of the predicted effects. It is cognitive effects like these which explain the generalizing and sweeping tendencies social cognitive researchers see as characteristic of prejudicial or racist discourse.

Hamilton and Trolier go on to note how social categories quickly become a focus for an associated baggage of beliefs, thoughts and value judgements about the people within the category. Benton and James do not just perceive two groups, Māori and Pākehā; they draw on a substantial body of ideas about the nature of these groups. But how is the content which becomes attached to social categories organized as a knowledge structure? In explaining this aspect, Hamilton and Trolier discuss the work conducted in both social and cognitive psychology on prototypes, schemas, stereotypes and object classification.

Stereotypes are 'sets of traits attributed to social groups' (Stephan, 1985, p. 600). James in her interview can be seen, for example, as generating and reproducing a classic racist stereotype, associating Māori people with 'fundamental laziness'. These associations, which link categories with presumed characteristics, are assumed by social cognition researchers to be the central feature governing the content of people's thoughts about social groups.

Hamilton and Trolier argue that the various contents of stereotypes, the particular associations of traits, are frequently and perhaps usually acquired as a result of socialization. James has learnt to talk in this way because of the social context in which she lives, where these types of prejudicial views are customarily expressed. However, Hamilton and Trolier also argue that the way our minds work, the way we process information, may *in itself* be sufficient to generate a negative image of a group. They point to several strands of evidence but, most notably, to the illusory correlation studies.

These experiments (Hamilton, 1981b; Hamilton and Gifford, 1976) suggest that pieces of information which are vivid, unusual and thus salient in some way may be associated together or become correlated in people's minds. For some Pākehā New Zealanders, for instance, witnessing undesirable behaviour, such as theft and drunkenness, may be a rare event. Some Pākehā may also know or come across very few Māori people, due to their minority status in New Zealand, particularly among the professional middle classes. The principle of illusory correlation suggests, according to David Hamilton, that if these two unusual events occur together and a Pākehā individual encounters a drunk or criminal Māori, s/he may well connect the two phenomena, and form a racist stereotype – 'Māoris typically steal and abuse alcohol.' Socialization into a racist culture may thus not be necessary. According to this view, racist stereotypes may simply result from a cognitive process of association.

Cognitive psychological work on object classification suggests that beliefs about social groups are likely to be organized in a mental hierarchy of basic groupings and then more fine-grain sub-divisions (Cantor and Mischel, 1979). Benton and James not only have a concept of Pākehā people as a whole but, on the basis of their experience with different members of their group, can divide Pākehā New Zealanders into sub-categories: 'the older generation', 'the younger generation', 'fine types', 'louts', 'South Islanders', 'North Islanders', and so on.

Each of these groupings may have ambiguous boundaries and so, for cognitive efficiency, basic, and the more superordinate, categories become organized around the mental image of a striking exemplar – the prototype. Prototype researchers might predict, therefore, that when Benton refers to the sub-category 'white Māoris', she has in mind a distinctive image, a representative example, whose features sum up what she takes to be the central attributes of this social group.

So far, therefore, this account of social cognitive research has focused on the process of categorization and then examined how categories might be surrounded with stereotypic schemas of knowledge, beliefs and expectancies about the characteristics of category members. In general, the cognitive effects and 'mistakes' thought to result from stereotypic schema parallel those assumed to result from categorization *per se*.

Thus Hamilton and Trolier might predict on the basis of their literature review that Pākehā people will pay more attention to the actions of those members of Māori groups who confirm their stereotypic hypotheses. Instances of behaviour which confirm the stereotype should be more memorable than disconfirming instances. Pākehā New Zealanders will interpret and evaluate the behaviour of Māori groups according to the light of their schema. They might be more likely, for example, to attribute the inadequate performance of a Māori job candidate to stupidity while attributing the poor performance of a Pākehā candidate to nervousness.

The picture can become confused, however, since research also suggests that Pākehā New Zealanders are likely to be impressed by and to remember information which is inconsistent with the expectations derived from their stereotypes. A young Māori male gang member, for instance, who behaves constructively and helpfully to a motorist in distress, as reported in this next extract from Sargeant, might stick in the mind, although it contradicts the more usual Pākehā stereotype of Māori gang members.

> Sargeant: . . . It's also quite recognized in New Zealand that if you have a breakdown in your car on the open roads the person most likely to stop is some lout on a motor bike with a black leather jersey and you know 'Blood suckers' written across (haha), he's the one that will help you, he's (0.3) craving for something constructive to do . . .

Finally, the social cognitive account suggests ways in which the social psychologist might work with people to reform prejudicial judgements and negative attitudes to other groups. Hamilton and Trolier argue that this is an area where much more research needs to be done, but they point to three competing suggestions about the process of cognitive change.

How might Pākehā people deal with information about Māori groups which disconfirm their general, negative, stereotypic schema? First, a 'book-keeping' effect (Rothbart, 1981) might occur. As contrary information accumulates, Pākehā individuals might gradually re-adjust their 'account books', modifying their schema and thus their discourse. Secondly, Pākehā people might undergo a 'conversion' under the impact of startling, and particularly vivid, new information (Rothbart, 1981), resulting in radical change as they suddenly see Māoris in a new light. Finally, Pākehā people might ingeniously fragment their cognitive structure, adding more and more 'files' to their systems (Crocker *et al.*, 1984). In the language of prototype theory, they might develop more and more sub-divisions in their category systems, as they find cognitive room for 'good' gang members and 'bad' gang members, in Sargeant's case.

Representation and reality in social cognition research

Once again the presentation of representation and reality here is mixed. On the one hand, social cognition researchers stress the constructive nature of human perception and thought. Categories and stereotypes 'create' perceptual effects. Yet this constructive activity is seen, as in the accounts of ideology we reviewed, as underpinned by the possibility of veridical perception (thus admitting the possibility of error). In practice, it is often very difficult to determine where social cognition researchers wish to place the boundaries between veridical and mistaken representation. And it is sometimes quite unclear whether a cognitive act should be seen as a 'mistake' or as a valid perception of physical reality (Edwards and Potter, 1992).

As we saw, in response to the kind of reasoning Benton and James display, Robert Miles questions the principle on which groups are divided, the descriptive adequacy of this method of distinguishing between people, and the meaningfulness of these particular kinds of social categories. Social cognition researchers would also want to question the adequacy of some descriptions of the characteristics of different groups as part of a general investigation of the validity of stereotypes. However – to a much greater extent than Miles – they take for granted the basic 'reality' of social categories.

Social cognition research, like cognitive psychology more generally, is characterized by what George Lakoff (1987) has described as a strongly 'objectivist' frame of reference. The social categories which structure thought about other people are seen as simplifications, but they are also taken as direct and accurate perceptions of features of the ways in which people are naturally divided in reality. Most social cognition researchers seem to take it for granted that whereas stereotypes may be mistaken, the social categories to which stereotypes become linked are based on empirical experience of others and thus reflect real and objective similarities and differences among the individuals encountered (Edwards, 1991).

In grouping people together as Māoris, for example, or as whites, it is assumed that Benton and James are responding to actual differences in skin colour, physiognomy and in characteristic behaviour. In this respect, if in no other respect, Benton and James are assumed to see the world accurately. Their categories are regarded as adaptive and legitimate to the extent they are based on the recognizable features of others (Hamilton and Trolier, 1986 p.129).

There are some elements of straightforward empiricism both in the accounts of ideology we have reviewed and social cognition research. People act in the world and, in both the ideological and social cognitive analyses, form a judgement about the nature of that world on the basis of their experiences and perceptions. Both Marxist theorists and social cognitive researchers raise the possibility of delusion and illusion. There, however, the similarity between the two modes of analysis ends (for detailed critiques of social cognition research see Billig, 1985; 1988; Condor, 1988; Edwards and Potter, 1992; Henriques, 1984; Potter and Wetherell, 1987; Tajfel, 1981; Turner *et al.*, 1987).

In the social cognition analysis, the perceiver remains a lone individual, forming, apparently in isolation, their account of 'racial' traits on the basis of the actual similarities and differences of the individuals s/he encounters. The social cognitive model of the representational process pits a self-contained individual against the complexities of the real environment. The individual's judgements thus reflect the struggle between the actualities of the world and the limitations of human cognition. Social cognition researchers do point to other forms of knowledge acquisition but the thrust of their approach and experimental procedures suggests that a collection of individuals might produce the same judgements, not because they talk and communicate with each other, but because each person faces the same set of stimuli with the same inbuilt cognitive limitations.

In the analysis of racist ideology offered by Robert Miles the individual, in contrast, stands with others, the other members of their social class. Through their joint practice and activities social groups work on and create a social environment which comes to structure their judgements. This material practice and subsequent set of social relations, along with the history of those relations, inexorably direct the attention of social groups to some features and to some behavioural patterns of other groups. In describing some people as part of the 'Māori race' and others as part of the 'European race', Pākehā people, in this analysis, are seen as taking part in social history and developing a partial set of images based on the economic interests of their group. The analysis of the history of ideas and categories is thus an essential component of Marxist analyses of discourse but a neglected aspect of the social cognitive analysis.

In line with the perceptualist emphasis, the social environment for the social cognition researcher seems to consist primarily of a set of sensory rather than socially organized facts. The argument seems to be that the categorizations produced by people such as Benton and James will be largely based on what they can see with their own eyes, unaffected by their economic or general social position. The social cognition tradition thus tends to work with a static conception of society and the social environment. Categorical differences, and 'racial' features, are a mere enduring fact of the physical world, there to be perceived and given cognitive significance in much the same way by any observer at any time in history.

In the absence of any social theory, the processes of change in judgements over time and the persistence of racism become particularly difficult to theorize. Social cognition researchers are reduced to stressing the cognitive 'utility' of prejudicial judgement and its inevitability. But why do Pākehā New Zealanders, such as Benton and James, have such a negative attitude to Māori New Zealanders in the first place? Most cognitive mechanisms are assumed to work in an essentially neutral manner in the sense that over-accentuation, biased generalization and selective remembering could just as easily result in excessively favourable images of Māori groups.

One answer is that cognition combines with socialization so that the package of beliefs associated with some groups is initially skewed in a negative direction because of the social context and this negativity is reinforced by cognitive procedures. But it is impossible to avoid the suspicion that, for some social cognitive researchers, the perceptualist and individualist model which organizes their work encourages a different answer. Hamilton and Trolier argue that cognitive processes should never be seen as the sole cause of discrimination but, none the less, that these processes can *in themselves* cause apparently discriminatory effects.

Their logic, and the logic behind the illusory correlation studies, suggests that some negative images result because Māori New Zealanders persist in behaving in such 'undesirable' and 'unacceptable' ways. They suggest that someone like Sargeant, for example, might be able to 'book-keep' more effectively, be 'converted', or generate a larger range of 'positive prototypes', if only Māori people would pull their socks up and offer more positive and 'disconfirming' images of their group. The argument implies that if there were better Māori role models on offer then white cognitions might be able to run in a more benign direction. If 'reality' was otherwise, there would be more 'evidence' available which contradicts stereotypic schema, and Pākehā New Zealanders might come to perceive Māori New Zealanders in a truly benevolent fashion. As Julian Henriques has commented:

> The black person becomes the cause of racism whereas the white person's prejudice is seen as a natural effect of their information processing mechanisms. (This works as a subtle double exoneration of white racism, no doubt all the more effective because it is not conscious.) (1984, p. 74)

Reading social identity

We have spent a considerable amount of time trying to unfold the suppositions of social cognitive research since these suppositions typify a great deal of
contemporary social psychology. They also partially structure the form of
analysis offered by the second social psychological approach we wish to
consider – social identity theory (Tajfel, 1981; Tajfel and Turner, 1985;
Turner, 1981; 1985; Turner *et al.*, 1987). Only partially, however, since in
contrast to social cognition research, social identity theory claims to develop a
truly social psychological account of intergroup relations. An account in
which social factors are not incidental or placed on one side but seen as
pivotal to psychological formation.

Like social cognition researchers, social identity researchers link the
problem of racism to the problem of biased and stereotypic judgement.
Racism is also seen as much more than this, however. Broadly, racism is seen
as a problem of ethnocentrism, of explaining how preference for one's own
ethnic and racial group is connected to a chain of discriminatory consequences. Racism is expressed not just in negative stereotypes but in other
forms of preference – evident in deeds, through the division and allocation of
resources, and through the general maximization of the differences between
groups.

Racist discourse, in this view, is discourse which favours ingroups and
denigrates outgroups; it is discourse which categorizes, evaluates, ranks and
differentiates between groups. The task of theory is thus to explain those acts.
Social identity theory focuses on intergroup relations as a general category.
Racism is one exemplar of intergroup relations as a whole. The goal of social
identity theory is to explicate the typical social and psychological processes
which produce intergroup conflict. This general account will then explain
local manifestations, whether that is racism, sexism or conflict such as that in
Northern Ireland based on religious categorizations.

How is the explanation mounted? How are psychological processes thought
to contribute to intergroup conflict? Why do individuals come to prefer their
own groups so strongly that their actions, discourse and representation of
events become marked by this favouritism? Tajfel and Turner trace the
causes to the psychological effects of identifying with a group. Ethnocentrism
is seen as one outcome of group membership. It is seen as a consequence
of perceiving social reality in group terms and as a phenomenon produced through aligning oneself to a group or being aligned in this way by
others.

Social identity theory assumes that it is possible to distinguish between two
kinds of social experience which lie at the ends of a continuum. First, at one
end of the continuum, there are those forms of social interaction best
characterized as interpersonal in nature; and then, at the other end of the
continuum, there are those forms of social interaction which take on an

intergroup character. Interpersonal interaction implies a particular mode of dealing with others and positioning oneself in relation to them. It is thought to be a mode of interaction in which individual differences are most salient, where responses are in terms of 'personal identity'. Tajfel (1981) defines personal identity as a sense of all those aspects of self which mark out someone as a unique and distinctive individual – separate from other individuals. Other people and oneself become categorized and evaluated as individuals – in terms of personality, temperament, likes and dislikes, habits and abilities.

In contrast to this, modes of social interaction which involve social categories and groupings of people are structured by social identity, or by one's sense of what is held in common with others in similar social positions. The switch from personal identity to social identity, or from interpersonal conduct to group conduct is thought to set in motion a chain of cognitive and motivational effects, and it is these effects which produce collective action and group behaviour, and which mediate intergroup conflict. When groups are involved and social identity is invoked, it is assumed the psychology of the individual will then become restructured on a number of fronts.

First, on the cognitive front, social identity theorists argue that all the effects of categorization described in previous sections will apply. Individuals will begin to accentuate differences between groups, for instance, and over-estimate the similarities and homogeneities of individuals within groups. A process of perceptual discounting of differences and similarities will begin to operate, sustaining the categorization of self and others through group membership (Turner, 1987b). Most importantly, as individuals begin to define themselves more and more in group terms, they become increasingly 'depersonalized'.

What Turner means by this is that individuals begin to see themselves as interchangeable with or equivalent to the other members of their group. What becomes apparent are not the divisions among group members, or individual differences, but the ways in which this group's characteristics are also one's own characteristics, and the extent to which the norms, concerns and interests of this group represent one's own beliefs, concerns and interests.

Social identity theory thus describes the process of group identification as a re-orientation of the psychological field. Objects of perception, other people, begin to appear in different lights, in terms of commonalities and differences at group rather than interindividual levels. The individual's self-concept becomes organized around characteristics, beliefs and traits assumed by the group as a whole and to this extent individuality is lost. Indeed, the individual not only disproportionately emphasizes what s/he has in common with the group, but actively begins to take on and assume group characteristics, in this way instantiating and reproducing the group.

More crucially, on the motivational front, individual self-esteem begins to be linked to the fortunes of the group as a whole. If a New Zealander begins to define themselves as Pākehā, and begins actively to 'stereotype' themselves in this way, defining self through representative Pākehā characteristics and attitudes, then to think well of this self it is necessary to be able to think well of Pākehā people in general, compared, that is, to other groups such as Māori New Zealanders or white Australians.

Intergroup comparisons between Pākehā and Māori, rather than comparisons with other individuals, become the arena in which individual Pākehā New Zealanders define their own self-worth. Since self-esteem is a desirable commodity, group members will be motivated to maximize the differences between the groups in favour of the ingroup, and will emphasize the positive distinctiveness of their own group on any dimensions which are valued such as prestige, monetary gains, ascriptions of intelligence and virtue, etc. Through emphasizing the merits of their own group and the weaknesses of Māori people, Pākehā New Zealanders can stress their own value and worth.

Social identity theory, therefore, would invoke this kind of process to explain the discursive patterns evident in the discourse of Benton, James and Sargeant discussed in previous chapters. These New Zealanders see the world in categorical and stereotypical terms because their social identities are, in these interviews, the most active element of their self-conceptions. They have been asked to position themselves in group terms and their self-esteem is thus linked to their discursive and rhetorical presentation of their group.

This does not mean that Benton *et al.* will always respond in this way. Indeed, social identity theory leaves open the possibility of a different form of social interaction between Māori and Pākehā, one based on personal identity, where what is salient is not race or group but personal and individual characteristics. It is possible, too, that Pākehā and Māori might join together in nationalism so that a superordinate group identity – New Zealander – restructures Pākehā and Māori representations of each other.

It is important to emphasize that in stressing the psychological effects of group membership social identity theorists are not dismissing other causes of intergroup conflict. Some forms of competition between groups and some patterns of ingroup favouritism and discrimination against outgroups are taken to be based on a clash of economic or other objective sets of interests. But Tajfel and Turner argue that the psychological processes underlying group identification are such that we can also expect what Turner (1975) calls 'social competition' to occur. That is, competition to maintain differentials and value distinctions in the absence of objective conflict. In the case of Māori and Pākehā New Zealanders both forms would probably be seen to apply. That is, real conflicts of interest lead to ethnocentrism and discrimination but this conflict is sustained by the psychological consequences of group membership which will operate willy nilly.

The ontology and epistemology of social identity theory

Social identity theory, like some other approaches we have considered, typically assumes that the empirical patterns and observable phenomena of social life are generated by a set of basic underlying processes. The task of the scientist is to derive the real causes from the superficial pattern. In this case the basic underlying process is thought to occur at the meeting place of the individual and the social. Social identity theory tries to describe the routes through which a social field of groups and group divisions becomes incorporated within the individual and is made to work psychologically, producing responses which sustain that social field.

The first step in any explanation occurs when the objects of explanation are specified. Once it has been decided that the task is to account for the inter-relationship of X, Y and Z, then a theory is already in place. In the case of social identity theory the raw material of explanation, and the prior ontological assumptions, are clear. The theoretical landscape is structured by the encounter between those two primal entities, the 'individual' and the 'social group'. Individuals are taken to be self-contained and independent organisms, with perceptual systems, distinct cognitions and motive systems. The social field, as Hogg and Abrams (1988) make clear, is understood in classic structuralist–functionalist terms. Society is 'hierarchically structured into discrete social categories which stand in power, status and prestige relations to one another' (Hogg and Abrams, 1988, p. 18).

The existence of social categories and groups, along with individuals, is thus taken for granted. The crucial question then becomes the terms on which these two entities will meet. Incidentally, discursive practice, but also behaviour and action, become seen as merely the expressions of this meeting, extruded from, and secondary to, the terms of engagement. Discourse, the words of others, is one way in which the social world may be presented to the individual, but is seen as merely reflective of categories and groupings already in place. Through interaction the individual expresses their psychological dynamic but discourse is again seen as merely symptomatic of this dynamic, the vehicle, one could say, for the psychological goods contained in the individual.

So on what terms do the 'individual' and the 'social group' meet in social identity theory? Turner (1987a) argues that social identity theory presents an 'interactionist' position. There are three main premises. First, psychological processes 'reside only in individuals'. The individual mind must play a 'determining indispensable role in the working out of social processes'. Yet social processes have their own reality and independent effects as 'distinctive emergent forms' (1987a, p. 4). The problem is, then, carving out a role for the individual which does not deny social reality.

Social identity theorists claim to do this through their emphasis on the way the psychological field is restructured in group situations. The shifts in identity and self-categorization, which we described above, are seen as responsive to external social reality, to the groupings already present in the social environment, but they also make possible the collective action from which social forms emerge. Individuals are different in groups and this difference is the very thing which produces recognizable forms of group action.

The social, therefore, structures individual perception, identity and action. In this sense society, understood as a system of group divisions, comes first; but it is the individual's psychological response to this social stimulus which allows the social to continue, which produces group action and which completes the circle. Social action is dependent on individual psychology just as that psychology is structured through social forms.

In many respects, therefore, social identity theory represents a considerable advance on social cognition research. It incorporates the main findings of this research but within a sociological frame – albeit a rather traditional one – and with a more complex notion of the social functions and consequences of individual acts of categorization. It is more difficult to accuse social identity theory of individualism, although we wish to return to this debate in the next chapter.

What social identity theory continues to hold in common with social cognition research, however, is a tendency to universalize the conditions for racism and a lingering perceptualism. Like social cognition research, it is assumed that all humans basically work in the same way. Categorization and some of the cognitive consequences of group membership are thus seen as universal and inevitable processes. The very notion of 'social competition' – intergroup conflict in the absence of objective reasons for that conflict – suggests that racism is seen as a default condition of human nature.

Tajfel and Turner argue that groups may express intergroup differentiation in various ways – not all groups will compete; but the way in which these theorists link self-esteem with positive group consequences suggests that alternative strategies will become seen as anomalous, self-defeating or pathological in some sense (Wetherell, 1982). The message for anti-racism is pessimistic. It suggests that because these types of group phenomena are expressions of a universal psychological dynamic, racism is more likely to persist than not, and, if racism did disappear, it would simply be replaced by some other grounds for group differentiation.

Ambiguities also arise concerning how the process of representation in relation to social categories is understood and the extent to which social identity theory shares the perceptualism of social cognition research. Turner's position here is an uneasy mix of acknowledging the socially constructed nature of categories and groups and emphasizing the foundational basis of individual perception. This unease, as we shall argue in the next chapter, derives from the failure to develop a theory of language, discourse and communication and a failure to consider categorization as a discursive practice (see Coulter, 1991; Edwards, 1991; Marshall and Wetherell, 1989; Widdicombe and Wooffitt, 1990; 1992).

On the one hand, Turner (1987b) argues that social categories and groups are 'pre-formed' – historically and culturally given in advance. However, the explanations he and his colleagues (see Oakes, 1987) advance for the salience of categories and for the processes of group formation seem to rely, as in social cognition research, on a model of a mute and solitary observer, restricted to the evidence of their senses, and caught within a perceptual rather than a social frame.

What will determine, for example, the identity and self-categorization an individual will adopt at any particular moment? It depends on the ' "relative accessibility" of that categorisation for the perceiver and the "fit" between the "stimulus input and category specifications" ' (Turner, 1987b, p. 54). What this seems to mean is that Anna James, for example, will choose to speak as a Pākehā, rather than choose to speak as a 'South Islander' or from some other identity because she has learnt 'what tends to go with what in the environment'. It also seems to depend on her 'current motives' (*ibid.*, p. 55). These two aspects will determine the accessibility of the category Pākehā or 'South Islander' in her mind. Whereas 'fit' refers to 'the degree to which reality actually matches the criteria which define the category' (*ibid.*).

Accessibility and fit only make sense if we imagine James standing to one side observing a social interaction, rather than actually participating in a conversation. Turner and Oakes seem to be suggesting that the way James will read a situation she is observing and the way she will position herself in relation to it will depend upon (1) what she wants to achieve, (2) her past learning about these types of situations which make some self-images more relevant than others and (3) the actual characteristics of other people in the situation.

The array of real similarities and differences between herself and others will determine whether James decides she is a member of the same group or social category as the other people present or sufficiently different from them not to belong. The concept of fit only makes sense if we assume that categories are presented visually and that people's main mode of interaction is structured mainly by gaze and not discourse.

A similar pattern holds when Turner invokes the concept of the 'meta-contrast ratio' to explain group formation and the 'emergent' nature of intergroup conflict. Turner and Tajfel argue that many of the negative (and positive) features of group behaviour will be apparent in the most minimal circumstances. Groups will discriminate against other groups in the absence of any material reasons for favouritism and even when it is against their interests to do so. All that is necessary for ingroup bias is the possibility of a group categorization, since all the psychological processes involved are triggered by this recognition. The concept of the 'meta-contrast ratio' is designed to expand on and explain this point.

Let us imagine Anna James in a small discussion group or perhaps required to make a judgement about a number of individuals; and let us say that the judging scale is such that James begins to notice that the difference between some individuals is less than some other individuals. Turner argues that in these types of conditions the pattern of similarities and differences will ensure that James will begin to form mental categories or cognitively group the individuals together. The meta-contrast ratio is the average of intra-category differences over the average of inter-category difference.

As the intercategory difference increases in relation to the intra-category differences, on any comparative scales which are relevant, Turner argues that individuals would become more likely to see people in group terms and to begin depersonalizing themselves and others as part of the predicted shift away from acting in terms of personal identity to acting in terms of social or group-based identity. Turner suggests that from these very minimal acts of perception groups can emerge and acquire a psychological reality. Further, once motivation is linked in to the cognitive system, discrimination becomes a real possibility.

Once again, however, this is an account dominated by perceptual process. We can only make sense of the meta-contrast ratio if we imagine that James exists in a kind of communicational black hole, simply sucking in perceptions of others and judging and evaluating on that basis. Indeed, the concept of the meta-contrast ratio takes as its model for social life the communicational paradigm found in psychological experiments. We have to imagine James as a solitary observer, recorder and evaluator of a social spectacle laid out for her benefit. This is not to suggest that some discursive account of accessibility, fit and the meta-contrast ratio could not be worked up, but it indicates the direction of theorizing here. In particular, it demonstrates the constraints imposed when a separate, self-contained, sensual but largely silent individual is taken as the starting point for theory.

Reading motives

In some respects, the third social psychological perspective we wish to discuss in this chapter, although a great deal older, can be seen as wider ranging in scope than the two approaches considered already. Authoritarian personality analyses of racism (Adorno *et al.*, 1950) tried to link, in a manner which is unusual in psychology, diverse bodies of social theory. Adorno and his colleagues describe their work as inter-relating the constitution of social relations understood through versions of Marxist theory with the constitution of subjectivity understood through neo-Freudian psychoanalysis.

The 1950 account of the authoritarian personality studies begins with this simple question: why do competing political ideologies have such differing degrees of appeal for different individuals (Adorno *et al.*, 1950, p. 2)? This initial question unites what prove to be the main themes of the authoritarian personality analysis – individual differences and the hooks of political rhetoric.

Adorno and his colleagues saw their task as explaining why some individuals found democratic discourse congenial, while others were drawn to fascistic and racist ideologies. Differences in susceptibility were related to differences in individual needs, in psychic organization and in the satisfaction of needs. Adorno *et al.* assumed there was a mesh between the content of an ideology and conscious and unconscious aspects of psychological structure. Thoughts, words, opinions, beliefs, actions, needs and motives thus became structured together into a complex whole.

Adorno *et al.* were most interested in the psychological basis of what they described as authoritarian forms of political ideology. This constellation of views was distinguished in their view by anti-democratic and conservative trends, and seen as the milieu or potential breeding ground for fascist and anti-semitic responses as well as for racism more generally. The aim of their studies was to identify regularities in the character structures and the psychic history of those who seemed drawn to authoritarian doctrines and thus discover an authoritarian personality for an authoritarian ideology.

There were some other strands, however, to their analysis. Adorno *et al.* claimed, first, that authoritarianism emerged not simply in political arenas, or in responses to other groups, but spilled over to other areas of individuals' lives. Authoritarian patterns of belief conducive to racism were seen as dynamically linked with other typical attitudes – to topics such as family life, sexual relations, self, others, religion and social life – and thus as just one aspect of a general philosophy of life. Secondly, Adorno *et al.* wanted to relate character structure to social structure. They argued it was no accident that some individuals developed personalities conducive to authoritarian ideology. These people were the victims of patterns of parent–child relationships, and ideas about child-rearing, found in certain social contexts, notably capitalist social formations.

> a basically hierarchical, authoritarian, exploitative parent–child relationship is apt to carry over into a power-oriented, exploitatively dependent attitude towards one's sex partner and one's God and may well culminate in a political philosophy and social outlook which has no room for anything but a desperate clinging to what appears to be a strong and disdainful rejection of whatever is relegated to the bottom. (Adorno *et al.*, 1950, p. 971)

The chain of cause and effect is complex – from the mores and habits prevalent in certain social circumstances, to parent–child interactions, to the formation of personality, to the expression of political ideology, which then once more sets the scene for the reproduction of these personality forms in another generation.

Adorno *et al.*'s research procedure involved assessing an individual through clinical interviews, projective tests and questionnaire responses and then deducing from these a set of motives, sometimes deeply repressed, which dictated the surface ideology expressed in the talk. The aim, in essence, was the clinical diagnosis of verbal and written materials, and their research was thus highly dependent on the interpretation and analysis of various forms of discourse. From their perspective the crucial questions to ask about any individual were these – what kind of man or woman is this? How do their opinions and group allegiances connect with their general world view, with their total personality and characteristic approach to life?

In their account of their research, Adorno *et al.* present detailed case-studies of two individuals which can be used as a model to indicate the form and nature of their investigation. We will focus on their account of someone they called 'Mack'. Mack is described as a typical instance of the authoritarian personality, and thus seen as particularly susceptible to racist ideology.

According to Adorno *et al.*, Mack's philosophy of life was distinguished by his respect for conventions, admiration of strong manly figures, respect for forms of authority such as the law and his denigration of the capacities of outgroups, who were seen as weaker and inferior to the powerful glorified ingroup. Adorno *et al.* argue that, particularly in men, these ideologies emerge in response to repressed hostility and as a reaction to fear of one's own weakness and dependency.

In Mack's case, these attitudes are traced back to a particular family dynamic. Mack's mother died when he was small and he was brought up by a strong but distant and perhaps punitive father. Adorno *et al.* argue that Mack respected his father as a figure of strength and authority, but felt also hostile and aggressive towards this rather remote figure who inadequately fulfilled Mack's needs for love, care and protection.

Adorno *et al.* conclude that Mack's dependency on his father meant his outward attitude had to be submissive. Both the hostility and the feelings of dependence became strongly repressed. The result, they suggest, is a personality dominated by a fear of weakness and a fear of dependency on others. Mack strives to present himself as 'manly' and 'self-sufficient', he wants to see himself as 'impregnable'. Continued respect for authority, and the projection of both weakness and hostility onto others become an important part of his psychic strategy. In Mack's case, these feelings are projected onto women and minority groups. He is not weak, they are; he is not 'power-seeking', they are. Certain types of 'dangerous others' thus take over these feelings. Mack can then safely despise others for their weakness and vent hostility outwards.

The links with broader social relations come through the process of later identifications with authority figures. Adorno *et al.* assume that authoritarian patterns and punitive discipline, along with the regulation of workers, and machismo attitudes are a necessary feature of certain forms of capitalism. As wider society becomes organized into certain modes of production, domestic life, too, becomes affected and re-constituted in a sympathetic form. Children then encounter attitudes in their parents and guardians which are a micro-cosm of the attitudes and forms of behaviour required in the work-place and society more generally. This meeting in the home of external demands with the demands of child-rearing leads to ideologies and practices of child-care which reproduce authoritarian patterns in segments of the next generation.

Clearly, like some forms of ideological analysis, the authoritarian personal-ity perspective works through argument against the person (Billig, 1978). In this case the personality of the subject is taken apart and found wanting; discursive positions are traced back to an individual's vested psychic interests. In both cases polite 'surface' expressions of concern are seen as disguising closeted real motives. The reading strategy with regard to discourse is to attempt to detect a system of needs through the slips and breaks in a subject's accounts.

We could apply the same kind of strategy to the Pākehā New Zealanders we interviewed. And we shall attempt here one reading along these lines to clarify further the type of analysis involved. This reading will use Sargeant, whose discourse first appeared in the Introduction (p. 5), as our target. Superficially, Sargeant's interview appears to be a typical example of politician's discourse. As the extract in the Introduction demonstrates, he is polite, seemingly rational, displays a worked out position on most topics, attends to the criticism of his political party, but tries to be solid in defence. Where is the personality?

In the extract presented in the Introduction, Sargeant worries that his attitude to Māoris might be seen as paternalistic, although he discounts the validity of this interpretation. Adorno *et al.* might begin at this point and assume Sargeant is indeed paternalistic and this mode of representing and dealing with Māori people reflects not just a political judgement but a habitual response on Sargeant's part to the complexities of social relations and judging others.

As evidence for Sargeant's preference for authoritarian ideology a number of themes across his interview could be picked out; the sum total of which could present Sargeant as a man deeply concerned with old-fashioned respect for authority, who distrusts permissiveness, who argues vehemently for individual freedom in economic and political life, but who also believes in Christian values of tolerance and responsibility for others. Respect for authority, for example, could be deduced from the following extract.

> Sargeant: In general there is a decline in respect for law and order and
> authority, that is common, it has occurred right throughout the world
> since World War Two, um, a decline in family life (0.2), decline in
> respect for authority, yes, the rebel decade in which young people
> really attacked many traditional concepts . . .

Sargeant's interview could be read, too, as displaying signs that he glorifies his own group, Pākehā New Zealanders, and sees them as superior to other groups. In this next extract, Sargeant describes the particular qualities of New Zealanders he venerates. Paradoxically, these turn out to be the opposite of a passive attitude to authority and include bloody-mindedness in the face of orders.

Wetherell: . . . do you think one can talk about a New Zealand national character in the way that we sometimes think there's a British national character or an American national character? If you can see one, what would be its good and bad features?

Sargeant: The good features, we (0.2) there are still traces of our pioneering background, after all we've only been settled by Europeans for just over a hundred years, um, therefore we tend to admire anyone who er who's courageous, adventurous. No-one in New Zealand is admired more than Sir Edmund Hilary, um, another man held in great veneration is war hero, Captain Charles Upham, (yes) he won the Victoria Cross twice. Um we have great respect for those sort of people. Bravery, courage, resourcefulness. We like to think the best of, the aspects of the best New Zealander are, as I talked before, tolerance, a person who gets on easily with all sorts of races, a person who, in whom there is no class consciousness, we are very very diff, far apart from the British class system and er we want none of that system.

Um (0.9) we like, we like to think, the New Zealander we like is what we'd describe as a decent joker, he doesn't need to be highly intelligent, um he doesn't need to be a fellow who will spend the afternoon at the bar of the pub all the time, but he can be a decent joker, a man you inherently trust. The New Zealand soldier in World War Two was a great soldier, um far better as a soldier than the American, the Australian, in line with the British Tommy who was a great soldier, but he was a great soldier for different reasons. He er the British Tommy was a fine soldier because he had instilled in him for generations that he must obey the upper class. The New Zealander is not like that, he was a, he was a great soldier because um he called up his pioneering sense of resourcefulness, and if his officer said, 'look, we're going to attack that hill', the New Zealander would say to the officer – 'Captain, don't be so bloody silly!' (hahaha), hahahah.

Sargeant's interview also suggests that he believes this superiority entails the duty of acting, as he puts it at one point in the interview, as a 'sort of mother, or big brother' to other less fortunate beings. But there are also hints of a punitive and deeply hostile attitude to other minority groups, described as 'stirrers', those who protest against Springbok rugby tours, for instance, or with whom he disagrees. These groups are described as 'over-stepping the mark', as going 'too far', as denying 'me my rights', and as 'bleating on television'.

In the next extract some of Sargeant's contrasting 'protective' attitude emerges in his desire to help 'lift up' Māori people.

> Sargeant: [discussing special provision for Māori groups] I think, I think we
> have to recognize the special needs of people like Māoris and
> Polynesians and make special provision for them. If we want to lift
> them up to provide them with the same opportunities as the
> European New Zealander.

Finally, there are signs of contempt for Māori groups which mesh with the
glorification of Pākehā New Zealanders, and it is in these moments of the
interview that racist themes emerge most clearly.

> Sargeant: The, um, the old Māori, only 150 years ago he was a cannibal, he
> was eating his enemies. He hasn't had the advantages of (yes), if we
> think the Western style of civilization is the ideal situation, he hasn't
> (.) had bred into him, generation after generation, er, the capacity
> to reason, analyze. Of course some do, not in the same proportion
> as whites.

Thus, like Mack, Sargeant does seem, as Adorno *et al.* might expect, to
represent Māori people and other minority groups as power-seeking, and he
expresses hostility towards them on that score. He also obviously respects the
independence, power and strength he attributes to the Pākehā New Zealand
ingroup. Adorno *et al.* might also conclude that there are signs in Sargeant's
praise for bloody-minded soldiers of a repressed rebellion against authority.
Sargeant certainly, too, sees Māoris as weak, but it is not clear that it is this
particular perception which produces his despising attitude.

What seems to distinguish Sargeant from Mack is the additional attitude of
paternalism, of self-conscious charity – 'lifting others up' – and his construction of Māoris and other groups as needing help, attention and special care –
the importance of acting as a 'big brother' to these groups. At several
points in his interview, he laid particular stress on the duties of Pākehā
New Zealanders and on the responsibilities of the economically well-off
to look after and improve the living standards of others. His general political philosophy emphasized the benefits and moral necessity of the welfare
state.

Racism accompanied by this form of 'benevolence' makes sense, as we saw
in Chapter 1, in terms of the history of the particular 'humanistic' ideologies
surrounding the colonization of New Zealand but does it make sense
psychodynamically? Perhaps not as a manifestation of the sado-masochistic
personality structure Adorno *et al.* identify, but other neo-Freudian analyses
could be applied to generate a plausible enough story.

Karen Horney (1946), for example, argues that one way people resolve a
neurotic conflict between, say, the desire to move towards others and also
move against them is through the construction of an ideal self which resolves
the conflict in fantasy. Thus, along these lines, it could be argued that
Sargeant's 'benevolence' and paternalistic attitude is a way of expressing both

contempt and hostility towards others without fear of punishment and also expressing some positive feelings while retaining a position of strength.

Discourse analysis as diagnosis

This reading of Sargeant's interview reveals not only some of the difficulties involved in producing a 'depth' reading of discourse, but also suggests the characteristic mode of discourse analysis required. Once again, discourse has acquired a representational and reflective status. To analyze the 'personality' in Sargeant's talk, the tensions, strains and contradictions evident in discourse become seen as representative of underlying psychic strains and inconsistencies. The flip side of this is that analysis has become insensitive to the practical role of the talk, the rhetorical strains and inconsistencies – and thus what is being achieved by it in terms of blamings, justifications and so on.

Adorno *et al.* suggest that thoughts, needs, actions and words are woven together, but thoughts and needs are given priority in this analysis. Motives organize words. Adorno *et al.* do not analyze how the words, the forms of discourse available to Sargeant, might equally come to constitute his subjectivity. The reading strategy required is thus a global one, where the analyst works intuitively from the broad brush message of the text, and pays relatively little attention to the immediate interactional context of the interview or to the active, purposive or functional nature of the talk designed for that context. The movement is from the surface of the discourse to supposed latent content.

Typically, authoritarian personality research draws connections between different realms of discourse. Thus Sargeant's direct expressions of racial theory become linked in this form of analysis to his discourse on welfare programmes, to his presentation of himself and his group, to accounts of his patriotic and religious views; and, if the material were available, links might be made to his sexual politics and family life. This generalization to Sargeant's broader philosophy of life has some advantages in light of recent developments in racist ideologies.

Frank Reeves (1983) and others who have mapped the changes in racist discourse over time have noted how references to biologically orientated racial theories are becoming relatively rare in domains such as contemporary UK political discourse. It is not that racism has disappeared. Reeves suggests that forms of legitimation have become more 'sanitized' and in some ways more covert. The analysis of contemporary racism thus needs to range beyond examples of biologism. In drawing connections between views on a number of related topics, authoritarian personality analyses, unlike some other theories of racism, are sufficiently flexible in this respect to follow ideological shifts. The problem is that these ideologies are then isolated in particular individuals.

We wish to retain Adorno *et al.*'s concern with 'philosophies of life' and similarly pay attention to the links between fascist, nationalist, conservative and racist discourse; but we also wish to advance Adorno *et al.*'s concerns, and look, too, at how racist legitimations can also work through social reformist, humanitarian and seemingly liberal discourse. As Part II of this book will make clear, the focus on authoritarian ideology and on authoritarians is too narrow. Racist discourse can be both authoritarian and liberal in form. Authoritarian points may be made in the midst of democratic discourse. The most apparently 'well-adjusted' in psychoanalytic terms may articulate their political views through the discourses of racism. Authoritarian personality research pathologizes both the ideology and the characters who endorse it, thus severely limiting the range of critical investigation.

Similar points have been made by those critics of authoritarian personality research (Billig, 1978; Minard, 1952; Pettigrew, 1958) who point to the pervasiveness of racism across all social groups, the rapidity of ideological change, and the power of social norms. All of these phenomena question the location of racist dispositions in the relatively enduring personality structures of authoritarians.

Minard's studies of black and white miners, for example, demonstrated how white miners, racist in one context above ground, become 'tolerant' and co-operative below ground, as social expectations varied. Pettigrew's research has illustrated how the prevalence of authoritarian character structures, as defined by Adorno *et al.*, remains relatively constant across Western societies and across regions of the United States, yet expressions of racism vary widely in different societies and in different states. Pettigrew concludes that other elements must thus be at work in determining ideological patterns.

Authoritarian personality analyses have, however, the advantage that they do not assume that all individuals work in much the same general way. In this respect this theory can be clearly distinguished from the universalistic assumptions of social cognition and social identity research. The focus is on how subjectivity is constructed differently in different social circumstances. Authoritarianism is seen as inevitable in some social conditions and once in place is seen to have an inevitable and enduring quality. But Adorno *et al.* also argue that as child–parent relations change in line with other social changes, then new 'types' of people will also emerge.

As a theory of identity, Adorno *et al.*'s work has some appealing and some problematic aspects. Individuals are seen as both variable and fixed in form – fixed in the sense that they acquire one character structure and become either an authoritarian or anti-authoritarian personality. Yet within the authoritarian character structure individuals are fragmented and crosscut by ambivalent and contradictory desires. Mack is seen as wanting to be both strong and submissive, for instance.

The theme of fragmentation is one we wish to pursue but we want to extend the argument to question Adorno *et al.*'s concept of a broad personality type.

We want to maintain Adorno *et al.*'s emphasis on the social rather than the instinctual or biological constitution of subjectivity but will argue that these aims are better realized within a theory of identity as a discursive and situated product. The next chapter will return to these points. Indeed, the major advantage of the authoritarian personality analysis, and the other perspectives reviewed in this chapter, is that they force the discourse analyst to confront questions of identity, the conceptualization of motives and the methodological procedures for reading these in discourse.

3

Discourse, power and subjectivity

This chapter will be concerned with two broad trends evident in the sociology and social psychology of racism reviewed in previous chapters. We wish to argue against confusing the study of ideology with the study of false ideas, and, secondly, we wish to dispute the tendency in social psychology for language to become a forgotten object, assigned an essentially neutral and mediating role between the 'individual' and their 'environment'. Although the four approaches we examined in Chapters 1 and 2 explain racism in sharply different ways, there is a surprising degree of unanimity in their general prescriptions concerning discourse. Reduced and simplified somewhat, the message taken from these sources seems to boil down to the following seven, largely implicit, injunctions:

1. Analyze racist discourse as a representation of reality and focus principally on the veracity of racist claims.
2. Treat racist ideology as a fixed system of ideas definable through its content.
3. Assume that the social field is a largely pre-defined structure of social groups and other divisions.
4. Assume, too, that psychological processes are contained within individuals.
5. Treat discourse as a medium which mainly expresses and reflects these pre-existing psychological and social realities.
6. Separate, in this way, discourse from action, discourse from subjectivity and discourse from social process.
7. Privilege some areas of science, including one's own account, while criticizing other areas.

In taking issue with each of these points we will be attempting to develop an alternative general framework for our own investigations, and an alternative set of prescriptions for analysis. It is important to stress that our goal in this and the next chapter is to derive an appropriate theory and method for the analysis of discourse alone – we are not seeking to theorize racism as a whole, or suggest that the analysis of discourse should replace every other analysis of racism. Discourse analysis has a bearing on other domains such as political economy, psychopathology and information processing, but the study of discourse, although highly relevant, is not equivalent to the study of those domains.

Our approach will assume that discourse is actively constitutive of both social and psychological processes. The psychological and social field – subjectivity, individuality, social groups and social categories – is constructed, defined and articulated through discourse. We shall thus suggest that action, the individual and the social, the subject-matter of social psychology, cannot be easily separated from discursive practice. Racism, we shall argue, needs to be seen as a series of ideological effects, with a flexible, fluid and varying content. Similarly, we shall suggest that all scientific claims, not just those currently disputed, should be open to critical attention, and that attention should turn from the veracity of racist claims to the processes whereby these claims become communicated as 'fact' and empowered as 'truth'.

In developing these arguments we will draw on currents of thought in linguistics, conversational pragmatics and semiotics which we have reviewed elsewhere (Potter and Wetherell, 1987), but we will also draw on a range of other sources. Notably, we have been influenced by some of Foucault's various formulations of discourse, power and truth, and by some recent attempts within Marxist traditions to work with new analyses of signification (e.g. Coward and Ellis, 1977; Hall, 1980; 1981; 1985; 1986; 1988a; 1988b; 1988c; 1988d). We will draw, too, on related developments in social psychology (e.g. Billig 1978; 1985; 1988; Billig *et al.*, 1988; Henriques *et al.*, 1984; Parker, 1992), and on some recent studies of racism which give a different priority to questions of representation and discourse (e.g. Billig, 1988; Centre for Contemporary Cultural Studies, 1982; Condor, 1988; Essed, 1991a and b; Gilroy, 1987; Hewitt, 1986; Reeves, 1983; Reicher, 1986; Seidel, 1988; van Dijk, 1984; 1987; 1991).

This chapter will be mainly concerned with developing the theoretical argument, while the next chapter will take up the more concrete questions of analytic practice. We begin with recent developments in the study of ideology and then work through our argument in stages, looking first at what it means to say that discourse is constitutive, then picking out some of the implications for the status of social science investigation and for questions of truth and anti-racist practice. The last half of the chapter will then take up a series of topics released by these new emphases: ideological practice, the construction of groups and subjectivities, and discursive power. Finally, we try to show

how our approach tries to work with the tensions which emerge if Foucault's concept of the genealogical study of discourse is allowed to intertwine with the concept of ideology.

Discursive practice

Some of the recent developments in Marxist studies of ideology, which we want to use to set the scene for our own investigations, were briefly noted in Chapter 1, although not developed there, since they contradict some crucial aspects of the basic frame of reference Robert Miles outlines. Althusser's (1971; 1977) work is the most notable example of these new developments, although this trend has been evident too in Stuart Hall's (1980; 1981; 1988a) various reworkings of Gramsci and is found in the work of Laclau and Mouffe (1985; 1987) and others.

One strand in this line of work is a set of powerful arguments for the constitutive and reflexive effects of ideological discourse. Ideology is no longer seen in these developments as playing an 'after-the-event' type of role (Hall, 1988c; 1988d), dictated by and justifying social relations assumed to be already in place, simply reflecting and determined by economic relations. Ideology and discourse become implicated in the very instantiation and maintenance of social and economic relations.

This is the emphasis which Robert Miles endorses in his work; and from this line of argument emerge studies of how ideology comes to act as a 'condition of existence' for the economic. As we saw, Miles describes how racist ideology facilitates the assignment of minority groups to exploitative roles in a division of labour through certain formulations of capacities, talents, roles and rights. Ideology becomes in these accounts, not a set of ideas which simply legitimate disadvantage, but part of the mechanisms which institute disadvantage.

Ideology, too, becomes seen as crucial to the reproduction of society, working through various specific institutions and 'state apparatuses' such as the media and the education system to ensure, for instance, a new generation of 'schooled' workers. We begin to see a shift, therefore, from the assumption that ideas are powerful simply as a consequence of their mental effects – powerful to the extent that they can successfully win hearts and minds – towards a view of ideology as a material process. Although it should be emphasized that the notion 'material process' here is not meant to imply that the operation of ideology can be reduced to a set of causal movements such as appear in the operation of a machine. Ideology becomes visible and forceful, seen as reshaping, in the most extreme case, geographical and physical landscapes, through the other social practices which are encouraged.

The notion of ideology as a set of rather ineffable ideas and systems of

knowledge is increasingly abandoned in these new theorizations as ideology becomes seen as primarily a form of practical action, instantiated in
policy statements, in the statements of political spin doctors, in memos,
in speeches, in documents, in newspapers, in conversations, accounts,
explanations, versions, anecdotes and stories. Ideology becomes transformed
from the categories and logic of thought into discursive practice. What
becomes apparent in this new formulation is that discourse is active,
compelling and a pervasive part of the fabric of social life. Moreover,
ideology ceases to be seen as an elegant coherent totality but as fragmented
and contradictory, with the very stresses and variations within it being crucial
to its operation.

In these kinds of discussions the rigid distinctions between economic base
and cultural superstructure, which had previously organized some Marxist
accounts of ideology, begin to soften. It emerges that discourse and ideological practice are inseparable from other social practices. Not just in the sense
that some words have concrete effects, but because it can be seen how every
feature of the conventional sociological landscape – social structures and
divisions, institutions, financial, military, health and educational practices – is
imbued with ideology and with discourse. Indeed, the very category system at
work here can be seen as one form of discursive construction.

Along with these new emphases go new analytic commitments. The old
ones, of course, still remain – to perform historical analyses and thus locate
contemporary discourse within some changing social, economic and political
context and to examine the power of ideology as rationalization and
justification. However, here is also pressure to investigate in a more localized
fashion how different political ideologies actively construct and create group
and class alliances and new types of identity and subject positions. To study,
that is, how ideological discourse becomes turned into popular discourse,
recognized as 'truth', and comes to work as effective rhetoric (e.g. Hall,
1988b).

In this outline of recent developments in Marxist theories of ideology we
have tried to pick out those aspects which seem to us to be particularly
congenial for discourse analysis and which set up a useful frame for our own
work. It also seems to us, however, as it has seemed to others, that these lines
of enquiry will be substantially undermined if, having established the
constitutive role of discourse, limits are then placed on this role.

Where we depart from Miles, and where Miles seems to depart from some
of these developments, is in his assumption that the constitutive effects of
discourse can at some juncture melt away leaving behind a simple, direct and
expressive relationship between the representation and the reality. Once the
constitutive role of discourse becomes apparent then simple distinctions
between distorted discourse and truly descriptive discourse become increasingly untenable.

Discourse and its objects

For Miles, ideology is probably best seen as equivalent to a sticky layer between the observer and social reality. In Goffman's (1981) phrase, he seems to assume that language is rather like custard or jam, an intrusive and congealing medium. Ideology becomes seen as a sort of temporary messiness mixed in with other social practices, a contingent complication in the lives of social actors, and a complication in analyses of social relations; but it is also assumed that with non-ideological understanding the surface can be wiped clean to afford a veridical representation, one which lets the real objects once more emerge.

Like Miles (and Goffman), we see language as an intrusive and sticky medium, but we do not accept that the surfaces can ever be wiped clean. Discourse, in our view, is not partially constitutive or only constitutive under some conditions but is thoroughly constitutive. Our accounts of objects always construct those objects in certain ways and this construction is inescapable. Some versions of reality may be infinitely preferable to others, and should be argued for and pushed forward whenever possible, but, in our view, there is no 'versionless' reality.

There are several points to make here about this argument. First, we are not suggesting that there is nothing but discourse – only that we come to know what there is in the context of some historically specific and socially contingent account. Similarly, we are not suggesting that there is a kind of 'unreality' to racism or that racism is simply accounts and words. If we think for a moment of how racism is made manifest. Words are central to that process but racism is made manifest, too, through physical violence, through material disadvantage, and through differences in opportunities and power. However, to understand that pattern, we have to develop some account, whether as social scientists, as politicians, as subjects of racism or as the initiators and beneficiaries. The crucial aspect, as always, is whose story will be accepted and become part of the general currency of explanation, whose version of events, whose account of the way things are?

Secondly, we do not wish to suggest that if discourse is thoroughly constitutive every account of social relations must be an ideological account. We do not wish to argue that ideological means simply constructed knowledge or should be synonymous with discourse, signification or cultural phenomena in general. The domain of discourse includes weather reports, as we noted in Chapter 1; it includes computer manuals, the words on the back of cornflakes packets. Sometimes it might be useful to analyze the ideological effects of accounts of nutritional ingredients and special offers but we are not condemned to do so by our stance on discourse. It is important to retain a distinction between analyses that construct readings in terms of ideology and those that do not.

For Miles, ideological discourse is distinguished by its entanglement with other social practices and power relations but, crucially, it is also distinguished by its falsity. From our point of view, ideology is equally distinguished by its involvement in power relations but, as we will try to show in the course of this chapter, the specification of falsity places too greater a constraint on, and actually hinders, the investigation of ideological practice.

Finally, our argument does not imply that social scientists should cease their speculations in other areas. We do not want to suggest that discourse analysis is the only possible social scientific activity given the constructed nature of the social landscape. Certainly, our claims give an edge and a prominence to the study of discourse; they make the study of discursive practice a central element of social scientific investigation. However, other objects, social processes and practices must also be accounted for and brought into being in social scientists' explanations and versions. Our study of racist social formations, such as New Zealand, will be a study of some aspects of the role and contribution of discursive practices; but that is not all that should be said about the New Zealand situation.

Communities, countries and nations emerge from the action of powerful material, economic and political forces. The nineteenth-century creation of New Zealand as an 'England in the South Pacific' involved movements of people and the organization of a political and economic infrastructure. These things are not just words – but they are not separable from words either. In our analyses in Part II of this book we will thus give accounts of New Zealand history which emphasize different kinds of social practices – migration, finance, wars. These practices can have their own most effective level of explanation, and we are certainly not wanting to suggest that they are *caused* by discourse. Yet they are inseparable, too, from a complex of discursive practices of understanding and interaction.

Overall, our general perspective on the role of discourse is neatly captured in Stuart Hall's point that:

> events, relations, structures do have conditions of existence and real effects, outside the sphere of the discursive; but that it is only within the discursive, and subject to its specific conditions, limits and modalities, do they have or can they be constructed within meaning. Thus while not wanting to expand the territorial claims of the discursive infinitely, how things are represented and the 'machineries' and regimes of representation in a culture do play a constitutive, and not merely a reflexive, after-the-event, role. This gives questions of culture and ideology, and the scenarios of representation – subjectivity, identity, politics – a formative, not merely an expressive, place in the constitution of social and political life. (1988d, p. 27)

Although we have tried to address some of the issues raised by this view of discourse as constitutive, other queries remain – what is the status of our own discourse as social scientists, what is the role of truth, and what are the implications here for anti-racist practice? We will take up these issues shortly.

First, we want to develop as an example the case of discovery. What are we actually suggesting here – that a country such as New Zealand, or any object for that matter, does not actually exist until it is discovered by speaking subjects?

We do want to argue that there is a crucial sense in which 'New Zealand' did not actually exist until it was discovered. Then, when it was discovered by Polynesian voyagers, by Abel Tasman and most recently by Captain Cook (and given various different names), it became several different objects. As Brannigan (1981) has pointed out for the discovery of America, there are sometimes a range of competing discovery claims. These are not claims to have discovered the same object; rather, the precise definition of what the object is is the *outcome* of the process of discovery, definition and articulation (Woolgar, 1988).

A constitutive perspective directs our attention to these processes of definition and articulation and the means through which one version of objects becomes established and alternatives undermined. Most obviously here, of course, in the American case, is the huge power asymmetry with the indigenous Indian groups who had to suffer Columbus's 'discovery'. In this context, the official story of the 'discovery' of America is inextricably linked to the varied resources that Columbus was able to mobilize on behalf of his particular claims, his explicit agenda of discovery, and to a range of notions about what counts as civilization and, indeed, humanity, and therefore who is competent to perform discovery.

Brannigan also makes the point that 'discoveries' may change their status over a period of time: Mendel is only taken as the 'discoverer' of modern genetics some time after the event; the Piltdown Man is initially taken to a be a missing link in human evolution but later understood to be a forgery. It is interesting to consider the 'discovery' of New Zealand in this way. Early Pākehā accounts draw on the idea that New Zealand was discovered by a European, either Tasman or James Cook. Yet the contemporary New Zealand 1990 Official Souvenir Guide specifically rejects the idea that Abel Tasman discovered New Zealand – such a Eurocentric construction has become problematic, not quite a forgery on the scale of the Piltdown Man, but certainly unpolitic as a claim.

Clearly, there is not some consensually agreed 'New Zealand' that either Māori or Pākehā groups are constantly stumbling across. The process of discovery is a process of constitution – defining what the object is. Take the land. What is the New Zealand landscape? Alps, fields, vegetation, grassy hills and so on – these seem obvious even if accounts of 'discovery' need to be hedged. However, this obviousness, too, is the result of a particular definitional system having become so established that it acts as part of common sense. Māori groups had a much more animate concept of physical land forms; while British settlers of the nineteenth century would be more likely to have viewed the land in terms of agricultural viability than through the modern sensibility guided by travel brochures and contrasts between the rural and the industrial (Williams, 1975).

Our perspective is not, we should stress, a form of subjectivism. The constitution of objects is socially organized and highly dependent on our existing forms of discourse and past discursive history. We are not suggesting that if someone thinks New Zealand does not exist then it does not; nor, as we noted earlier, that all there is to reality is ideas. New Zealand is no less real for being constituted discursively – you still die if your plane crashes into a hill whether you think that the hill is the product of a volcanic eruption or the solidified form of a mythical whale. However, material reality is no less discursive for being able to get into the way of planes. How those deaths are understood (see Hirst and Woolley, 1982), and what caused them is constituted through our systems of discourses.

The status of scientific accounts of racism

The view that discourse is thoroughly constitutive leads us to a particular kind of stance on the role and status of scientific accounts. In brief, we assume that no scientific account of reality should be privileged or placed in some non-social realm of pure representation or pure description. This argument seems to us to be particularly crucial when the scientific accounts in question are accounts of race and racism. We think there are differences between the discourse of scientists and the discourse of lay people but these differences are contingent rather than absolute. Differences depend on the social and political context in which science is typically conducted, the resources scientists can usually mobilize and the different canon to which scientific discourse belongs which gives science its own specific history and discursive antecedents.

In line with his general position on representation and reality, Miles, as we saw in Chapter 1, wishes to distinguish strongly between types of science. Like Althusser (1970; 1977), he wishes to accord a special status to some scientific accounts of race which are seen as trustworthy and as properly in touch with the real, and deny that status to other scientific accounts. We saw in Chapter 1, for example, how Miles (1989) places some scientific studies of race in a historical and political context. He wants to argue that the biological analyses of nineteenth-century science were forms of mistaken ideology sustaining racist analyses. On the other hand, it is clear that he wants to treat modern population genetics as fact and as a resource for defining racism. Similarly, Althusser wishes to distinguish between mystificatory bourgeois science and genuine non-bourgeois science.

How can the ideological and the factual roles Miles attributes to science be reconciled? As Anthony Giddens (1979) has pointed out, the notion of a clear-cut epistemological break between ideology and some, but not other, forms of science is particularly difficult to sustain. Giddens presents his arguments in the context of a critique of Althusser but the points apply equally to the approach to racism Miles develops.

Giddens argues that the imposition of the labels 'scientific' and 'ideological' by virtual decree is not a successful way to avoid what he sees as the crucial problem of relativism. Althusser (and Miles) wish to guarantee the privileged status of Marxism through aligning politics to science. Additionally, Miles wants to privilege those areas of biological and psychological investigation which support his case. However, Miles fails to offer any convincing criteria by which we could decide that X theory of population genetics was an expression of ideology while Y theory of population genetics was part of a non-bourgeois scientific practice, accurately capturing the reality of social relations and social interests. Without these criteria, the splitting of science from ideology becomes, according to Giddens, a matter of dogmatic assertion open to claim and counter-claim.

Unlike Giddens, we do not see so many dangers in relativism, and the assertion of claim and counter-claim seems to us one of the most usual modes through which science is conducted. However, we agree that strong distinctions between ideological science and non-ideological science seem doomed to failure. We prefer to see social science in general, and indeed the biological and natural sciences also, as fields of discursive struggle. Part of the struggle concerns what is to be accepted as 'factual' and part concerns the interpretation of these 'facts'. The rules and forms of this struggle differ from lay discourse but in both cases plausibility has to be fought for and actively established.

The sociology and history of science (see Bloor, 1976; Collins, 1981; Gilbert and Mulkay, 1984; Latour, 1987) demonstrate that what is counted as true and false changes regularly, suggesting that it would be ill advised to take any current view as definitive and timeless. This history also indicates how 'the facts', almost irrespective of their content, have been regularly mobilized to bolster the causes of racism and sexism. It seems sensible to leave open the possibility of examining both the social construction of error and the construction of what is currently accepted as true. We need to be very wary of treating any possibly relevant scientific finding or theory as a criterion for judging what is, or is not, a racist claim or argument. That scientific view may change, and will itself be a product of complex social processes. It would also result in the absurd situation that the same speaker's utterance might on one day be deemed racist, but on another, after some prestigious scientific journal has rolled off the presses, become quite acceptable and legitimate.

What, then, are the differences we see between lay discourse and our own and other social scientists' analyses? As is probably obvious, we assume that the social scientist's account of events (including our own) is equally a discursive construction. We see ourselves as in the business of developing representations, theories and concepts which account for and make sense of other people's representations. Whether you place a representation within the realm of science or within the realm of the everyday seems to us a matter of convention emerging around particular institutions.

As we noted, however, these conventions and differing institutional locations are the source of some important contingent differences between lay and scientific discourse. It makes sense here to talk about the 'politics of representation' (Hall, 1988d). The two can be distinguished in terms of the apparatus and institutions or in terms of the 'machinery' of representation in which they are located. Social scientists, for instance, sometimes have the leisure for refinement of terms, can sometimes draw on a particular specialized discursive history, frequently utilize different conventions for debate, and sometimes have additional resources for research.

Our accounts of others' discourse need not, although they often do, supply practical rhetorical solutions for pressing problems of categorization and self-presentation in the everyday. Scientists' accounts are sometimes, although not always, less obviously supportive of ideological practices. In our case and in the case of most social scientific studies of racism they are also designed to be critical of those ideological practices. In this weak way they could be described as potentially part of a different social apparatus, involved in a different discursive fray, and as part of a discursive practice potentially geared to different ends.

Truth and anti-racist practice

One of the main difficulties with what we are calling representational analyses of racist discourse – the analyses found in some accounts of ideology and in most of social cognition research – is that what is assumed to be 'true' becomes in some sense non-social, beyond investigation, while falsity or error become open to study and are seen as quintessentially social phenomena. As in social psychology, social influences are often only brought in when some negative action, or some piece of error or 'misrepresentation' needs to be explained.

We wish to propose a different kind of study where the way claims are made out as factual becomes a topic of investigation. Instead of following the logic of Miles and Althusser's positions and treating as the crucial question the truth of certain facts, we can ask how these facts are constructed as facts and the consequences these particular constructions might accrue (Edwards and Potter, 1992; Potter and Edwards, 1990). We agree, in other words, and this point will be developed in more detail later in this chapter, with Foucault's broad argument that one way to undermine a 'truth' is not to counterpose it with another 'truth' but to examine the discursive process by which true and false statements become distinguished.

truth isn't outside power, or lacking in power: contrary to a myth whose history and functions would repay further study, truth isn't the reward of free spirits, the child of protracted solitude, nor the privilege of those who have succeeded in liberating themselves. Truth is a thing of this world: it is produced by multiple forms of constraint. And it induces regular effects of power. (Foucault, 1980, p. 131)

It may seem to many that if we abandon a view of discourse as merely faithfully reflecting or failing to reflect reality, we are also abandoning some of the best weapons of anti-racist practice. The contrasting of racist claims with 'the real facts' has been and will probably continue to be extremely important in establishing the moral and scientific authority of anti-racism. The argument that a claim is unscientific has become a powerful form of rhetoric in most cultures; but in our view it is simply that: a powerful rhetorical device.

A correspondence approach to racist discourse which examines the truth or falsity of racist claims should not be seen as an automatic guarantee of effective anti-racist practice. Social psychology, in particular, is littered with accounts of this kind; accounts of prejudice, for example, which, if anything, have often undermined anti-racist practice with their under-developed concepts of the social nature of the 'real'. Anti-racist practice, in our view, is distinguished by its politics and values not by its epistemology. The argument that 'truth' needs to be created as well as 'discovered', and our stress on the active and 'interested' nature of discourse and scientific description, does not absolve the social and biological scientist from ethical and political commitments. This emphasis, in our view, has the reverse effect. It should intensify and clarify the demand for these things.

The refusal to privilege some types of account on epistemological grounds – relativism, as it is often called – should not be seen as a morally or politically vacuous stance, or as rhetorically ineffective. There is still the imperative to establish the claims of some versions over others. This struggle is reinforced by the knowledge that racist discourse is not ephemeral but powerful in constituting social formations in ways which are oppressive for certain social groups. We do not, therefore, see any contradiction between a view of discourse as constitutive and a view of discourse as ideological – where the commitment to studying ideology is also a commitment to the critique of some positions, some of the ways in which power is exercised and some forms of argumentative practice.

So far we have focused on rather general theoretical claims; but we also want to suggest that a constitutive view of discourse is a pragmatic choice which frees up new productive topics of analysis and allows new approaches to old topics. We turn now to this claim – looking first at what is entailed by a shift from ideology to ideological practice, then at the construction of social groups and the construction of subjectivities and finally at the relationship between power and discourse.

From ideology to ideological practice

One of the dangers with a focus on representation and reality and on truth and falsity, in our view, is that it can sometimes lead to a neglect of the actuality of ideological practice and to an often obsessive concern with defining the content of racism in an *a priori* fashion. Traces of these tendencies can be seen both in the work of Robert Miles and in research on the authoritarian personality.

Miles (1982; 1989), for example, argues that if social scientists are to use the concept of racism then they must have a clear specification of its analytic content. Much of his own theoretical work is thus advanced through considerations of the appropriate criteria for racism and he criticizes other social scientists such as Hall (1978; 1980), Fanon (1967) and the Centre for Contemporary Cultural Studies (CCCS, 1982) for their apparent evasiveness on this front. Authoritarian personality work follows a similar procedure whereby the ideology in question is defined in advance and then subjects are studied for signs of these beliefs.

The crucial role Miles gives to definition follows logically from his framing of ideology as false and distorted knowledge. The designations 'true' and 'false' necessarily focus attention on the *content* of knowledge, on the propositions, claims and evaluations contained within a system of thought. To label something false, it is necessary to identify the claims which deserve this label. As we saw in Chapter 1, Miles wants to define racism as an ideology containing certain (false) doctrines. Analysis thereafter becomes a process of comparison. If a piece of discourse also contains doctrines X, Y and Z, then it can be labelled racist.

It seems only good practice to work in this way and begin analysis with a clear description and account of one's theoretical concepts. Why, then, do we want to resist this emphasis on propositions, this stress on the content of ideology and the prior definitive specification of racism? An example from our own studies might make our objections clearer. When we first approached the analysis of our interviews with Pākehā New Zealanders we looked for evidence of racism following the kind of definition Miles and others offer. We looked, that is, for arguments which gave significance to phenotypical and/or genetic characteristics, which placed groups in a hier-archy and which linked this hierarchy and the phenotypical division to the allocation of resources.

We found many examples of this kind of reasoning and the incidence increased as we looked at parliamentary records from ten, twenty and thirty years previously. It was also apparent that the exploitative treatment of Māori people was justified through many other forms of discourse. Yet these other types of arguments could not easily be recognized as racist in terms of the criteria Miles offers. Sometimes Pākehā New Zealanders explicitly disavowed any differential valuing of characteristics attributed to Pākehā and Māori people; sometimes they claimed that any differences were purely social in origin; and sometimes supposed Pākehā characteristics were seen as strongly negative compared to the positive nature of Māori groups. But, all the same, the general rhetorical effect in these cases could be read as protecting Pākehā interests.

The force of the points made by the CCCS against prior definitions of racism became clear in an immediately practical way. We began to sympathize with definitional slipperiness. According to Miles, the CCCS sees racism as 'contradictory and constantly undergoing transformation' (Miles, 1989, p. 64) and 'warns against "extrapolating a common and universal structure to racism, which remains essentially the same, outside of its specific historical location" ' (Hall, 1980, cited in Miles, 1989, p. 65). This focus on variability meshes with the changing patterns of racism we could detect in the discourse of Pākehā New Zealand and which others have noted in British political discourse (Barker, 1981; Reeves, 1983).

If racism is not to be defined in terms of its distinctive content, as a particular knowledge system, then how do we recognize it? Miles argues that the CCCS fail to provide any criteria for identifying the characteristics historically specific racisms have in common. As a consequence, he suggests, we have no way of distinguishing racism from other ideologies such as sexism or nationalism.

It is indeed difficult to separate racism from nationalist and sexist discourse since they are so often intertwined. Miles, too, finds this tricky. His own definition of racism (see p. 16, Chapter 1) does not solve the problem and could be applied equally well to some sexist claims as to some racist claims. Sexist claims similarly frequently work on the basis of phenotypical divisions, create group hierarchies and allocate resources on that basis. None the less, it is possible to hold a distinctive conception of racism – not as an intrinsic property of certain forms of discourse – but as one effect of discursive practice and other social practices. Racist discourse, in our view, should be seen as discourse (of whatever content) which has the effect of establishing, sustaining and reinforcing oppressive power relations between those defined, in the New Zealand case, as Māori and those defined as Pākehā. As such, its identification and analysis can be particularly subtle – such consequences are rarely spelled out or treated as explicit goals.

We want to endorse, therefore, a shift from the study of ideology *per se* to the study of ideological practice and ideological outcomes. Racist discourse is discourse which has the effect of categorizing, allocating and discriminating between certain groups and, in the context of New Zealand, it is discourse which justifies, sustains and legitimates those practices which maintain the power and dominance of Pākehā New Zealanders.

It is very important in our view that the multireferential nature of arguments and interpretative resources be acknowledged. Some lines of argument (egalitarianism, for instance) can be used to justify the exclusion of black groups from some resources and can also be used to oppose racist practices. Arguments can be mobilized in many directions and the analyst needs to be able to follow these paths where they lead rather than decide in advance that some routes are closed. It is for this reason that we place our over-riding stress on the study of discourse in action rather than language as an abstract system (Potter *et al.*, 1990).

We acknowledge that there are some interpretative resources which will constitute social action in racist ways on nearly every occasion they are deployed. However, to focus on these is to ignore the other, sometimes more flexible, resources which characterize a good deal of 'modern racism'. It also ignores the perhaps rare occasions in which biological essentialism, for example, has been successfully mobilized for anti-racism or anti-sexism, and those much more frequent occasions where successful anti-racist practice has relied strongly upon common-sense phenotypical characterizations without deconstructing these first.

The first point we wish to establish, therefore, is that strong distinctions between true and false representation, although productive in some respects, also systematically exclude some forms of very useful work. We take Miles's point that careful theoretical and analytical work is required in studies of racism; but this intellectual labour should take place, in our view, around the conceptualization of the categories for analysis, *not* around the objects of that analysis. Conceptual work should focus on the method and theory for analyzing ideology and social action; it should not try to specify the propositional claims of ideology in advance. The specification of these claims makes sense if ideology is defined as false representation, but it seems to us to be largely wasted effort and indeed, given the pace at which racism is currently changing, leads to a theory and method which would need constant revising.

A refocus in studies of racist discourse away from questions of correspondence does not simply increase our scope as social scientists, it is important, too, for anti-racism. Attempts to define the content of racism on an *a priori* and global basis can be positively dangerous, and can sometimes have an ideological and rhetorical effect counter to that intended. Miles (1982) has claimed that some social scientists reinforce racism through their continued use of the ideological categories 'race' and 'racial'. Yet it is also clear how contemporary politicians, partly in response to the successful academic and popular casting of certain propositions as racist, become skilled at what Frank Reeves (1983) has described as 'sanitary coding' and the 'disguise' of racism; that is, precisely the operation of racist discourse without the category race.

Even relatively blatant fascist propaganda and blatant advocates of racism (such as Le Pen in France) have learnt to modify their discourse so that on some occasions racism can occur without biological categorization and the more familiar paraphernalia of 'advanced' and 'primitive', 'negative' and 'positive', 'superior' and 'inferior' distinctions. Given this flexibility of the enemy, and the way debates move on, it seems sensible not to commit oneself to one exclusive characterization of racist claims. There is a danger of being silenced when racist discourse continues to oppress but no longer meets the main characteristics of social scientific definitions of racism.

Constructing social groups

Hall (1988a) argues that one of Gramsci's major contributions to the development of Marxist theory was to point to the way in which hegemony, and the overthrow of hegemony, depends on various 'wars of position' or 'wars of manoeuvre'. Central to these battles is the active construction of alliances and the definition of groups and forms of solidarity through discursive and other practices. Some constructions of class and other social and economic relations are not, Hall argues, automatically self-evident through their 'truth', they have to be actively made salient and brought into 'truth'.

One major contribution discourse studies should be able to make in the area of racism is the analysis of these kinds of constructions around groupings such as race, culture and nation as well as class and gender, and we shall attempt an analysis of this kind for groupings in New Zealand in Chapter 5. Yet this kind of analysis is effectively blocked by the prescriptions of the approaches we reviewed in previous chapters. Miles, for example, is interested in the construction of race, but places class relations or groupings based on production relations within the domain of truth and the real and thus beyond certain kinds of study.

Social cognition research is not generally interested in these kinds of questions but even if they were thought relevant, it is quite difficult to see how they might be handled. As we saw, there is considerable ambiguity here. Social categories in social cognition research are seen as cognitive productions and cognitive constructions but these constructions seem to be based on a real array of similarities and differences which sum up human physical and natural differences. There is certainly no sense in this work of social groups and categories as social, historical, political and economic as well as cognitive productions.

The position social identity theory takes is more complex and we will return to that shortly. First we wish to underline the importance of these issues through examining Paul Gilroy's (1982; 1987) critique of Miles's sociology of racism. Gilroy focuses on the class reductionism evident in Miles's theory and vividly picks out the implications for the strategies of black groups in Britain. He points to the ways in which Miles's theoretical and empirical analyses come to neglect the actuality of black political organization. Gilroy traces this absence to the general lack of interest Miles displays in the methods through which black groups come to recognize and describe themselves and come to act through these self-characterizations.

To be consistent with his characterization of race as a mistaken and purely ideological category, Miles is forced to castigate black activists who organize around common experiences of race and racism. This kind of political activity, in his view, mistakes ideological relations for real relations and thus must be counterposed by collective action on the basis of class or production relations. Gilroy notes how Miles is constantly required to place theory above practice, slighting the variable meanings and uses of race in practical politics and everyday resistance, and sticking rigidly instead to theoretical definitions of correct practice.

Gilroy argues that it is no accident, mistake or mere irrelevance that black groups in the United Kingdom have organized their resistance to racism on the grounds of the common experience of race rather than any common class position. He agrees with Miles that this may not make genetic or biological sense in terms of contemporary science but points out that racial methods of self-description cannot easily be brushed aside as 'false constructions' or delusions and indeed should not be dismissed in this way.

The dispute becomes sharpest over the appropriate political strategies for anti-racism. Miles locates the main source of change within the economic sphere and in the response of the working class to capitalism. Racism, he seems to be saying, has some autonomy as an ideology but its effects become particularly pernicious when tied to the development of capitalist social relations. Furthermore, racism is simply perpetrated and continued if anti-racist groups persist in using the false terminology of ideology: understanding themselves and others through the concepts of 'race'.

Effective anti-racist strategy, Miles suggests, comes through a struggle to transform the production relations which organize both the black and white working class. His stress on the primary and real (non-ideological) nature of class relations leads Miles to question the homogeneity of black groups. A Māori shop-keeper, he might argue, for instance, has a very different set of economic interests from a Māori factory worker. It makes little sense, in this economic context, to develop a pan-Māori anti-racist movement, whereas it must make sense for Pākehā and Māori members of the working class to join together. Class action of this kind would in some way resolve the problem of racism.

Gilroy would agree that capitalist relations of production intensify racism and particularly disadvantage black groups, but he has a more complex and pragmatic perspective on anti-racist practice. Gilroy suggests that cultural forms have more weight than Miles allows. Consequently, anti-racist strategy must take into account the forms of the autonomous organization of black groups. It is important to work with and to study the way groups define themselves. The experience of racism can produce a cohesive, effective and even a powerful platform as Māori people, in the New Zealand case, recognize some crucial joint interests, despite their different positions in an economic hierarchy.

Gilroy's point is that it is not useful either politically or within social science to reduce race relations to class relations. For Gilroy, talk of race and races sometimes works as an ideology, and sometimes works as a counter-ideology, or as a form of resistance. Miles, in his view, pays some attention, but not enough, to the flexibility and varying manifestations of cultural and political forms, and thus does not give enough credit to the openness and independent effects of realms of meaning.

Does social identity theory cope any better with this kind of argument and with the actual constructive practice of black groups and those white groups in opposition? This theory, unlike most social cognition research, does assume that the boundaries and attributes of social groups are historically and socially constructed. Recent social identity work (e.g. Haslam, 1990; Turner, 1991) argues, too, that the object of study should be the 'judgemental field', where the identity of the perceiver, the character of the perceived and the frame of comparison are seen as continually interacting and continually connected. In these recent accounts social identity theory is presented as an explanation of how group members are likely to respond to a complex and changing social and material reality, forming judgements on the basis of the comparative interplay of self/other and frame of reference.

This emphasis seems to mesh with the ambitions of discourse analysis in the sense that we too wish to study how categories become constructed in different social contexts and how the method of construction creates a subjectivity for oneself and for those defined as Other. Yet social identity accounts still understand this process in largely perceptual terms. The topic is the identity of the perceiver and the (real) character of the perceived. The frame of reference which unites these seems to be understood in mainly perceptual and cognitive terms. The consequence, as we noted in Chapter 2, is an impoverished account which seems to owe more to the vagaries of what is possible in laboratories than the actual flexible and discursive character of social interaction in the rest of social life.

Further, social identity theory displays a strong tendency simply to take social groups as givens in practice and to treat them as unexamined terms – as static features of a pre-defined macro-sociological landscape understood in a structuralist-functionalist manner. This tendency reflects a desire to work with a notion of a relatively rigid division of labour among the social sciences, and with what seems to be a 'building block' understanding of knowledge accumulation (e.g. Turner and Giles, 1981). The realm of the social is thought to belong to the sociologist, the economist and the political scientist; it is not for a social psychologist to cross the lines of demarcation. The task of the social psychologist is seen as explicating the relations between the individual and the social, and once that knowledge is complete it can be inserted as a building block into the edifice of the social and biological sciences.

The problem here is that we cannot just assume that the nature of the social landscape is the problem of some other social science discipline. There certainly has to be some division of labour. We are not proposing, for example, to discuss in our empirical work on New Zealand, the details or even the broad outline of the macro- or even micro-economic situations; but we do wish to suggest that the *discursive* process through which social groups are constructed and made real should be seen as a crucial social psychological topic. It should be central to social psychological analyses of racism precisely because the process of negotiation, of subtle positioning, of active constitution of group characteristics in changing social circumstances implicates psychological process and the construction of subjectivity. The domain, that is, social identity theory wishes to describe as the 'individual'.

Constructing subjectivities

One of the key planks in social identity theory is the assumption, noted in Chapter 2, that 'psychological processes reside only in individuals' (Turner, 1987a, p. 4). This assumption makes perfect sense if strong distinctions are maintained between the 'individual' and the 'social', and if perceiving, judging, evaluating and the planning of actions are assumed to be entirely mental operations – events located solely in individual minds. The individual comes to be seen as a somewhat detached and self-contained entity, and the social becomes defined as an *external* landscape, a structure of groups and group divisions outside the individual, which need to be incorporated into subjectivity in some way.

We wish to take an alternative view of psychological process and subjectivity in our work on racist discourse, one which sees the psychological field as constituted through the social domain of discourse (Edwards and Potter, 1992). As a first step, we want to suggest that the very notion of the 'individual' displayed in social identity theory, is itself a discursive (cultural, social and historical) construction. As the history of racism shows, what it means to be an individual, indeed what it means to be human, is understood through cultural and social practice.

As various anthropologists, cultural and social psychologists (e.g. Geertz, 1984; Harré, 1983; Shweder and Bourne, 1984) have argued, the modern idea of individuality, the idea which social identity seems to take as a scientific verity, is a product of a series of complex social and economic changes in Western societies. This conception of individuality can thus be contrasted with the sometimes very different accounts of subjectivity and personhood found in other cultures subjected to different histories and social organizations.

Social psychology, in theorizing human nature, tends to build on, discover and reflect the common sense of Western culture. The specific assumptions concerning the nature of 'individuality' operating here have been summarized by Paul Heelas.

> An Englishman [*sic*] assumes, without undue reflection, that he is a unique individual, complete with a mind and an unconscious realm, and perhaps a soul or spirit, which are distinct from his physical body. Our indigeneous psychology focuses on the inner, private, self: on emotions, states of consciousness, will, memories, the soul (if one is a Christian) and so forth. It also focuses on the self as agency. We regard ourselves as being capable of acting on the world, exercising our will power, and we feel that we have the ability to alter many of our psychological attributes (as when we 'make up our minds to be calm'). A number of expressions, in fact, focus on the powers of the self with respect to itself – e.g 'self-determination', 'self-possession', 'self-respect' and 'self-assurance'. (Heelas, 1981, p. 4)

The notion of personal identity found in social identity theory and presented as the contrast to group identity is clearly strongly influenced by this conception of human nature. Individuals acting 'interpersonally', as individuals, are assumed to be mainly concerned with personal uniqueness. Actions in this sphere of identity are assumed to be controlled by a more or less integrated system of personality characteristics and temperamental traits. This philosophy of the individual owes an obvious debt to the individualism apparent in liberal political traditions of thought (Hall, 1986; Smart, 1983).

Social identity theorists could argue that in defining personal identity in this fashion, they are simply responding to the way in which personal identity and individuality have already been socially constructed. When personal identity is salient to individuals they act out their (socially constructed) conception of individuality. It is the case that their theory could be seen as responsive to social construction in this sense but liberal and modern Western individualism is also implicated in the very substance of social identity theory, in the way the theory defines its object of study as the 'individual' and the 'social' and the way in which psychological processes in general are understood.

The argument for the discursive constitution of subjectivity is more extensive, however, than an argument about the sources of contemporary notions of personhood. We also want to note the ways in which the kinds of 'cognitive processes' at the centre of social cognition research and social identity theory have to be seen as linguistic achievements: for example, however much categorization is considered a cognitive event, it is also an event established in discourse and represents a type of discursive action (Edwards, 1991).

Take, for instance, this use of categories in another extract from our interviews with Pākehā New Zealanders. In this extract someone we have called Joan Wood gives her response to recent attempts in New Zealand to establish a 'renaissance' of Māori culture.

> Wood: I think we'll end up having Māori wars if they carry on the way they are. I mean no it'll be a Pākehā war (yes). Um (.) they're making New Zealand a racist country. Um but you know you usually feel, think, that racism is um (.) putting the, putting the darker people down but really

they're doing it the other way around, I feel. Um, everything seems to be to help the Māori people, um, you know. I think at the moment sort of the Europeans sort of they're just sort of watching and putting up with it, but they'll only go so far. Um you know we've got Māori friends out here, uh who we have into the house, you know they're friends, um but when things happen when they suddenly say oh they're going to make Māori language compulsory, um it is, it's antagonizing and the Māori friends that we've got, they don't agree with it. OK you've got your extremists there too, the ones who feel, you know, that everyone should learn it but um I think the average Māori sort of perhaps is worried too.

There are a number of categories introduced in this strongly racist account of recent events: 'average Māoris', 'Māoris who are friends', 'Māoris who can be invited into the house', 'Europeans', 'the Māori people', 'extremists'. This pattern of categorization no doubt depends on some 'cognitive events', just as speech depends on a physiology of mouth movements and on brain chemistry. Yet, clearly, the meaning of these categories, their function and thus their social and psychological significance is established within their discursive context. Indeed, the meaning and the definition of these categories will change as the discursive context changes.

The category 'Māori friends', for example, accomplishes a substantial amount of rhetorical work in this extract. It is used to establish Wood's own 'credentials' – she is not a bigot, she does have Māori friends, and she does invite Māoris into the house – and also the authenticity of her argument – her view must be right if some Māoris are equally convinced. In other discursive contexts the entire connotation and meaning of this categorization might well change. 'Māori friends' or 'average Māoris' in some other discourse may become very different entities as they become placed within alternative systems of contrasts, opposites and differentiations.

It may be that Joan Wood carries around in her head a relatively fixed set of cognitive schema which include categories such as 'average Māori'. We could see her discourse here as the outcome of the triggering of that category system. We could assume that the categories and system of contrasts are established mentally as a result of a perceptual process and then merely expressed discursively, in words. Instead of this view, we think it is more useful to see categories as actively constructed in discourse for rhetorical ends. As those ends change so too does the construction of groups.

Categorization and similar cognitive events can be seen as entirely mental events but they are also, very obviously, forms of social action established through discourse. The process of categorization, and thus the psychology of categorization, reside, not just in the mind, but, we would suggest, within discourse as part of a collective domain of negotiation, debate, argumentative and ideological struggle.

The same argument extends to other areas of subjectivity – motives, personality, intentions. Identity – who one is and what one is like – is established through discursive acts. Identity in talk is a construction, an achievement and an accomplishment; and, of course, this construction and accomplishment is both private and public. Subjectivity is organized discursively as a public act of self-presentation, but introspection, private accounting for oneself and self-description, are no less discursive. In this sense discourse straddles the boundaries usually erected between the objects of internal worlds and the objects of external worlds. Identity, argues Hall, 'is formed at the unstable point where the "unspeakable" stories of subjectivity meet the narratives of history, of a culture' (1988c, p. 44). Internal stories and private accounts are often 'unspeakable' but they are none the less discursive. Indeed, the very distinction between public and private is a discursive construction which we would not want to take at face value – much 'private' material may be so designated because of issues of etiquette and accountability rather than because it exists in an epistemologically sealed realm (Coulter, 1991; Edwards and Potter, 1992).

We do not want to suggest that discourse simply plays a facilitative role here, as one further site in which a pre-constituted identity is expressed. We want to argue that the identity and forms of subjectivity which become instantiated in discourse at any given moment should be seen as a sedimentation of past discursive practices. A sense of identity and subjectivity is constructed from the interpretative resources – the stories and narratives of identity – which are available, in circulation, in our culture. This subjectivity is also constrained, of course, by other social practices. Some accounts of self are more readily available to some than others.

An important aspect, therefore, of the study of racist discourse is the examination of self and other constructions. Edward Said (1978), in his investigations of the discourses of Orientalism, argues that one of the means through which knowledge of the Oriental was established in the West was through the dramatic figures (and emblematic objects) which came to structure the discursive field of Orientalism. In the case of New Zealand, the construction of the Other (Māori people) has, in many respects, been less formalized; but there, too, there are the theatrical figures of the 'good Māori', the 'extremist', the 'cannibal', 'the gentlemanly Māori' and so on. There are also the 'subject positions' of Pākehā New Zealanders through which racism becomes spoken – there is the 'tolerant individual', 'the realist who faces up to hard truths', the 'disinterested purveyor of facts' and the 'unashamed bigot'.

One of the main difficulties with the authoritarian personality analysis and other approaches which link racism to individual differences is that the range of subject positions connected to racism becomes limited to one or two 'types' which become fixed enduringly to individuals. We are not suggesting that there are no 'individual differences' or that there is no continuity to identity. Identity is not formed from scratch every time a person speaks. Continuity comes from what we described as the sedimentation of discursive practice over time. Identity can only be constructed from those narratives which are available, and discursive practice, as we noted, intertwines with other social practices. Those enmeshed in one set of social relations will thus construct identities from rather different resources than those enmeshed very differently.

The picture of identity emerging here, however, still places greater emphasis on fluidity, flexibility and variability than found in authoritarian personality and similar accounts. Given the relative mobility of ideology, it seems sensible not to conclude that one character structure, established early in the life of the subject, is productive of racism. What was most evident in our empirical investigations (see Chapter 8) was the way in which some of the 'opposites' of authoritarianism – 'tolerance' and the refutation of feelings of prejudice – have come to form part of the standard identity work found in racist discourse.

Discursive power

One of the main advantages of reconceptualizing subjectivity and identity in the manner we have just outlined is that some connections between power and subjectivity become opened up in a new way. It becomes possible to talk, for example, of 'subjectification', as a double process whereby people become subjected and regulated through the kinds of identities assumed in discourse. That is not all there is, of course, to power; but this dimension is one which could be central to social psychological investigations of racism.

As a way into these questions, this section examines the conceptions of power and social process found in Foucault's work. The account we will present relies mainly on those sources which have focused on the tensions between Marxist and Foucaultian analyses of social relations (e.g. Beechy and Donald, 1985; Clegg, 1989; Hall, 1988a; Minson, 1986; Poster, 1984; Said, 1984; Shapiro, 1988; Young, 1990); but we will also draw on the excellent, more general, commentary on Foucault's theory and methods provided by Dreyfus and Rabinow (1982). Our discussion will range quite widely across Foucault's arguments – looking not just at power and subjectification but also, to establish our own position further, at his views on history and the role of social analysis.

Foucault is probably best seen as a historian of science, although this designation also proves too narrow. His main themes concern what he calls the 'dubious sciences' – the human sciences – specifically psychiatry, medicine and criminology. His general procedure within this domain is to take a clump or complex of knowledge and related institutional practices and ask about the 'grid of intelligibility' which makes this complex possible (Dreyfus and Rabinow, 1982, p. 121). What are the statements here, how are they placed in relation to each other, what do they order and what objects and subjects emerge as a consequence? How, in other words, is knowledge constituted and what else is created in the process?

If this was Foucault's only interest then his work would be of minor significance for the concerns of this book. But Foucault's attempts to explicate the discursive formations of the human sciences also led him to question the process of 'doing history', to question the objects of social scientific explanation and to develop new analyses of power and its mode of operation. It is on these fronts that his work engages with Marxism, with particular relevance for investigations of ideology.

Very crudely, the contrast between Marxist and Foucaultian perspectives concerns whether one prefers versions of history which try to specify who did what to whom and why, or versions which are more concerned with how the 'what', 'whom' and 'why' are constituted. It is a matter, too, of locating power with specific agents, structures and social classes or dispersing power throughout social formations. It also involves whether one defines powerful discourse through its authors (so that powerful words are simply the words of the powerful), or whether the power of discourse becomes evaluated through the kinds of authors or subjects it creates.

To take the question of historical accounting first. Marxist historical narratives are frequently described as essentialist narratives, compared, that is, to Foucault's anti-essentialist accounts. What this means is that, from a Marxist perspective, history comes to involve tracking down origins and real causes. It involves telling, if not a teleological account, certainly a story with a unifying theme. This is typically a story of power struggles between groups and the resolutions of these struggles. History is the account of social classes in relation to each other, where some stories of the nature of reality are questioned but where other accounts of reality remain to form the truth.

Foucault argues that these themes, and this emphasis on discovering order, are particularly clearly exhibited in the ways in which ideology has been conceived. Ideology, Foucault suggests, always implies the possibility of a non-ideological gaze at history. It assumes that someone somewhere (usually the speaker) can see through the smokescreens of delusion to describe what history is really about. Someone will be able to say who is actually dominant, where the real interests of the subordinate lie, and will be able to definitively fix the lines of power around the fortunes of different groups.

In opposition to this, Foucault sees any knowledge, including historical knowledge, as constituted through discursive formations. It is for this reason that he wishes decisively to abandon ideological accounting. History is always a version. There is no stance or platform 'outside' discourse, or, in Foucault's later work, power/knowledge. He does not think it is possible, therefore, to take the privileged vantage point the concept of ideology seems to imply. Further, he wants to substitute for this kind of historical narrative a study of vantage points in themselves. The result is what Foucault calls archaeological or, later, genealogical studies which look at how the conditions for knowledge, including historical knowledge, become produced.

As many have pointed out, Foucault's stance here is best seen as strongly anti-hermeneutic (e.g. Shapiro, 1988). The task of the hermeneuticist being to discover from fragments and remaining parts the nature of the whole which generated these relics. Hermeneutics searches for the hidden and obscured meaning and Marxist accounts of ideology are similarly concerned to detect through the rubble and remainder of history the real shape of the story. In contrast, Foucault wants to dismiss the possibility of this kind of revelation.

The more appropriate task, from his point of view, is to suspend judgement about real meanings and examine instead the knowledge formations which lead to meaning being framed in this way. As we noted earlier, this leads to a distinctive position on truth. Foucault's concern is with how truth (powerful knowledge) is brought into being. He wants to study how truth is formed, not discover truth.

As Dreyfus and Rabinow have pointed out, Foucault's own histories become as a consequence of his stance stories of 'strategies without strategists'. Since Foucault is opposed to finding some principle which would give direction and purpose to history, he must also reject the intentionality or functionality which frequently structures Marxist accounts. As we saw, Marxist accounts of the history of New Zealand try to detect the ways in which particular discourse and ideologies serve the interests of some Pākehā New Zealanders. It is not supposed that Pākehā New Zealanders deliberately act in concert but we can certainly investigate how Pākehā discourse legitimates their exploitation of Māori people and is designed to that end. We can see history as having, from this perspective, a *direction of domination*, where that direction is intimately linked to the fortunes and interests of a certain group.

Foucault is interested in studying patterns of domination and talks of the organized effects of power, but, to specify strategists and their directions, is, in his view, to posit some supra-mentality, or some group, outside the ensemble of practices or discursive formations. It is to discover, after all, an essence and a line to history. Foucault's approach is thus nihilist in the sense that he focuses not on function, purpose and intention but simply on the shape of 'meticulous rituals of power'.

> The genealogist sees that the battle of domination is not simply the relationship of rulers and ruled, dominators and dominated. . . . These meticulous rituals of power are not the creation of subjects, nor simply a set of relationships; nor are they easily located in specific places; nor is there an easily identifiable historical development that lies behind their emergence. . . . History is not the progress of universal reason. It is the play of rituals of power, humanity advancing from one domination to another. (Dreyfus and Rabinow, 1982, p. 110)

One important consequence of this epistemological position is that social science, and specifically sociological analysis, loses its familiar landscape and demography. If we are no longer to talk of groups and the power they wield, and if we can no longer define history as the story of who did what to whom and why, then what is there to say? Foucault replaces conventional terms of analysis (the state, classes, groups, social actors, structures and agents) with the study of power *per se*. In effect, he reverses the usual sequence where the social scientist first identifies the main interest groups and looks at how these exert pressure on others. Foucault makes power the prior term and sees how agents, objects and subjects are the effect of various rituals.

More specifically, Foucault places centre stage, as the new object of analysis, discursive formations in his earlier work and, later, ensembles of practices or fields of force relations. The discursive formation or the apparatus of practices Foucault studies is impersonal; meaning that it is not seen as the property of one or other social group. Discourses and practices are not representative of particular groups or their interests, but are seen as having a dynamic and momentum of their own, through their principle of organization. It is this dynamic and organization which becomes the target of study.

So far our account of Foucault's work has been largely negative, structured by the positions he opposes. To see why there is some benefit to these epistemological moves it is necessary to outline the scope and range of Foucault's alternative conceptions of power; to see what insights emerge when fields of force relations become the explanandum. The best procedure here, however, is to continue (for the moment, at least) describing the accounts Foucault rejects.

Foucault develops his theses on power through a contrast with what he describes as sovereign, juridical or repressive conceptions of power (Clegg, 1989; Minson, 1986). It is his identification and rejection of these conceptions which is the most distinctive aspect of his contribution. Sovereign conceptions, Foucault argues, assume as an implicit or explicit model the kind of force which rulers or monarchs might be supposed to direct against their subjects. This is a vision of a negative legislative power mainly concerned to prohibit certain unwanted actions. It is also a power exerted in particular epsiodes of domination and which becomes quiescent or disappears when there is nothing 'out of order'.

Sovereign power is not just concerned with prohibition and repression, it is also a conception of power as located and originary. Those who theorize power in this way assume that power is possessed; it is a force exerted by those who have it, those in authority, against those who do not. As Foucault describes it, this is a power which is levied against subjects where there is a deduction in the forces and resources of its object (Minson, 1986). As Minson points out, if power is understood in this frame then the crucial questions become the identity of the dominating force and the legitimacy of its assertion.

Power, too, becomes seen as causal in what Clegg (1989) describes as a conventional A acts on B manner. One set of forces contends against an independent and competing set. This is primarily, also, a power located outside discourse and knowledge where words and ideas become, if not peripheral to the operation of power, conceived as one weapon or mode of expression among several.

In opposition to this account, Foucault proposes an analytic scheme which relies on descriptions such as 'productive', 'positive', 'dispersed', 'permissive', 'continuous', 'anonymous' to replace 'prohibitive', 'negative', 'unitary', 'legislative', 'episodic' and 'originary'.

> It seems to me now that the notion of repression is quite inadequate for capturing what is precisely the productive aspect of power. In defining the effects of power as repression, one adopts a purely juridical conception of such power, one identifies power with a law which says no, power is taken above all as carrying the force of a prohibition. Now I believe that this is a wholly negative, narrow, skeletal conception of power. . . . If power were never anything but repressive, if it never did anything but to say no, do you really think one would be brought to obey it? What makes power hold good, what makes it accepted, is simply that it doesn't weigh on us as a force that says no, but that it traverses and produces things, it induces pleasure, forms knowledge, produces discourse. It needs to be considered as a productive network which runs through the whole social body, much more than a negative instance whose function is repression. (Foucault, 1980, p. 119)

Foucault argues that to grasp the nature of modernity it is necessary to understand the novel consolidations or technologies of power which characterize modern times – specifically, disciplinary power and bio-power. Conceptions of sovereign power are, he suggests, misleading in this context and, worse, productive of those very force relations which they attempt to grasp in thought.

Modern power, in Foucault's view, works through knowledge, not apart from discourse, in some other realm. The human sciences he studies do not simply establish new 'grids of intelligibility'; they are one feature of new forms of regulation and control. Modern rituals of power are in some ways less obvious rituals, less clearly repressive and coercive – in some ways less physical and more mental.

The rituals of recent times centre on self-regulation and on the production of docile bodies – ordered and made productive in institutional settings such as the army, the factory and the prison. Power comes to work through the identification of new categories of people and new methods of assessment and surveillance of populations. These observational procedures are tied to the growth of forms of knowledge in psychiatry, medicine and the social sciences and to the emergence of new administrative procedures organizing the counting, classifying and naming of populations. Power develops through 'normalization', through defining what is usual and habitual and to be expected, as opposed to the deviant and exceptional.

This is a form of power which produces subjects, creates certain kinds of self-knowledge and 'truths' about oneself. One consequence of power is thus the process we referred to earlier – 'subjectification', or becoming subject to particular knowledges of aspects of the self. Power, therefore, is not necessarily repressive in Foucault's view, in the sense of acting against some human essence or resistance; it works in part through constructing what it means to be human in the first place. Power is not just a negative prohibition, but can be recognized when a subject willingly says 'yes' to some mode of behaviour, or sees this mode as particularly expressive of their real identity. Regulation occurs when force from 'outside' works as self-discipline from 'within'. Foucault, as a consequence, is most suspicious of those moments of apparent 'liberation' and 'permissiveness', when subjects feel positively empowered.

In effect, power becomes fragmented in this account, not a unilateral property of certain groups or the state, although it becomes embodied in these places, but dispersed through various social practices, rituals of normality and administrative machines. Power, as a consequence, becomes implicated even in acts of resistance. There can be no simple divisions between homogeneous power for and homogeneous power against. This is so because resistance to some domination frequently occurs within the terrain already set, and through the very agenda which shapes the domination. Foucault argues that to oppose one term with its opposite is often to continue the structuration and discursive practices through which power works.

The object and target of power in Foucault's account cannot thus become the human individual or the social group, as usually understood, since he argues the shape of these is constituted through power/knowledge relations. Foucault is left, as Dreyfus and Rabinow point out, with a much vaguer conception of the object of power, the 'body', human and social, which provides a kind of raw material on which power works. Power comes to be defined as the procedures through which this mute body is shaped into forms of subjectivity, categories of people, types of population, and given voice.

In contrast to Foucault, from many Marxist perspectives power is best understood in 'personal' terms – not just as one social actor against another but as a commodity possessed by certain social groups and exerted over other groups. Just who will be powerful is seen as predictable from production relations and from the intertwining of these with politics. Capitalism, for example, differentially empowers those who own the means of production and disempowers those without these means. Power is in this sense homogeneous, unitary and authored. The actual exercise of power can, however, take several forms. As colonial history indicates, domination can be directly physical, military and coercive; but, consent to domination can also be manufactured in less bloody ways, and this is where ideology becomes important.

If a dominated group can be successfully persuaded of the thesis that its interests correspond with the interests of the powerful, then consent has also occurred, but the blows struck become mental rather than physical. Oppressive social relations can be maintained with an illusion of solidarity and can operate through the mystifying premise that society is working for the benefit of all. Crucially, the powerful can also become persuaded that they are acting in everyone's interests, and thus also become reconciled to the power exercised in their name.

In this view, therefore, ideology and discourse become seen as one weapon among several which some social classes can direct at other social classes who can then be seen as the targets. Power thus has an object and has also gained an agent, although, as Chapter 1 demonstrated, not necessarily a self-conscious and deliberate agent. Power, in this way, tends to be placed largely outside discourse, as something prior to and other than the discursive. Ideological discourse is the means through which power and class interests are expressed. It is, however, secondary to power.

What is also clear is that while some Marxist accounts of power relations conflict with Foucault's emphases, there is much greater overlap with some of the recent developments in Marxist accounts of ideology discussed earlier in this chapter. These accounts are similarly concerned with processes of subjectification. Althusser, for example, in developing a strongly structuralist account of subjectivity, also argued that human subjects are the outcome of ideological processes.

That is, our very sense of being an agent, an 'I', an integrated centre of experience is an effect of the imaginary relations established through ideology. Others, society, the state reflect back to us an image of our coherence and subject status. In becoming 'interpellated' in this way, Althusser suggested, we become regulated as citizens and subjects of law; but, he says, this recognition of ourselves is a misrecognition. People are incoherent subjects who are 'artificially' cohered by ideology. Foucault was Althusser's student, and here we begin to get some sense of a family history of these concepts.

Genealogy and ideology

This review of competing and overlapping social theories and accounts of power has suggested the possibility of a choice. On the one hand, following Foucault, we could see our task as analyzing those ensembles of practices which bring into being the objects (groups, structures, subjects) of contemporary New Zealand, and we could understand power through this lens. Or, in a much more familiar vein, we could discuss the social functions of ideology in our analyses, talking of strategies of domination, of the way the interests of one group – Pākehā New Zealanders – are served by their discursive formulations.

We wish, in fact, to do both; to combine, alternate and intertwine genealogical and ideological modes of analysis. Indeed, from the practical standpoint of doing analysis a sharp contrast between these two modes is hard to sustain. Foucault and the concept of genealogy draw attention to some crucial topics and his emphases mesh broadly with the framework developing throughout this chapter. However, we also agree with the assessments of Foucault's work offered by some Marxist critics (e.g. Clarke, 1991; Hall, 1988a). Too much seems to be lost when the subjects of history are replaced with rituals of power. One kind of essentialism seems to have been replaced by another, but this time the directive force (power) is dislocated to become a type of Hegelian Spirit wandering through time.

Interestingly, Larrain (1979) has made much the same point concerning Althusser's account of ideology as a general mechanism for the production of subjects. Larrain argues that Althusser also constructs a new type of transcendental entity – ideology as the great Subject in which human subjects recognize themselves. In Larrain's view, Althusser substitutes ideology for Hegel's concept of the Spirit moving through history. Historical class ideologies and their constituted human subjects (practical ideologies) become the manifestation of general ideology working its way through time.

To follow Foucault is to rule out certain, sometimes very productive, ways of telling history, but to follow some Marxist accounts is to exclude, as we have tried to demonstrate, certain investigations of class identification and studies of the mobility of discourse. We see, therefore, discourse analysis as necessarily involving a double movement. A satisfactory account of a piece of discursive material must, in our view, move backwards and forwards between what could be described as the 'established' and 'constitutive' aspects of discourse. Our account must examine, as Foucault and others suggest, the specification of reality and the social in discourse – how agents and subjects are formed, how the social world is grouped and categorized, how material interests and the nature of relevant objects are determined. Analysis must look at how power, particularly persuasive and rhetorical power, the power to formulate and be believed, is generated in the process.

We also must examine, however, how a new piece of discourse is established and gains its plausibility in terms of what is already there, already in place. Discourse does take place in history, it feeds off the social landscape, the social groups, the material interests already constituted. In analyzing establishment it is possible to talk of directions of domination, of past campaigns which author present campaigns, of interests which are served, of power which is located and possessed, and to invoke some of the functional apparatus and articulations of practices, so well described in Marxist theory.

Hall (1988a; 1988c) has described this mode of analysis which tries to talk of both the constitution of groups and groups as constitutive, as deconstruction and reconstruction, as a commitment to walking forwards while looking backwards. As he notes, there is a danger of falling into a pit, or at least of stumbling along with a very strange gait; but much, too, can be gained from weaving rather than marching.

4

Analyzing racist discourse

In the last chapter we argued against a number of central features of dominant sociological and social psychological accounts of racism, and particularly with some of their often inexplicit assumptions about the operation of discourse. This chapter has two main tasks: first, it will lay out some of the principal analytic concepts required for the empirical investigation of racist discourse and consider some of the practicalities of such work; second, it will outline a brief account of New Zealand history and social structure to form the backdrop to the specific studies that form the second part of the book.

Before starting on these tasks, however, we wish to consider briefly the context in which the term 'discourse analysis' arises and the particular inflection we adopt. In recent times a range of quite varied styles of research has been developed under the rubric of 'discourse analysis'. The work we have conducted has very little in common with some of these. In particular, there are important theoretical and analytic disagreements with speech-act-orientated studies of conversational coherence (e.g. Coulthard and Montgomery, 1981) and so-called 'discourse processes' work on story grammars and the like (e.g. van Dijk and Kintsch, 1983). The former are wedded to a rather mechanistic notion of turn sequences and the latter to a cognitively reductionist idea of coherence (see Levinson, 1983, for a critique); neither is directed at the sorts of issues that form the focus of our current study.

In contrast, as the previous chapter will have made clear, we have been strongly influenced by developments in 'continental' discourse analysis such as that of Foucault and other post-structuralists, as well as various strands of thinking in the sociology of scientific knowledge. Some of this latter work is specifically discourse-orientated; some not. We have also drawn substantially on work in the ethnomethodology and conversation analysis tradition, which itself is sometimes characterized as part of a broader field of discourse

analysis. These traditions are far from generally compatible – and at times their proponents are openly hostile to one another. However, we have found that if we want to use studies of discourse to develop a genuinely social psychological approach to racism, all three have important arguments and insights to offer.

Given our position on the rhetorical organization of discourse, and scientific discourse more specifically, it seems important to also note the disciplinary context which has structured our investigations. Our own concerns are structured through the academic context of social psychology. Although we frequently attempt to subvert them, we are none the less working within problematics which have stressed fiercely empiricist rationales for research. The context in which our study is situated is thus quite different from post-structuralism. Where that tradition has been 'analytic' (and the term itself is problematic from this perspective), it has focused overwhelmingly on images and texts, often from literature and philosophy. What post-structuralism has not done is address everyday discourse – people's talk and argument – nor has it been concerned with materials which document interaction of one kind or another. In some ways, therefore, our general aim is to pursue post-structuralist questions with the analytic fervour of social psychologists, but in a domain of materials which have been most thoroughly explored by ethnomethodologists and conversation analysts.

Finally, before starting, we should emphasize that it is not possible to do justice to the complicated issues involved in analyzing racist discourse in a single chapter. Our own approach to discourse analysis is described most completely in Potter and Wetherell (1987, Ch. 8); while Potter and Mulkay (1985) specifically address the issue of conceptualizing and analyzing interview materials, Wetherell and Potter (1988; and Potter *et al.*, 1990) address questions about the understanding and identification of discourses or interpretative repertoires, and Potter and Wetherell (forthcoming) focus on methodological issues in the analysis of the detailed rhetorical construction of discourse. In addition, van Dijk (1987; 1991) makes important points about the analysis of specific racist materials, although they are not always entirely congruent with the approach we have taken. Our task here will be to provide a general overview to the analytic approach used and also to highlight those elements which are distinctive to this particular study.

Discourses and interpretative repertoires

The arguments developed in the last chapter were strongly influenced by some of Foucault's claims about the role of discourses in the construction of various realms of objects and subjects. Discourses in this sense and in this tradition are seen as historically evolved, making up an important part of the common sense of a culture as well as providing the structure for the operation of institutions such as human science, education and the law. While endorsing much of the general value of this theoretical account, this definition of discourses raises some important issues about analytic practice that have not always been satisfactorily resolved, particularly by those wishing to import these ideas into psychological contexts.

One of the dangers of this view is that the social practices of discourse use often disappear from sight altogether; and Dreyfus and Rabinow (1982) spend some time documenting Foucault's lack of interest in actual linguistic performance. The study of discourses can thus become something very like the geology of plate tectonics – a patchwork of plates/discourses are understood to be grinding violently together, causing earthquakes and volcanoes, or sometimes sliding silently one underneath the other. Discourses become seen as potent causal agents in their own right, with the processes of interest being the work of one (abstract) discourse on another (abstract) discourse, or the propositions or 'statements' of that discourse working smoothly and automatically to produce objects and subjects (see, for example, Parker, 1992). In contrast to this, we wish to place much more emphasis on discourse as social practice, on the context of use and thus on the act of discursive instantiation.

This emphasis has two closely connected consequences. Firstly, it encourages us to treat as primary what may be called the 'action orientation' (Heritage, 1984) of discourse. The sense of texts or talk is not seen as derived from their abstract meaning or organization but from their situated use. By the same token, the nature of the use to which any text or talk is put is not derivable from the abstract or dictionary meanings of the terms used. Secondly, a focus on discourse as social practice has led us to analyze discourse in terms of its entry into the world of practical affairs: everyday conversation and texts. This means that rather than attempting to derive 'discourses' from some set of materials, and then consider how those discourses work together and against one another in the abstract, the focus is very much on the implementation of those discourses in actual settings.

For these reasons, we have found it preferable to talk about interpretative repertoires rather than discourses *per se* (Gilbert and Mulkay, 1984; Potter and Wetherell, 1987; Wetherell and Potter, 1988). By interpretative repertoire we mean broadly discernible clusters of terms, descriptions and figures of speech often assembled around metaphors or vivid images. In more structuralist language we can talk of these things as systems of signification and as the building blocks used for manufacturing versions of actions, self and social structures in talk. They are some of the resources for making evaluations, constructing factual versions and performing particular actions.

Interpretative repertoires are pre-eminently a way of understanding the *content* of discourse and how that content is organized. Although stylistic and grammatical elements are sometimes closely associated with this organization, our analytic focus is not a linguistic one; it is concerned with language use, what is achieved by that use and the nature of the interpretative resources that allow that achievement.

To develop an example, one important theme in Pākehā discourse, as Chapter 5 will demonstrate, is the notion of 'culture'. In our analysis of this discourse we began with a file of more or less elaborate extracts from texts and interviews where the notion of culture was applied in the context of Māori affairs or politics. Our starting point here was our own general understanding of the concept of culture (of course, not all extracts used the word itself). However, in further readings of this file and as our understanding of the materials we had collected developed more generally, we started to be able to distinguish two distinct constructions of culture.

On the one hand, it appeared that culture could be constructed as *heritage*: traditions, rituals and values passed down from earlier generations. This is something that Pākehā respondents treated as important to preserve, in much the same way that the last few mountain gorillas would be:

> Shell: I'm quite, I'm certainly in favour of a bit of Māoritanga. It is something uniquely New Zealand, and I guess I'm very conservation minded (yes) and in the same way as I don't like seeing a species go out of existence I don't like seeing (yes) a culture and a language (yes) and everything else fade out.

On the other hand, culture could be constructed as *therapy*: Māori people, particularly young Māoris, were seen in this construction as estranged from culture, which they needed to rediscover to become 'whole' again.

> Pinter: . . . it's a culture, you know they're family orientated people and um you know they come to a city and they get stuck in a rented house in some dingy suburb and what chance do they have? (yes) They lose their identity, they lose their will, they lose (Wetherell: their family connections) exactly, they're nothing. And their society's rooted in the land and family and elders, they lose that or they lost it and I think they're getting it back.

If we considered these two sorts of constructions of culture in the abstract it would be easy to see them as fitting snugly together; but typically the two constructions were applied in rather different contexts where they manufactured different objects and subjects and often implied competing kinds of upshot for social policy. The first was often used in general discussions of Māori language while the second was common in discussions of crime among young Māoris or in talk about educational failure. It is not that respondents could not reconcile these two constructions, it is that they were doing different sorts of work with them in their discourse.

Moreover, these culture repertoires have something of the status of a socially accepted cliché. In Billig's (1987; 1991) terms, they act as 'commonplaces', sets of taken-for-granted and commonly used value terms in a culture. Although many alternative constructions to those emphasizing culture are available in our materials, it was very rare to see these culture repertoires explicitly undermined. As such, they provided a basic account-ability: having constructed a version in these terms no more need be said, no further warrant need be given.

One of the advantages of considering constructions like culture-as-heritage as interpretative repertoires is that it suggests that there is an available choreography of interpretative moves – like the moves of an ice dancer, say – from which particular ones can be selected in a way that fits most effectively in the context. This emphasizes both the flexibility of ordinary language use and the way that interpretative resources are organized together in developed ways. It shows the way the tectonic image breaks down in studies that focus on discourse use in practice. It is not the *term* 'discourse' which is a problem – indeed, we ourselves often use it as an alternative to interpretative repertoires – it is the tectonic *assumptions* that have often been brought with it.

It is important to explicate some of the analytic nuances at work with the notion of interpretative repertoire. Although some of the most developed research examples up to the present time come from research on scientific discourse (Gilbert and Mulkay, 1984; McKinlay and Potter, 1987; Mulkay, 1985; Potter, 1984), they are in some ways atypical. The empiricist discourse of science is closely identified with access to, and work within, science as an institution. Indeed, Mulkay (1984) has argued that the nature of the institutional settings of science may be constituted out of this discourse.

The sorts of repertoires we are addressing in the everyday talk of New Zealanders, however, do not have this feature of defining institutional membership. Nor do they have the sorts of specific and formalized socializa-tion procedures associated with science training. The use of culture as heritage or therapy, say, may mark a particular occupational or institutional identity for New Zealanders, but it does not necessarily do so; nor is it part of an explicit and systematic training package. Repertoires of this kind are fluidly drawn on in the course of a wide range of conversational topics. People in lay talk have access to a compendium of different interpretative resources which they blend together to produce a wide variety of different effects.

When we examine the argumentative patterns in ordinary discourse we do not find, therefore, the focus that comes from the requirements of scientific accountability, nor the neat organization which might be expected from a person working from a consistent set of beliefs and attitudes or a single model of the world. Rather, what we see is a fragmentation. Billig calls this the 'kaleidoscope of common sense'; a shifting pattern of resources where *explanans* and *explanandum* (premises and inferences) regularly swap places (Billig, 1992), where shifts are fluidly made between arguments from principle and practice (Litton and Potter, 1985; Wetherell *et al.*, 1987) and where, as we shall see, 'liberal and egalitarian values' are selectively drawn on and reworked, sometimes to racist and authoritarian effect.

There is a final issue that is important to note here, explored first at the end of Chapter 3 in terms of the debate between genealogical and ideological analyses of discourse. In this more specifically analytic setting the debate appears in terms of the status of agency and strategy: are we seeing agents strategically using discourse or are discursive forms playing themselves out through the actions of individuals? Our position here is to some extent to have it both ways. On the one hand, we are working at a level of analysis where we are not concerned with participants' intentions or strategic cogitation – we see it as possible to do perfectly coherent analyses of discourse and its consequences without considering how far actors are in control of what they are doing (Potter and Wetherell, 1987). Moreover, one of the features of post-structuralist argument is to emphasize that subjects are themselves constituted in discourse. On the other hand, it is often useful analytically to treat accounts *as if* they are designed to achieve strategic goals. As we argued in the last chapter, we want to develop a discourse analysis which might utilize a double movement between styles of reading that emphasize the constitution of subjects and objects and those that emphasize the ideological work of discourse.

As well as causing problems for the tectonic analysis of discourse, this more flexible, practice-based view of discourses has an important methodological consequence for more traditional psychological methods for dealing with open-ended materials. It seems unlikely that these complicated patterns of social practices will be easily accessed through identifying particular sets of words, and then coding and counting them. Such a traditional content analysis would not reveal the interpretative work done by these resources.

Put at its baldest, to show that a particular respondent alludes to some construction of 'the nation' on three occasions, or in 5.72 per cent of their recorded discourse, is not necessarily going to tell you anything at all about racism; indeed, it may be positively misleading. What is needed instead is an approach which addresses the use of repertoires in context, the way concepts of 'race', 'culture' and 'nation' are mobilized, paying close attention to their specific construction, to their placement in a sequence of discourse, and to their rhetorical organization. It is to these latter features of a discursive approach that we now turn.

Rhetorical construction

One of the points we have emphasized in the previous section is that interpretative repertoires do not have special powers which govern the conditions of their use. Rather, they are available as resources to be used in a range of contrasting and sometimes surprising ways. We have described them as one of the principal building blocks out of which accounts are constructed.

The metaphor of construction is an important one in discourse analysis. In addition to stressing that accounts themselves are manufactured, the metaphor of construction emphasizes the role of discourse in constructing objects and subjects.

We discussed this 'constitutive' role of discourse in some detail in the previous chapter. Our concern now is with what this means in analytic practice. As it stands, the metaphor of construction is somewhat vague and open-ended. It alludes to a wide range of literatures with different goals and assumptions but does not in itself specify particular processes or specific analytic objectives. For this reason it is worth spending some time clarifying what construction might mean in the context of an analysis of discourse. We can usefully start by distinguishing three senses of the term construction.

First, and at its most basic, the notion of construction alludes simply to the referential property of language. Any referential term or descriptive phrase can be considered to 'construct' an object in the sense that participants come to be concerned not with the words but with the invoked objects (see Grace, 1987). Even at this most simple of levels, however, using the idea of construction has some sense, for it points to the pervasiveness with which we deal with the world through discursive versions rather than through 'direct' experience (of course, the idea that there could be any such thing as merely direct experience has been severely tested by Wittgenstein and other linguistic philosophers).

Post-structuralists have come at this problem from another direction, giving a second and more satisfactory take on the notion of construction. They have been interested in the way forms of talk and writing give an effect of realism. Their general analysis has realism as a product of a historically developed familiarity in the use of discourses, or what we have been calling interpretative repertoires. Barthes's (1975) analysis of the workings of a realist literary text is probably the best-known post-structuralist account of realism, with its notion of a Balzac short story being constructed out of a weave of different interpretative codes which combine to give the illusion of solidity and mere description. Shapiro summarizes the general post-structuralist view as follows: 'to the extent that a representation is regarded as realistic, it is because it is so familiar it operates transparently' (1988, p. xi).

As it stands this account begs a variety of questions. Why should certain discourses take on a familiarity denied to others? How widely are a set of discourses shared across the members of a culture? Why are some familiar discourses nevertheless treated as unsatisfactory and unconvincing? And how can a previously familiar and accepted discourse be overturned or simply fall into disrepute? In many ways the post-structuralist account is an outline sketch waiting to have the colours filled in. Nevertheless, it provides a powerful stimulus for considering what might be significant in a set of analytic materials. In particular, it provides a way of understanding important patterns and organizations that cut across particular occasions of discourse use.

This post-structuralist perspective, then, gives one account of the workings of interpretative repertoires to construct real-seeming versions. The very obviousness of such versions makes them seem literal and not versions at all. Repertoires such as culture-as-therapy, and others we will explore in later chapters, provide a reassuring and solid common sense to discourse; their use does not have to be further accounted for.

Although we take this particular post-structuralist focus on the production of realism to be capturing an important part of the operation of repertoires we do not think it is sufficient as it stands as an account of construction in general. These first two accounts of construction treat it as a relatively automatic process: in the former case because of the referential properties of words, in the latter because of the transparency of familiar forms of sense making. However, there is a third, rhetorically based, sense of construction which treats realism as something that is *achieved* through the way text or talk is put together. It does not contradict the other two senses, but it emphasizes features which they underplay.

In this view, texts and talk are organized in specific ways which make a particular reality appear solid, factual and stable. To accomplish this they draw on a range of devices and techniques, and they can be more or less effective in this task. This is a topic of study where ethnomethodologists and conversation analysts have made a more sustained contribution than post-structuralists. This difference is probably a product of the former positions' focus on interactional materials, and on the way versions are managed in situations of dispute such as courts, in contrast to the post-structuralist emphasis on documents, texts and images.

When we consider rhetorical construction in this third perspective, then, we are addressing more than the simple referential property of words, and something over and above the idea that there are familiar types of sense making that form a taken-for-granted basis for understanding and accounting. We are addressing a range of specific discursive features through which versions are warranted. These include a variety of effects derived from categorization and particularization, the use of combinations of vivid and systematically vague formulations, the mobilization of various narrative techniques, constructions involving consensus and corroboration, and various basic rhetorical forms such as lists and contrasts (see Atkinson, 1989; Edwards and Potter, 1992; Smith, 1990; Woofﬁtt, 1992).

The specifically rhetorical meta-theory at work here also emphasizes something that is under-developed in the ethnomethodological and conversation analytic tradition. It emphasizes that versions are not only constructed to make an argument; they are also constructed *against* alternatives (Billig,

1987; 1991). This idea is more familiar in post-structuralist thinking where there has been more concern with the sense of present texts being produced by contrasts with absent structures of various kinds. Rhetorical theory thus gives a more central place for conflicts and tensions than conversation analysis. In terms of specific research technique, it directs attention to the way a particular version or argument is designed, often in a highly inexplicit manner, to undermine one or more competing alternatives. The general point is that arguments and factual versions are often constructed against some absent Other.

We can illustrate what this notion of rhetorical construction means in practice by considering another extract from one of our interviews. This was conducted by a respondent we have called Jones, a 22-year-old customs officer born in the United Kingdom but who emigrated to New Zealand with his parents when he was a child. This extract concerns crime and race, and it concerns as its topic not just Māori groups but groups of Polynesian migrants to New Zealand whom Jones describes as Islanders.

Wetherell: Do you think New Zealand can be described generally as a violent society? In terms of crime rate and

Jones: Yes, it has got a very high crime rate (.) Um (.) Yes, I think so. It's not as bad as some places though (.) but the crime rate is going up.

Wetherell: Uhm. Why do you think, what's responsible there and what could be done about it? (pause)

Jones: To really answer that you'd have to look at (.) the type of crimes you've got, ah, and who's committing them.

Wetherell: Yes. Uhmm.

Jones: There have been you know ideas put out, what is it, that the majority of rapes are committed by Islanders or Māoris and a lot of house burglaries I would imagine are committed by kids and the majority of the kids that are hanging around in the streets are Islanders, they're not the Māoris, well it's unfair to say the Māoris because the Māoris I know are quite nice really (yes). Māoris (.) are quite good it's the Islanders that come here and can't handle it

Wetherell: Yeah. Yeah, so it's partly sort of immigration, it's related to immigration?

Jones: Umm. Yeah, we don't, seeing them coming through off the aircraft at night, half of them can't speak English, um (.). If they can't speak English they're not going to be able to get a job, they're going to go and be in their little communities and (.) they're not going to contribute anything to the country. And they're going to get frustrated and they're going to get bored. And they're gonna, you know, there's nothing for them to do so the kids are going to start hanging around in the streets. At home Mum and Dad can't speak English and so the kids can't speak English. They go to school and suddenly they are confronted with English – 'we can't speak that, and so what do we <u>do</u>?' – <u>nothing</u>. And so by the time they get to fifteen they just drop out, they have had it up to here with school and it's not the school's fault. They have <u>brilliant</u> <u>lives</u>, they have <u>brilliant</u> <u>lives</u> back in, <u>family</u> lives back in the Islands, that's where they should be.

Again, without wanting to burden our text with too much detail at this juncture, there are a number of features which illustrate some of the work done by rhetorical construction and the constitution of versions.

A considerable amount of rhetorical work goes into developing this particular ideologically charged account. To understand this work we suggest it is most helpful to view the speaker as caught in a dilemma of stake or interest. Such a dilemma is present when performing any potentially offensive, problematic or sensitive action which could be reacted to as interested, biased or motivated (Edwards and Potter, 1992; Pomerantz, 1984; Potter *et al.*, forthcoming; Wooffitt, 1992). The dilemma takes its specific form here in the attempt to manage a highly racist and obnoxious account without being heard as racist and thus disqualified.

In this extract, the dilemma is managed by constructing evaluations as part of the world, as a bad thing which is simply being described, rather than an expression of personal negative attitudes to this group. The discourse is organized in various ways to avoid a prejudiced or racist identity. This is most obvious in the construction of friendship with Māoris – Jones comes close to adopting the cliché that some of his best friends are Māori people! More subtly, the account fabricates an elaborate and layered causal narrative about language skills, unemployment and community and individual alienation (for more detail see Potter and Wetherell, 1988a). This means that not only is highly blameworthy behaviour constructed in the account for Māori and Islander groups, but also reasons for that behaviour. This serves a double task: at one and the same time it attempts to establish the factuality of the version and it attempts to display the criticism as not blindly prejudiced but based on understanding.

We are not, of course, suggesting that rhetorical constructions of this kind are always successful in managing the dilemma of stake. Far from it. Such rhetorical constructions often have their concomitant techniques of rhetorical destruction, and attempts to establish a version as merely factual can be undermined by a range of approaches designed to display versions as interested, contentious, biased or whatever (Billig, 1987; 1991; Edwards and Potter, 1992).

The general point we want to emphasize is that there is a lot of detailed rhetorical work going on in racist discourse which is central to the mobilization of meaning and the development of argumentative practice. Part II will try to describe some of this strategic work, but we will place most emphasis on the overall pattern of discourses or interpretative repertoires. Our aim is to map the broad sweep of sense making about race that goes right across a culture, to characterize the dominant discourses of majority group members in New Zealand and to indicate some of the most important ways in which those discourses are deployed. At this juncture we need to consider some of the nuts and bolts of research needed to make that ambition achievable.

Interviews and documents

When we embarked on this study our specific research decisions were a product of a number of both negative and positive considerations. First of all, we were concerned not to produce yet another psychologically reductive study of racism. We were not attempting to see how racism could be understood as a product of cognitive biases or stereotypes; nor how it could be produced through the psychological dynamics of child-rearing. Another feature here was a concern to separate the study of racism from the specific study of authoritarianism or fascism. Such research plays an important part in understanding and combating racism; yet if racism is equated with authoritarianism attention is drawn away from the mundane racist practices of majority groups which have practical effects through the workings of political legislation, the courts, schooling, social work, service provision and so on. Finally, we were committed to avoiding the common tendency of psychologists to study the victims of racism rather than the perpetrators (see Bhavnani, 1988; 1991; Condor, 1988, for critiques).

If these were the negative considerations, our positive goal was to focus on the discourse of the Pākehā majority group. We have drawn primarily on two sorts of materials. Firstly, we collected an archive of documents. These included newspaper reports of relevant matters, including a comprehensive collection of reports relating to the controversial Springbok rugby tour of 1981, magazine articles and various histories of New Zealand. We sifted through Hansard for records of parliamentary debates about race and Māori affairs. Finally, we collected a body of material concerning the commemoration of the 150th anniversary of the Treaty of Waitangi – the moment when New Zealand became a British colony.

The second, and larger part of the study involved carrying out open-ended interviews with a total of eighty-one Pākehā New Zealanders. These were mainly middle-class professionals: people such as teachers, doctors, farmers, company managers, the self-employed and politicians. While we make no claims that our sample mirrored the composition of New Zealand society, they were of varying political affiliation, relatively evenly spread between the two main political parties, National and Labour. They covered most age ranges from eighteen upwards and were roughly balanced in terms of gender. (See Appendix 1 for further details of the sample and methodological procedures.)

Most were interviewed as individuals or couples, although two groups of final-year school students were interviewed together. In many ways we would have preferred to have participants' everyday, unsolicited talk about race –

what they said over family dinners, in discussion in pubs, in the course of doing their ordinary jobs. However, the technical and practical difficulties in collecting a large, comparative body of such material led us to do interviews instead.

The advantage of doing interviews is that it allowed us to explore a relatively standard range of topics with each of the participants. Although the interviews were conversational, and often ranged widely over two or more hours, the interviewer (Wetherell) worked from the same schedule of questions and comments in each case. Also, the interviews were designed to allow the same themes to be addressed in a variety of different contexts. Issues of rights, the nature of racism, essential features of Māori culture and so on recurred many times in terms of specific questions about the causes of unemployment, disputes over land and the likely future evolution of New Zealand. This was particularly valuable because it allowed us to explore the diverse interpretative repertoires that participants brought to bear on issues and some of the effects that could be produced by combining them together in different ways.

It is important to stress that interviews are not understood in the same way in discourse analysis as they are in many other research areas (see Potter and Mulkay, 1985; Potter and Wetherell, 1987). The orthodox requirement of an interview is that it produces clear and consistent responses that can allow the researcher to make inferences about underlying beliefs or previous actions. Ideally, its status as a piece of social interaction should be minimal, and having asked their clear and unambiguous questions in the correct manner the interviewer's part should be of no further interest in the research.

In contrast to this, in discourse work interviews are treated as a piece of social interaction in their own right. The interviewer is contributing just as much as the interviewee, and the interviewer's talk is just as interesting as that of the interviewee. Both are constructing versions which draw on a varied range of interpretative resources; both are analytic topics of interest. Viewed in this way the orthodox idea that interviewers should be as neutral and uninvolved as possible becomes highly problematic. Rather than having little effect on the respondent, such interviewing tends to generate a particular style of rather formal interaction.

Following the logic of the discourse analytic approach, our interviews were conducted in a much more active and interventionist manner. On the one hand, this involved the interviewer being an animated conversationalist, commenting and providing the sorts of 'back channel' 'ums' and 'yes' responses that are characteristic of informal talk. On the other, this involved being prepared to be much more straightforwardly argumentative than would be appropriate in an orthodox research interview: offering counter-examples, questioning assumptions and so on. In this way we hoped to access some of the wide range of different sorts of arguing and thinking that the participants would have produced outside the interviews.

It is worth briefly commenting at this point on issues of empowerment and influence going on in the interaction between researcher and participant. Important arguments have been made about the researcher's duty to avoid recreating wider exploitative relationships with their participants and, at the same time, to avoid legitimating racist or otherwise problematic assumptions (Bhavnani, 1991). In this case our respondents, as members of the most affluent section of the dominant majority group in New Zealand, were hardly in need of empowerment.

The issue of legitimating racist ideas in the course of interviews is a more difficult one. It is certainly the case that, at times, participants made obnoxious and obviously racist arguments as well as deploying many more subtly racist ideas. To have terminated the interview at that point or expressed strong disagreement afterwards would have been a clear expression of dissent. Yet, in the context, we doubt that the direct effect of this would have been very great; and the cost would have been the loss of materials intended to form the basis for a much more widespread critique of racism. Moreover, this kind of direct, immediate intervention depends on the interviewer having a clear grasp of the full implications of the interaction while it happens. Although this might be straightforward in the rather rare cases of direct and unhedged racism, much of the time what is going on is far less easy to read, and many judgements need the benefit of hindsight.

Transcription, coding and analysis

As is almost essential in this type of study, all the interviews were tape-recorded. The tapes were later transcribed in their entirety. This procedure follows from the idea that the interview is a conversation, with two contributors, each equally important (Burgess, 1984; Mischler, 1986). To have transcribed just the respondent's talk would have been to buy into the orthodox view of interviews as a measuring instrument. The transcription used a cut-down version of the Jeffersonian system commonly used by conversation analysts (see Appendix 2). This included speech errors, pauses and gross changes of volume and emphasis, but ignored most features to do with speed, breathing and intonation.

As a first step in analysis, and to make this very large body of transcript more manageable, we then performed a series of codings. This involved searching through the material for a number of themes. Some of these arose from the concerns which had stimulated the study in the first place – but others emerged from the powerful and vivid experience of interviewing this large group and from reading the individual transcripts. Others still were prompted by considerations arising from our archive of documents. Such codings are distinct from the analysis itself. They are designed to make the job of analysis easier by being able to focus it on relevant issues.

Stretches of talk from the interviews were copied across into files if they bore any relation to the theme of interest. Often we annotated these extracts at the time to assist later analysis. The selection was inclusive. We preferred to err on the side of having irrelevant extracts included rather than relevant material excluded. This was also a cyclical process. As our understanding of a particular theme developed we would find it necessary to go back to the original materials and search through them again for instances that we could only now see as relevant. Often themes would merge together – some of the chapters in the second half of this book relate to a number of coding files – others would disappear as we started to see them as incoherent or as more usefully represented as subparts of others. Although we did not directly code the range of documentary materials in this way, we regularly cross-referenced such materials as reminders for later analysis.

One of the difficulties in talking about discourse analysis method is that the category 'method' comes from a discourse developed for quantitative, positivist methodologies such as experiments and surveys. Method in those settings consists of a distinct set of procedures: aggregating scores, categorizing instances, performing various sorts of statistical analysis and so on. It is sometimes tempting to think that in discourse work there is some analogous set of codified procedures that could be put into effect and which would lead to another set of entities known as 'the results'. Yet to see things in this way would be very misleading – although, given the authority which accrues to these procedures, it is sometimes tempting to try.

Another point of departure from the way analysis is understood in more traditional studies concerns the procedures through which claims about the data and the research conclusions are justified. In much orthodox work, to be seen to carry out the procedure of analysis correctly and comprehensively is *itself* part of the justification of results. Thus the impression of the solidity of a finding is reinforced through the operationalization of the variables, the appropriate stratification of the sampling, the appropriateness of the statistical analysis and so on.

In discourse analysis, in contrast, the analytic procedure is largely separate from the warranting of claims. How you arrive at some view about what social practices are taking place in a domain of discourse may be quite different from how you *justify* that conclusion. For example, in this study, as we will discuss below, our analysis was importantly guided by the sorts of subtle knowledge that a cultural member possesses; yet this knowledge is not in itself the warrant for the veracity of the analytic conclusions. Much of the work of discourse analysis is a craft skill, something like bicycle riding or chicken sexing that is not easy to render or describe in an explicit or codified manner.

One of the central elements in analyzing discourse with the aim of identifying interpretative repertoires is to search for variability (Potter and Wetherell, forthcoming; Wetherell and Potter, 1988). Variability is important because it is a signal that different ways of constructing events, processes or groups are being deployed to achieve different effects. Patterns of variation and consistency in the form and content of accounts help the analyst to map out the pattern of interpretative repertoires that the participants are drawing on. More broadly, it is a way of helping to reveal the different ways in which discourse is orientated to action. For example, it was typical in our interviews for respondents to move between ideas and claims that might be described as racist and others that could be thought anti-racist. Such variation is particularly problematic for those social psychologists who work with some form of attitude theory. How should these many confusingly variable interviewees be classified? Are they basically anti-racist liberals who have picked up one or two racist ideas? Are they racists trying to present themselves in a more liberal manner? Or should some sort of mid-point or average be computed: so many racist utterances balance out so many anti-racist ones?

What is a methodological problem for attitude theory is all grist to the mill of discourse analysis, for in discourse analysis the analytic goal is not to classify people but to reveal the discursive practices through which race categories are constructed and exploitation legitimated. We do not expect individuals to be consistent in their discourse – indeed, it would be very surprising if they were. Instead, we expect their talk and writing to vary as they draw on different repertoires to do explanation and justification in different contexts and to make their claims accountable.

Understanding, ethnography and discursive consequences

> The starting point of critical elaboration is the consciousness of what one really is, and 'knowing thyself' as a product of the historical process to date which has deposited in you an infinity of traces, without leaving an inventory.
>
> (Gramsci, 1971, p. 324)

There is one respect in which this study of racist discourse is rather different from other discourse analytic work we have conducted. This is due to the important role it gives to ethnographic understanding in making sense of our materials and, in particular, in identifying some of the ideological consequences that flow from this talk and writing.

Ethnographic understanding can never be entirely eliminated from research. At its most basic, an analyst has to have a basic comprehension of what the words in a language mean to make sense of a text or transcript. For example, in our discussion of Jones's account of 'Islander' crime we were treating a range of central terms and assumptions in his discourse as problematic. Yet, at the same time, we could not have got the analysis started without familiarity with basic words like 'and' and 'the'. We also needed to have some conception of what a world is like with streets and aircraft, what sorts of things crime can be and so on. In addition, we needed some basic knowledge of the sorts of activities that people do, things like compliments and blamings, and even the knowledge that people are entities that do activities in the first place.

None of this means that we cannot start to make *any* of these things problematic by making them a focus for analysis. Indeed, at times the process of analysis is largely based around critically interrogating one's own taken-for-granted assumptions and expectations (Potter, 1988). We are not suggesting that this conversation with oneself during analysis has been silenced because of the importance placed on ethnographic understanding here. Nor should we pretend to be working with an ethnographic *tabula rasa* (for different positions on the relation of ethnography to conversation analysis see Hopper, 1990/1; Moerman, 1988).

Although accepting that analysis is conditional on a range of ethnographic assumptions, one of the things we have tried to do in past studies is avoid having analytic conclusions dependent on unexplicated assumptions of this kind. In concrete terms, for example, when we have tried to analyze the 'effects' or consequences of particular pieces of discourse we have done this through considering their upshot in particular documents or stretches of talk. We examined the way a certain construction of community paves the way for a specific policy recommendation (Potter and Reicher, 1987) or the way versions of personality could be used to legitimate police actions (Wetherell and Potter, 1989).

The current study is significantly different, largely due to its ambition to capture the ideological operation of a wide range of different interpretative repertoires operating in a culture. This involved us being concerned with the upshots of discourses, the logic of particular discourses, and the ways in which they could be blended together. Yet we commonly did not have complete examples of such things available in our materials. Nor were the interviews situations where we could always follow through the broader processes that we were interested in. Much of our analysis has thus involved a complex and not always easy to describe process of sense-making.

In this case, then, the role of the analyst's own ethnographic understanding is vital. Primarily this comes through two routes. One of us (Wetherell) is a Pākehā New Zealander, a 'member' of New Zealand culture, who has grown up with these discourses and, in post-structuralist terms, her sense of self, values and place in the world is partly constituted out of them. Such members' knowledge is often very difficult to make explicit, of course. It is frequently so obvious as to be transparent. However, the process of interviewing here makes a second crucial contribution to the study, providing a further way of developing ethnographic understanding.

Interviewing can be seen as a way of developing a 'participants' comprehension' of a culture (Collins, 1983). In this case, the interviews not only allowed us to record a range of accounts, drawing on a wide variety of different interpretative repertoires, they also provided an arena for reflexively considering the nature of local ethnographic knowledge, for they involve the researcher becoming a participant all over again. This is not something straightforwardly captured on the tapes and transcripts, although its consequences are seen in the easy fluidity of these many different conversations. Rather, it is a development of a skill, a more conscious and theorized understanding of how to be a cultural member.

This heightened ethnographic insight is traded on heavily in the analytic chapters that make up the second part of this book. However, this does not mean the study has abandoned the discourse analytic perspective to become a more orthodox interpretative anthropology. The general theoretical perspective is very much a discourse analytic one; talk and texts are not being used as symptomatic of underlying psychopathology in the manner of much social psychological work, nor are they being used as the basis for a reconstruction of events and histories in New Zealand society. The focus is squarely on the discourse and its operation.

In addition, our emphasis on ethnographic knowledge does not mean that readers are being asked to take claims and conclusions on trust because they are guaranteed by a special participant's knowledge. In the course of the chapters in Part II the argument is made using a wide range of extracts and documents for support which provide many opportunities for us to evaluate claims critically. More generally, as we noted in the Introduction, many of the ideological themes and dilemmas that we explore in the second part of the book are not unique to New Zealand but are features of many Western nations. As such they provide the opportunity for many readers critically to assess the plausibility of the various claims. Nevertheless, New Zealand has its own specific history – and before we embark on analysis, some understanding of this will provide a helpful background.

Putting discourse in context

> Border: . . . you say to people in New Zealand – 'history' – they reply, 'oh, did we have one?' . . .
>
> The shadow of the land is to the Queen, but the substance remains to us.
>
> (Nopera Panakareao, 28 April 1840, cited in McCreanor, 1989a, p. 37)

The previous sections of this chapter have considered various aspects of the methodological framework guiding the discourse analysis we practise. Above all, we have tried to emphasize the *active* nature of discourse analysis as a process of developing, testing out and justifying interpretations and readings of texts. Following this format, Part II of this book will attempt to identify patterns of meaning in the documents and transcripts we have chosen to study and will attempt also to formulate some of the most prevalent argumentative and rhetorical practices through which these interpretative repertoires become mobilized as part of public and interactional domains.

However, since we are concerned in this study not only with ethnography and genealogy but also with ideology, we will, in addition, be attempting another kind of interpretative activity in Part II. One which connects the discursive pattern we can read in our materials with the patterns we can read into the social context. Our readings of discourse will try to emphasize the social significance and social consequences of certain versions, accounts and narratives. As John Thompson (1984) has pointed out, the study of ideology, if the term is to be at all distinctive, must involve an interpretation of the position of a story, account or version of events within a field of power relations.

In Thompson's view, the analysis of ideology should involve three stages: first, the social scientist must describe the social field, history and social relations relevant to the area of investigation; then engage in some systematic linguistic analysis of the pattern of discourse; and finally, in an interpretative or hermeneutic act, connect the latter with the former. This final moment of analysis is vital, Thompson argues, if we are to argue confidently that certain forms of discourse are implicated in the sustenance and maintenance of particular social patterns.

Thompson's scheme for analysis is a useful one, and at various points in Part II and in this last section of this chapter we will try to present accounts of New Zealand's history and social relations as a context or backcloth for our interpretative connections. Thompson's notion of stages is, of course, also an idealized scheme. Having questioned the idea of doing history in Chapter 3, we do not want to now suggest that 'what happened', the social context 'surrounding' discourse, can be described in any simple or neutral way as a convenient frame for our analyses. The stages of analysis are entirely intertwined and all, in our view, are interpretative – all involve constructive readings.

Indeed, if one assumes that discourse and the social context are entirely interpenetrated, then the practical analysis of ideology can never be a tidy procedure. We prefer to see it as a case of multiple resources, where a range of accounts and versions of events are used to make sense of other accounts and versions in order to develop an argument and to make a case about some body of material.

In spite of these caveats, we want, in the last part of this chapter, to do some general context-setting of the type Thompson recommends. Our aim is to develop an introductory 'pre-story', a very brief overview of some of the social context in New Zealand to orientate readers less familiar with the outlines of British intervention and its consequences. Our story will focus mainly on the discursive and political ambiguities surrounding the 1840 Treaty of Waitangi, the 'founding document' of New Zealand.

The struggle between Māori and Pākehā in New Zealand has been largely a struggle over the boundaries of the 'shadow' and the 'substance' Panakareao refers to above, and it is these boundaries, along with the basis of British intervention, which the treaty sought to define. We have relied for our version of this context to Māori–Pākehā relations on a number of contemporary historical sources, notably Claudia Orange's (1987; 1990) work, on Peter Cleave's (1989) account of the 'sovereignty game', on *The Oxford History of New Zealand* (Oliver and Williams, 1981) and the more recent *Oxford Illustrated History* (Sinclair, 1990), and on the introduction to the Treaty of Waitangi that Yensen *et al.* (1989) have developed for Pākehā readers.

The other comment which introduced this section, from a 17-year-old male school student we interviewed, suggests that many Pākehā New Zealanders may share our general scepticism about the process of 'doing history'. Their doubts, however, seem to rest on the assumption that 'proper' history should go a long way back, and should be like the history of Britain as conventionally told, consisting of successions of kings and queens, battles, laws and acts extending into the very distant past. New Zealand is seen as a 'young' country in this respect, and indeed, from a Pākehā, and entirely Eurocentric, perspective, that is so. New Zealand was first introduced to Europe (and named) in 1642 through Abel Tasman's voyages; 'discovery' was then consolidated by Captain Cook in his visits of 1769, 1773 and 1777. However, archaeological evidence and Māori oral traditions suggest that the country was first settled by people from Polynesian islands such as Hawaii, Rarotonga and Tahiti between 1,000 to 2,000 years ago (Biggs, 1990; Davidson, 1981).

Māori cultural and social life was organized on a hierarchical tribal and kinship basis. Individuals were placed within extended family systems, broadening outwards, organized by systems of authority which were largely hereditary or dependent on particular prowess. Despite the tribal divisions patterned across the country, and the conflicts and competing loyalties between these groupings, Māori people could be recognized by themselves and visiting Europeans as homogeneous in terms of language, cultural practices and origins. Material subsistence and social organization were arranged on a communal basis with well-developed systems for defining and determining consensus.

Although Captain Cook saw himself as claiming parts of New Zealand for King George III, until 1840, New Zealand was treated as an independent state, the province of the Māori people, under the general overview of the British colony in New South Wales. Fifty years of European interest in New Zealand and contact with Māori preceded British annexation in 1840, beginning most obviously with coastal sealers, whalers and traders in the

1790s, intensifying with the arrival of missionary groups in 1814 and with the development of commercial, shipping and colonial interests in the 1820s and 1830s.

Māori people during this period were dominant – their numbers were estimated at between 100,000 to 200,000 – while European visitors were mostly transient and not so much interested in settling as in plying a cross-Tasman trade in flax and timber as well as sealing and whaling, trading also goods (guns, clothes, tobacco, etc.) to Māori groups. Estimates suggest that in 1830 there were only 300 Europeans who could be described as resident in New Zealand, although by 1840 that number had increased to 2,000. Māori tribes organized their agricultural production to meet the new demands for trade in food for the settlements and set up various joint enterprises in flax and ship building with European groups.

Orange (1987; 1990) argues that the representatives of the British Crown that Māori groups encountered as they first began travelling to Sydney, and some even to London, including their contacts with the first official British Resident in New Zealand, James Busby, fostered an image of Britain as a benevolent protector of Māori interests, a neutral force whose concern was largely to govern, control and regulate the behaviour of those Europeans who visited and settled in New Zealand. The Crown, for a variety of reasons – to protect trade, due to the numerical dominance of Māori groups and due to humanitarian concerns for native peoples that were becoming fashionable in Britain – adopted a conciliatory stance, mediating between would-be settlers and traders and Māori interests, exchanging hospitality and compliments with Māori chiefs. From a Māori perspective, therefore, this was the tenor of relations with Britain leading up to the events of 1840, with some tribes now experienced in sustained contact and with vested interests in this contact, while others had little experience of European groups.

On the British side, there was a multitude of voices over these years. The British Colonial Office in London was reluctant to undertake the expense and problems of a new colonial venture, while British groupings in New South Wales could see more clearly the advantages but felt impotent to address the problems of ownership, and the growing difficulties of land claims. There were also concerns that the situation and control over European renegades would degenerate, and concerns too that France and the United States might pre-empt British claims through establishing their own colonies. All of these motives encouraged the petitioning of the British government for direct intervention.

Simultaneously, there were powerful voices from missionary groups and their backers in Britain seeking to consolidate their 'civilization' and conversion of Māori people through a more formal British presence, although one which would also recognize Māori ownership and self-government of New Zealand. And from an opposing perspective there were newly formed land companies in Britain, whose goals were the acquisition of land and the formation of colonies through the sale of this land at a profit. The interests of Europeans in New Zealand were changing from groups seeing themselves as trading with independent groups of Māoris to groups who saw New Zealand as their potential home and base for operations.

In response, the British Colonial Office finally despatched William Hobson to New Zealand in 1839 and gave him the task of negotiating British sovereignty and the development of a British colony. Initially, New Zealand was to be a Crown Colony, a dependency of New South Wales, and Hobson was to be the lieutenant-governor of any land he could establish sovereignty over; all previous land claims and sales were to be suspended unless proved valid by the Crown, who would also act as the sole land purchaser in the future and agent of land transactions. The expansion of government in New Zealand and the establishment of the Crown were to be funded by the sale of land acquired by the Crown from Māori groups to European purchasers.

Hobson went about his task by first drafting a treaty and convening a meeting of a range of Māori tribes – the Confederation of tribes. This confederation had previously been loosely organized by Busby (the British Resident) as part of an attempt to introduce local self-government among Māori groups. A translation of the treaty into Māori was drawn up by a local missionary and then during two days of discussion the treaty was described to the assembled chiefs, their views were elicited and they were urged to sign. On 6 February 1840, at Waitangi, forty-six chiefs eventually signed the Māori translation. After meetings around the country, where the treaty was presented to other Māori tribes, 500 signatures were eventually collected and in May 1840 Hobson proclaimed British sovereignty over the North Island of New Zealand by Māori cessation and over the South Island by right of discovery.

The treaty itself and its presentation to Māori groups involved a delicate set of discursive compromises with sufficient ambiguity so that each party emerged with their own version of promises made and their consequences. Hobson's goal was presented in the first article of the English translation of the Māori text of the treaty – 'the chiefs of the Confederation and all chiefs who have not joined that Confederation give absolutely to the Queen of England forever the complete government over their land' (Yensen *et al.*, 1989, p. 29). This wording, however, is immediately undercut by a guarantee in the second article of the treaty inserted by James Busby, who helped Hobson draft the treaty and who was aware that Māori chiefs would not easily sign away their power and control. In the English text this guarantee reads as:

> Her Majesty the Queen of England confirms and guarantees to the Chiefs and Tribes of New Zealand and to the respective families and individuals thereof the full exclusive and undisturbed possession of their Lands and Estates Forests Fisheries and other properties which they may collectively or individually possess so long as it is their wish and desire to retain the same in their possession.
> (Yensen *et al.*, 1989, pp. 30–1)

In addition, there are crucial ambiguities evident in the translation between Māori and English versions of the treaty indicating the difficulty of meshing very different cultural understandings of property ownership, government and sovereignty. In Māori 'full exclusive and undisturbed possession' was rendered as 'te tino rangatiratanga', which translates more broadly not simply as property ownership but rights of control, cultural and political independence (McCreanor, 1989a). Similarly, the Māori term used for government is likely to have been interpreted as referring only to civil government, a 'governor's authority', rather than sovereignty and control in any more pervasive sense. It is from these confusions that the question of who owns the 'shadow' and who owns the 'substance' of the land can arise.

Indeed, the drawing up of the Māori text was commensurate with the way the treaty and British motives were introduced to the chiefs at Waitangi, both in the written preambles and in the speech-making of the day. Māori chiefs were told that the main motive was protection of their rights and to stem lawlessness, keeping Europeans under legal control, while extending the benefits of British citizenship to Māori people. As the signing approached, one of the missionaries present objected to Hobson that the Māori chiefs were, for these reasons, not aware of the import of what they were signing. Out of this muddle, however, the new British colony of New Zealand emerged.

The story of the next period is one of gradually increasing Pākehā colonization and dominance and increasing Māori resistance and disenchantment. Māori attempts to assert their rights seemingly guaranteed by the Treaty of Waitangi and to organize their own affairs were outweighed by increasing Pākehā power and presence. Although some of the migrants to New Zealand came from other European countries – notably, the area around Yugoslavia – the great majority of settlers were British in origin. From 1845 to 1872 the tensions of settlement resulted in armed conflict, with the 1860s dominated by outright war over land issues between certain Māori tribes, the British army and settler militias. Much Māori land was confiscated in the process. Land sales also proceeded apace, and, as Sorrenson puts it, 'in fifty years the greater part of New Zealand had been purchased by the Crown or European settlers, much of it at nominal prices' (1981, p. 187).

Sorrenson notes that, by 1891, Māoris made up only 7 per cent of New Zealand's population, and their numbers were declining due to poverty and lack of immunity to diseases (such as small-pox, influenza, tuberculosis and measles) introduced from Europe. Māori people retained less than one-sixth of New Zealand and from being 'the main agricultural producers of the 1840s and 1850s . . . were now relegated to a precarious subsistence on the fringe of a rapidly expanding European agricultural economy' (1981, p. 192).

New Zealand became self-governing with its own (male Pākehā) elected assembly in the 1850s, and, as Cleave (1989) argues, this transition to self-government marked the shift on the Pākehā side to a practical interpretation of the Treaty of Waitangi almost entirely in terms of the first article. In the early years of the colony after 1840, when Pākehā settlers were in a relatively insecure position *vis-à-vis* Māori groups, the Crown had attempted to balance Māori concerns and rights against settler claims. Political discourse and the stance of British officials was, formally at least, dominated by the notion of the Crown as 'protector' and mediator, with the Crown conscious in its negotiations with Māori chiefs of Māori rights guaranteed in the second article of the treaty; but certainly by the late nineteenth century, this reading of the treaty had been all but submerged.

The position of Māori people in modern New Zealand has remained grim, particularly in terms of socio-economic prospects and in terms of cultural and social autonomy. In 1986, persons of Māori descent made up 12 per cent of the population, marking an increase over the low point of the late nineteenth century (*Report of the Royal Commission on Social Policy*, 1988, vol. 1, p. 50). Until the Second World War, Māori people were largely rural but the changes brought by New Zealand's actions on the European and Pacific fronts, along with the general post-war economic expansion, led to urbanization. Sorrenson (1990) reports that whereas only 11 per cent of Māori lived in urban areas in 1936, by 1961 the figure was 38 per cent, rising to 78 per cent in 1981. Urbanization largely increased Pākehā cultural hegemony, and Sorrenson argues that 'urbanisation and economic development were merely converting the bulk of the Māori work-force from an unemployed proletariat rural to an urban one' (1990, p. 340).

The 1988 'April Report' of the Royal Commission on Social Policy documents the extent of the skew in the distribution of occupations, income, educational history, crime figures and employment prospects. According to the authors of the report, Māori and Pacific Island Polynesian workers are more than twice as likely as members of other ethnic groups to be in production, transport and labouring occupations requiring few or no formal qualifications (vol. 1, p. 129). Whereas only 3 per cent of Māoris were employed in 1981 in professional, technical, management or administrative positions, 17 per cent of Pākehā New Zealanders were employed in this way (Sorrenson, 1990, p. 345). As a result the income for Māori workers is substantially below those of non-Māori workers (April Report, vol. 2, p. 617). Māori workers are also substantially more likely to be unemployed, particularly young Māori (vol. 2, p. 620), and while Māori make up only 12 per cent of the population, Sorrenson notes that since 1979, they have comprised over 50 per cent of the prison population.

The movement towards Pākehā hegemony in New Zealand has been a one-sided struggle since the mid-nineteenth century. Despite its one-sided nature, the debate within Māori communities over the best methods of resistance and adaptation has never ceased. Some Māori concluded that assimilation with Pākehā society (the official government policy for most of this century) was the only option, others have fought for a range of alternative strategies, for autonomy and for sovereignty. In recent years, Māori groups have had considerable success in attempts to obtain some honouring of treaty guarantees and the spirit of the treaty under Labour governments of the 1980s, although governmental response has been hedged, too, by economic considerations (see Kelsey, 1990) and by the mixed ideological messages of recent 'multiculturalist' social policy which we will examine in detail in Part II.

The events of the nineteenth century set the political and social context for modern New Zealand and they set the context, too, for the discourse we will analyse in Part II. In making sense of current Māori–Pākehā relations, the middle-class Pākehā sample we interviewed are also making sense of their history and the circumstances of colonialism. Their discourse is ideological, we will argue, to the extent that it can be seen as an attempt to justify, incorporate and 'normalize' this history and the current position of the Māori people.

Part II
Discourse in action

Preface

Part II has three main aims. Each chapter takes up a major theme in Pākehā New Zealanders' discourse concerning Māori–Pākehā relations and tries to show how the social landscape has been ordered in each case. As a second aim these investigations try to exemplify the theoretical and methodological principles developed in Part I and attempt to introduce some more specific analytic tools along the way. Finally, each chapter relates the discursive patterns we identify to important theoretical debates within the social psychology of racism or, alternatively, to similar patterns in the discourse of social psychologists.

Chapter 5 examines the construction of social categories and communities, studying the formulation of Māori and Pākehā as 'races', 'cultures' and as members of one 'nation'. Chapter 6 looks at how Pākehā New Zealanders account for social conflict and social influence and for the 'social body' more generally. Chapter 7 analyzes the construction of practical politics around the issues of land rights, language and affirmative action. The final chapter then looks at accounts of prejudice, discrimination and racism. These topics cover, in our view, the major strands in the contemporary ideological project of Pākehā New Zealand.

Each chapter draws on our interviews and the public discourse of politicians, commentators and journalists. Using discourse analysis as a method of social critique, we try to demonstrate, for each arena, how the discourse of Pākehā New Zealanders legitimates. That is, how colonial history and current forms of Māori disadvantage are justified and rationalized, how inequality is normalized and rendered 'safe', and how diversity and continuing conflicts are subdued and consensus manufactured.

Part II can be seen as a series of case-studies in which we develop the new social psychology of racism outlined in Part I. As part of this attempt to instantiate a new approach, some chapters develop a contrast with existing social psychological literatures. Chapter 5 compares discourse analytic approaches to social categorization with traditional social psychological approaches; while Chapter 7 critically examines new American attitudinal research and the 'symbolic racism' tradition from a discourse analytic point of view. Chapter 6 compares lay accounts of social influence and social theory to the accounts found in some areas of social psychology. Similarly, Chapter 8 discusses the overlap between lay accounts of racism and the social psychology of prejudice. We try to apply our findings not only to debate with other social psychologies of racism but also to examine the ideological nature of aspects of the discipline itself.

We hope our three aims of documentary, critique and exemplification do not prove conflicting. Our intention is to speak in these chapters to two audiences: to fellow New Zealanders concerned with systematically exploring a shared 'lived ideology' and to social psychologists interested in how discourse analysis investigates racism and tackles a particular empirical example.

5

Constructing community: 'race', 'culture' and 'nation'

What we are dealing with here are in the very widest sense communities of interpretation, many of them at odds with one another, prepared in many instances literally to go to war with one another, all of them creating and revealing themselves and their interpretations as very central features of their existence. No one lives in direct contact either with truth or with reality. Each of us lives in a world actually made by human beings, in which such things as 'the nation' . . . are the result of agreed upon convention, of historical processes, and above all, of willed human labour expended to give those things an identity we can recognize. (Said, 1981, pp. 41–2)

Whenever an actor speaks of 'us', s/he is translating other actors into a single will, of which s/he becomes spirit and spokesman. S/he begins to act for several, no longer for one alone. S/he becomes stronger. S/he grows.
(Callon and Latour, 1981, p. 279)

The year 1990 was important in New Zealand's history. The Commonwealth Games were held in Auckland (always a cause for celebration), and 1990 also marked 150 'years of nationhood'. It became a year of 'commemoration' based on the sesquenticennial anniversary of the signing of the Treaty of Waitangi in 1840. New Zealanders were constantly invited to remember that 1990 was going to be 'Huia Tuia Tui Tuia' and 'Our Country, Our Year' and, as one song had it, that 'the combination was simply indestructible'. More broadly, the 1990s were described as consolidating the era of multiculturalism introduced during previous decades. Ethnicity as well as nationhood was to be celebrated, sustaining a Māori 'cultural renaissance'.

These exhortations and opportunities to identify with one's nation or culture, with their underlying stress on shared community, are organized around several basic categorizations of New Zealanders. These provoke important questions. What is at stake when people are ordered by ethnicity and culture rather than by race, for example, or when they are classified by nationality rather than social class? Who is at the locus of these invitations to celebrate? Indeed, who is being invited and who is doing the inviting?

This chapter focuses on the everyday logic of group descriptions and categorizations. To talk about group relations in any society, whether as a social scientist, a lay member or as a politician, involves the formulation of a common language which defines the objects of the demographic landscape. It defines who is being dealt with; and what kind of people these are. Similarities and differences are articulated, and boundaries erected between groups.

In the sections which follow we will try to show how the descriptive methods of race, culture and nation generate their own distinctive ontologies, psychologies and social theory. Discursive orderings based on race find very different kinds of groups, and posit very different demographies, from discursive orderings based on culture. The categorization of nation implies a very different theory of identity from the subject position constructed within race, and each ordering encourages a contrasting model of intergroup and broader social relations.

Each of these methods of constructing a story of intergroup relations has a history and not just in New Zealand but in social science. This chapter is based on the premise that race, culture and nation are not natural phenomena but constructed categories. Modern accounts of groups are closely related to current social arrangements and must build on past discursive achievements. Categories change and what was once ideologically useful and persuasive can become obdurate and awkward material stubbornly resisting the reworkings of later generations. For example, when instructing William Hobson to negotiate a treaty with the Māori people in 1840, the British Colonial Office, on some occasions formulated his task as dealing with an independent Māori nation (Orange, 1987; Yensen *et al.*, 1989). Yet in the 1990s this representation of the Māori people as a national group is most unpolitic from a Pākehā perspective, for talk of a Māori *nation*, which draws on the interpretative resources of citizen rights and popular sovereignty, questions the very status of Pākehā New Zealanders (Awatere, 1984). Now in the commemorative booklets and official statements it is deemed that nationhood in New Zealand only began with the signing of the treaty, nationhood is now just 150 years old, and Māoris are reframed as a *cultural* rather than a national group.

Similarly, the categorization 'New Zealander' once referred to just Māori people. James Boswell, for example, describes, in a classic construction of the 'primitive Other', how Captain Cook once gave him 'a distinct account of a New Zealander eating human flesh' (Ryskamp, 1963, in Orsman and Moore, 1988, p. 132). Boswell remarks that he felt a vague stirring to go and see a people living in such a different state. The distinction was also often made in the nineteenth century between the New Zealander, meaning Māori people, and the British settler. 'Whatever may have been said of the New Zealander, he is one of "nature's gentlemen", both in feeling and deportment, and is, to the full, as sensible a man as the settler' (Earp, 1853, in Orsman and Moore, 1988, p. 242). Over the last hundred years or so, however, British migrants have come to recognize themselves as, pre-eminently, *the* New Zealanders, and on this basis can self-confidently distance themselves from the 'Poms' or the new British migrants of the twentieth century. Indeed, in the course of this century white migrants have established themselves as 'the' national group, while Māoris have been relegated to contrastive categories: they are a race or a culture. In fact, for many of those we interviewed it was ambiguous whether Māoris are New Zealanders at all. The reference of the term has become synonymous with white European, and a variety of further distinctions are often drawn on in everyday talk to indicate whether references to New Zealanders are narrow or inclusive.

Our analysis, therefore, will try to tease out the ideological labour which different group descriptions accomplish. Although we focus on discourse and on the signification of groups, we are not trying to argue that acts of imagination and rhetoric are all that are required to bring a nation or a culture into existence. Communities, countries and nations emerge from the action of powerful material, economic and political forces. These clearly constrain and organize signification. The nineteenth-century creation of New Zealand as a replica 'England in the South Pacific' involved large-scale movements of people, military action and the establishment of an economic infrastructure.

Nor do we wish to argue, however, as Part I of this book made clear, that international relations and military movements are independent of discourse (Der Derian and Shapiro, 1989; Edwards and Potter, 1992); the semiotic penetrates all of these realms. Material possibilities may structure the plausibility of different discursive orderings of community but it is also the case that categorizations of race, culture and nation come to organize these material possibilities and transform them into politics.

Our account is organized chronologically. We shall argue that whereas once race seemed to be the most effective and prevalent legitimating tool, the ideological baton has now been handed to culture and nation. The analytical line we are pursuing has been strongly influenced by the work of Robert Miles on the category of race (1982; 1987; 1989), by the studies of Jakubowicz (1981) and Yuval-Davis (1986) on ethnicity, and Benedict Anderson (1983) on nation. Our analysis owes a particular debt to Edward Said's (1978) notion of imaginative geography and his emphasis on the construction of 'imagined communities', a term elaborated by Anderson (1983).

The premises of race

The following sections try to clarify the 'ontology', 'psychology' and 'social theory' contained in discourse on race and examine its application as ideology. Put another way, we are reversing the standard realist focus on how language captures and describes a recalcitrant world; our concern is with how a particular discourse produces the world and how it invokes a realm which for the participants is real. We shall argue that references to 'races' still abound in the talk of Pākehā New Zealanders, but that full-blown racial explanations – with their emphasis on superiority and inferiority and their agricultural metaphors of stocks and breeding – have become an embarrassment.

This version of community has ceased to be prevalent in the discourse of New Zealanders; yet it is of more than historical interest, for it helps throw light on the organization of current discourse about intergroup relations which is partly a response to, and transformation of, this prior discourse. It also shows the contingency of people's taken-for-granted common sense; what was an entirely natural and obvious way of understanding the world (indeed, for all intents and purposes it *was* the world) has, in a relatively short period of time, become embarrassing and strange. We shall document its working in two periods of New Zealand history: Victorian New Zealand and during one of its last policy applications in the 1960s.

The following collection of extracts from our interviews all display a racial formulation of Māori people, Polynesian migrants and, more rarely, Pākehā New Zealanders. Some extracts attempt to 'praise' Māori people but the premises on which these 'positive' accounts are based are racist and deeply offensive.

Knight: The Māoris seem more advanced than the Aboriginals.

Stones: The Māori ha . . . is a classy person. You know he rivals the European in a lot of ways. You know he has got, uh, he built a society that was a good society, and, uh, you know, he made things, he was aggressive enough, he, he has certain traits almost of a European, uh, whereas the people from the Islands tend to be a little a, a gear lower.

Davison: The Māori on the whole isn't a leader, uh, I think that the Māori that is leading in this way probably has a lot of Pākehā blood. Cause there are no pure-bred Māoris in New Zealand and that probably, you know, that's the reason why.

Sargeant: The, um, the old Māori, only 150 years ago he was a cannibal, he was eating his enemies. He hasn't had the advantages of (yes), if we think the Western style of civilization is the ideal situation, he hasn't (.) had bred into him, generation after generation, er, the capacity to reason, analyze. Of course some do, not in the same proportion as whites.

Couch: You'll find a great number of people in New Zealand who have a sprinkling of Polynesian or Māori in them.

Bradman: To be able to sing well seems to be a general trait. . . . Yes it
            seems you've got to be, um, how can I say, you know, either a
            Māori or a Negro or something to be able to bop dance. It's
            very interesting that it always seems to be the darker people.

Border: I think there's a tribal instinct if you like.

Munman: . . . there's wonderful Polynesian people and wonderful Māori
            people who are hard workers and family, probably more family-
            orientated than a European, but the gang team work comes
            from a hereditary factor within their own communities.

Bird: It's this innate shyness they've got. When they get to the top
            they usually disgrace themselves.

A. Bickerstaff: New Zealand born people are not a violent race, I feel that
            we're a friendly, kindly race, but I feel that as immigrants are
            coming in and interbreeding I think it has become . . .

Pinter: It's only when I'm overseas that I really sort of look at other
            indigenous races and I sort of say, 'my goodness, you know, the
            Māori is a, you know, and educated, you know, noble, you
            know good-looking er person.'

Mills: I had a friend in Motueka who's um say, almost full-blooded
            Māori.

Dixon: Perhaps the fact that really the Māoris as the Aborigines and
            black Africans and I suppose to some extent even the Indians,
            we've, we've really asked them in about 150 years to encompass
            centuries and centuries of social evolution.

Irvine: Hmm. Well once again, er, I think, I think it must go back into
            the hereditary part of the Māoris that they are not accustomed,
            and their forebears have not been accustomed, to sitting down
            and studying (mmhmm). They are people of the land really (yes)
            and therefore it's probably come through their make-up, or their
            genet genetic make-up that that studying is a bit foreign to
            them.

James: I think that the only possibility, you see, OK you're talking
            about um (0.2) you're ignoring genes, and alright we we have a
            lot a lot of intermarriage, I mean none of the Māoris are pure,
            and um they do have a racial trait, a characteristic that that I
            don't know whether it's going to be dominant or not, but they're
            basically a lazy people, um and OK with a bit more

intermarriage maybe that will be lost to a larger extent with a bit of the old Protestant work ethic thrown in, it might improve them . . .

As these extracts illustrate, race as a classification works with people as biological objects. Group belonging is articulated through physical origins. For some, genes are the crucial biological entity; for others, the biological division is encapsulated in the shorthand of 'blood'. The blood possessed by Māoris is said to dictate, in a mysterious way, personality, temperament, ability, outlook on life and social organization.

This determination of psychological and cultural traits forms the crux of race discourse. Group characteristics determine individual characteristics. As a psychology, race is thus rigid; it is presented as a strong constraint. Nature rooted in the body cannot be easily changed, unlike the characteristics given by culture. There is an inevitability about race summed up in the notions of instincts and inheritance. Race is not something that can be easily shrugged off.

Racial groups, in some of these extracts, are thought to be organized into hierarchies running from civilized superiority to primitive inferiority, according to the quality of the blood. Some Māoris are considered to be pure bloods, others as having mixed blood as a result of intermarriage. In the latter case, the quintessential racial traits can be seen as 'diluted' by 'superior' mixtures.

Obviously, this social theory is conservative in the sense that change is either seen as undesirable and impossible or as proceeding extremely slowly, in the case of Dixon's comments above, through a gradual process of evolution. However, race discourse also allows for different groups to be congratulated. The 'white races' are celebrated as a matter of course; but Māoris, too, can come in for praise, for being one of the more 'advanced races'. A common comparison is made with Australian Aborigines; Māori people were thought to be more promising raw material for civilization. Some 'savages', according to these accounts, can aspire to nobility.

The careful placing of Māori people in a racial hierarchy can indulge nationalist sentiment. 'Our' Māoris have the dubious distinction of being the best 'primitive race' in the world. Jack articulates this complex emotion in the following anecdote.

Jack: We were in an underground station in London and we had our Air New Zealand bags over our shoulders . . . and a man came up to us and started to chat . . . he said how badly the Māoris were treated in New Zealand . . . . And I looked at him and said, 'I'm sorry but that's a lot of rot.' And he said 'What do you mean?' I said 'Māoris are not treated like that, and they're very intelligent people.' I said, 'Actually we have a son-in-law who is in the head office of the . . . department in the capital and he has Māori blood in him' . . . . I'm quite positive many (foreigners)

liken them to Aborigines . . . and I've said to people, 'Look I
believe when white people arrived in New Zealand, they found a
very advanced people, otherwise they wouldn't embrace Western
culture so quickly and readily.'

Race discourse can sometimes permit a utopian vision of social progress.
Several of those we interviewed referred to the idea of a 'melting pot', and
looked forward to the emergence of a 'coffee-coloured' people who would
live in mutual tolerance. In this, they echoed the sentiments of a former New
Zealand Prime Minister of the 1960s and 1970s, Sir Keith Holyoake.

Holyoake: A race will evolve a century hence which will be brown skinned,
much the colour that many people seek to acquire on the beach
in the summer.

(New Zealand 1990, p. 65)

H. Kenwood: I'd like to think that New Zealand could go on as it is and
ultimately become you know an integrated population. I listened
to a talk many many years ago and this is what was um, this
person who was on the programme was saying that in fact this is
how it would become an integrated population, and that uh you
know we'd all be or our children, our children's children, you
know, would all be a coffee colour. That you know they'd
intermarry etcetera and ultimately you know the race would be
assimilated.

Dixon: I wish we could all stop thinking about Māori and Pākehā and
think about New Zealanders (mmhm) and to hell with what
colour people are. I'm sure that when another couple of
generations have gone by that we're all of us going to be a bit
brown or a bit white as the case may be, ha ha (yes). You know I
do think that um since the Māori birth rate is a great deal higher
than the Pākehā this will happen.

This vision expresses a desire for a painless remedy. It is assumed that cultural
characteristics and social positions are transmitted genetically. So, if the
genes are the same, diversity and conflict of interests must disappear.

Our interviews suggest that race continues to be a formidable method for
formulating groups and communities in New Zealand. Race is still 'everywhere' in the discourse of Pākehā New Zealanders; but it is also the case that
racial accounts persist mainly as a kind of residual sediment. Certain tropes,
metaphors and images have been retained, such as the concept of 'blood', but
the detailed analysis of social relations through racial theories has been more
or less abandoned. About two-thirds of our sample made racial references of
the type noted above, but very few developed sustained arguments based on
race discourse alone.

Victorian racial interpretation

Whatever its contemporary status, the description of groups as biological types or species has been extremely influential in both New Zealand and the United Kingdom. Banton (1987) argues that the belief in white racial superiority reached its heyday in Western Europe in the two decades before the First World War; but for Victorian colonizers, as well as for Victorian scientists, it was an equally powerful common sense. New Zealand was annexed and settled at a time when this particular discourse and system of classification was at its most taken for granted.

Race was the principal lens through which relations between the Māori people and white migrants were viewed throughout the nineteenth and early twentieth centuries. A fierce debate over exactly what kind of race the Māori belonged to stimulated the intellects of local amateur and professional anthropologists as well as their colleagues in Europe. Some argued that because the Māoris were such a 'fine race' they could be the lost tribe of Israel, or Mediterranean or Aryan in origin (Sinclair, 1986). They were described both as mongoloid and as caucasian in appearance. The suggestion that there were red-haired Māori encouraged the view that some might be a long lost tribe of wandering Scots (MacDonald, 1989).

The historian James Belich (1986) has described how the theories of race circulating in Victorian England produced a dominant framework of interpretation for historians, journalists, politicians and military strategists of the period. He calls this framework the 'doctrine of fatal impact', and his analysis demonstrates how race discourse became woven into early practices to justify exploitation and inequality.

A central tenet in British dealings with the Māori was the assumption that a superior race must win out against a group understood as more primitive. Impact with the 'elevated' was seen as inevitably fatal for the 'primitive' way of life. Superiority was defined as the possession of 'higher mental and military faculties'. Māoris should simply fade away in the face of this superiority or would quickly assimilate as best they could to the new 'civilized' society. As Belich notes, this outcome was presented as a simple and uncontrollable law of nature. It was often seen, from a humanitarian perspective, as a sad, rather than a triumphant, fact.

> The Māoris are dying out, and nothing can save them. Our plain duty, as good compassionate colonists, is to smooth down their dying pillow. Then history will have nothing to reproach us with. (Dr Isaac Featherstone, 1856, in Sorrenson, 1977, p. 8)

> The Māoris . . . look forward with a fatal resignation to the destiny of the final extinction of their race. They themselves say, 'As clover killed the fern, and the European dog the Māori dog, as the Māori rat was killed by the Pākehā rat, so our people also will be gradually supplanted and exterminated by the Europeans. (Dr Ferdinand von Hochstetter, 1865, in Sorrenson, 1977, p. 8)

The doctrine of fatal impact provides a solid defence of colonial activities. One cannot be responsible for a law of nature. If primitives are being supplanted by a group on a higher plane then, even if the process is painful, all is well and good. However, the doctrine had more specific consequences.

Belich also argues that the discourse of race covered over and obscured Māori resistance to British rule, presenting as inevitable something that was in fact touch and go until the 1860s or so. In his alternative, 'revisionist' history of the period, he suggests that Māori actions should not be seen as the desperate struggles of a subordinated and dying race but as one of the most successful acts of resistance against British rule in the empire. We should reread New Zealand history not as a story of the unavoidable and unfortunate decline of one group but as a struggle for power between Māori and Pākehā which Pākehā eventually won due to their superior material resources.

The doctrine of fatal impact became severely strained during the New Zealand Wars of 1845–72, when groups of Māori fought against British and local settler armies over ownership of the land and the applicability of British rule. Local material conditions and the military practices of the Māori were such that British armies were frequently beaten, even when the Māori were outnumbered.

Accounting for these defeats was a taxing problem for contemporary journalists and military personnel. How could a 'superior race' fail in this way? But explanations were found. Indeed, the image of the Māori as courageous and chivalrous and as one of the 'finer races' dates partly from this time. The images of white, civilized, rational warfare and irrational, unplanned, disorganized Māori savagery were carefully nurtured and protected. When armed conflict was over, it was once again easier to take white victory for granted and imagine that racial history could not have been otherwise. The doctrine of fatal impact provides one example of the ideological potential of race discourse. We turn now to another example – the use of this form of discourse in 1960s New Zealand.

Race in 1960s New Zealand

In New Zealand's political history there are few documents or policy statements which explicitly lay out a model for intergroup relations. One important exception is the Hunn Report of 1960 which tried to systematize the principles on which the Department of Māori Affairs should be based and develop a 'policy for the races'. Analysis of this report indicates the form in which nineteenth-century interpretations of intergroup relations persisted into the twentieth century. The report also marks a transition between older racial discourse and newer cultural interpretations and for this reason is worth looking at in some detail. The report embodies some of the contradictions emerging in public discourse of the time.

Hunn's report has often been presented as a progressive step in the history of Māori and Pākehā relations (Spoonley, 1988). It advocated integration as the social policy for the future rather than the assimilation and eventual disappearance of Māori culture. It signalled a change from the tacit acceptance that Māori culture should be quietly allowed to die away. It also considered and decisively rejected segregation and the South African model of apartheid.

Integration was defined as follows: 'Integration: To combine (not fuse) the Maori and pakeha elements to form one nation wherein Maori culture remains distinct' (1960, p. 15). Hunn's emphasis on cultural maintenance and cultural plurality captures some of the new elements entering public debate; but culture is understood in this report through the perspective of race and Hunn's representation of Māori and Pākehā as racial communities encouraged and reflected a particular understanding of the practice of integration.

Throughout the report Māori and Pākehā are referred to as racial groups. Māoris are described, for example, as a 'virile race' (p. 17) and the problem is defined as integrating 'the two species of New Zealander' (p. 14). Hunn argues, from a social Darwinist perspective, that only the 'fittest elements' of Māori culture have 'survived the onset of civilisation' (p. 15) and these practices are features of the 'ancient life' of the Māori (p. 15).

Indeed, his claim demonstrates the way Darwin's theory of evolution became incorporated into racial theories. Darwin questioned the idea that species and thus races were fixed and unchanging types; but this argument became transformed in race discourse to the thesis that, although races evolve, some are more evolved than others (Miles, 1989). The fittest will therefore win out in any struggle. Clearly, this idea informed the doctrine of fatal impact also.

Hunn portrays the Māoris as a group on an evolutionary journey. The endpoint of this journey defines the beginning point for integration.

> When the first Europeans arrived in New Zealand about A.D. 1800, the Maoris
> were in much the same condition as the Ancient Britons at the time of the
> Roman invasion in 55 B.C. In the short century and a half since then, many
> Maoris have overtaken the Pakeha lead and adopted the 1960 pattern of living
> in every way. A few others, the slowest moving members of the race, have
> probably not yet passed the 1860 mark. There is least a century of development
> between the most advanced and the most retarded Maoris in their adjustment to
> modern life. (Hunn, 1960, pp. 15–16)

The themes are familiar. It is seen as inevitable that a superior white civilization should subordinate primitive Māori culture. The term 'advanced' is unselfconsciously applied. Hunn suggests the process of evolution will normally be slow-moving, and so some Māori people should be praised for completing their journey up the ladder in a short time.

Although Hunn's stress on the 'primitive' and the 'civilized', the 'advanced' and the 'retarded' would have been familiar to any Victorian, there are some differences from earlier racial discourse. Hunn not only introduces the new variable of culture; he unfailingly presents the Pākehā mode of life, not as a set of racial traits, as the 'higher faculties' of whites were understood in the previous century, but as simply the modern way of life. One feature of race accounts in twentieth-century New Zealand is an increasing onesidedness in attribution of the term.

> Here and there are Maoris who resent the pressure brought to bear on them to conform to what they regard as a pakeha way of life. It is not, in fact, a pakeha but a *modern* way of life, common to advanced people (Japanese, for example) – not merely white people – in all parts of the world. Indeed some white people, everywhere, are not able to make the grade. Full realisation of this fact might induce the hesitant or reluctant Maoris to fall into line more readily. (Hunn, 1960, p. 16; emphasis added).

Māoris continue to be a race but Pākehā New Zealanders become representatives of an international modernism. Their identity lies in the way the world happens to be now rather than in their distinctive blood. This move was common in our interviews also. Race now appears as a way of talking about *other* people rather than oneself. In that respect it is like the label 'ideological'. 'Other people have ideologies, I have truth'; 'other people belong to racial groups, I'm simply normal'.

Those we interviewed often found it difficult to define and specify their racial group, or the race which contrasts with Māori. A biological or racial account of characteristics minimizes individual autonomy and individual achievement. If you are offering a positive evaluation of your group's characteristics you want to be able to take responsibility for that positivity. Positive traits are best viewed as something *you* produce rather than your genes. Pākehās tended generally to locate themselves or speak from 'outside' race.

This is a useful move ideologically. As a consequence of the events of the Second World War it has become more untenable for a group to claim racial superiority. Also, presented as races, Māori and Pākehā could have a dangerous equivalence; the merits of one race can be debated against the merits of another. The standpoint of the modern might prove more unassailable, a value in a different equation.

What price, then, integration understood in this framework? Hunn is explicit about the task of the Māori Affairs Department, quoting with approval an editorial from *The New Zealand Herald*.

> The painless absorption of the fast-growing Maori population into the economic and social structure of the European is *the great problem* facing both races in New Zealand today . . . . The Maori must be educated for his new role in the city, not only in his personal behaviour but vocationally. (Hunn, 1960, pp. 78–9; emphasis in the original)

Hunn adds that the goal of Māori welfare is: 'To assist the Maori, particularly the younger generation, in adapting himself to the new culture, each according to his ability' (1960, p. 79). It is becoming clear what the policy of integration or combining two cultures might mean in practice. Hunn is explicit. He sees integration as a stage on the road to assimilation and the echo of the doctrine of fatal impact is clear. Assimilation is inevitable because of the presumed racial and hence cultural inferiority of the Māori.

> The Swiss (French, Italians, Germans) appear to be an integrated society; the British (Celts, Britons, Hibernians, Danes, Anglo-Saxons, Normans) are an assimilated society. In the course of centuries, Britain passed through integration to assimilation. Signs are not wanting that that may be the destiny of the two races in New Zealand in the distant future. (Hunn, 1960, p. 15)

Hunn's report illustrates both the strengths and weaknesses of a racial formulation of community when applied as ideology in the twentieth century. On the one hand, the emphasis on inevitability and hierarchy usefully represents oppressive social relations and the hegemony of one group as part of a natural and universal process. The doctrine of fatal impact justifies and makes the best of a bloody struggle. The enemy is weakened if they can be portrayed as rather inadequate and pathetic survivors of an outmoded way of life.

On the other hand, is this formulation, however persuasive and humanitarian it might appear to Pākehā advocates, going to persuade Māori people that their best interests lie in 'joining in'? The race account was to become more and more marginalized as the 1960s and 1970s unfolded. Critics successfully brought the notion of racism into play and mobilized against race discourse both in science and in political arenas.

The social problems of maintaining order and allegiance to the state do not go away, however. In the next section, we will look at an alternative discursive strategy, developed most obviously from the 1970s onwards, which makes culture, not race, the focal point of community.

The premises of culture

From the 1970s onwards, and certainly during the 1980s, the utopian programme in government and administrative circles was no longer the coffee-coloured people or even the transformation of Māoris into 'brown-skinned Pākehas', but national harmony through mutual acceptance of cultural differences (Barber, 1989; Spoonley, 1988).

The shift from race to culture reflects discursive shifts in Western democracies more generally and the development in social science, during the 1950s, of new theories of identity and sociological analyses of discontent. It is also a response to material change, a search for solutions to the new social problems of Māori urban migration. Also, crucially, it is a reaction to the efforts of Māori people, during the 1960s and 1970s, to reset the agenda and make a pan-Māori culture the ground for resistance and social change (Greenland, 1984; Simon, 1989; Spoonley, 1988). There is some debate within anti-racist politics in New Zealand over exactly how culture should be applied as a strategy for resistance (Webster, 1989). We will focus, however, on how culture has been coopted and nuanced by Pākehā New Zealanders.

We could identify two distinctive strands in culture discourse: 'culture as heritage' and 'culture as therapy'. Each proposes a slightly different psychology and social theory and so we will deal with them separately.

Culture as heritage

Culture defined as heritage becomes traditional and unchanging. It refers back to some golden and unsullied time of the constant re-enactment of rituals and values. Culture is seen as ancient, it is the past, not the present or the future, and so the correct response becomes preservation and conservation while the appropriate emotions emerge as nostalgia, grief at loss, 'hanging on', collecting and saving. The emphasis is on memory and faithful reproduction.

Shell: I'm quite, I'm certainly in favour of a bit of Māoritanga. It is something uniquely New Zealand, and I guess I'm very conservation minded (yes) and in the same way as I don't like seeing a species go out of existence I don't like seeing (yes) a culture and a language (yes) and everything else fade out.

Williamson: I think it's important they hang on to their culture (yeah) because if I try to think about it, the Pākehā New Zealander hasn't got a culture (yeah). I, as far as I know he hasn't got one (yeah) unless it's rugby, racing and beer, that would be his lot! (yes) But the Maoris have definitely got something, you know, some definite things that they do and (yeah). No. I say hang onto their culture.

Māoris in this formulation become museum keepers. Theirs is the privilege and the burden of heritage. They are the custodians required to hold the archaic for the national psyche. This task is presented in this form of accounting as a major responsibility. Māori people must not clumsily misplace or contaminate this precious commodity of the past. It must instead be polished and perfected and fixed in amber.

But how does 'culture as heritage' acquire an ideological thrust? Cowlishaw (1988), in her critique of Australian anthropological analyses of aboriginal culture, argues that this form of discourse 'freezes' culture. The emphasis on the archaic and on the 'pure' culture of the past neatly separates culture from politics. The study of ethnic groups becomes segregated from the study of the systematic exclusion and oppression of minorities. In fact, the modern members of an ethnic group become almost an irrelevance. The new social practices they develop in dynamic response to changing conditions are never identified as cultural strategies but as degraded forms of activity in danger of contaminating their pure culture. Only those hidden in backward rural areas who identify with the past (and who take their cue from anthropologists) can be seen as the authentic actors of ethnic culture.

Similarly in New Zealand, culture as heritage discourse suggests Māori political practice should remain 'unpolluted' by the modern. Radical Māori activists are often accused of being out of tune with their culture and, particularly telling, of being out of tune with their elders: the elders being the 'true' repository of what it means to be 'properly' Māori. A divide-and-rule strategy applies with some Māori becoming co-opted as the ethnic politicians and spokespeople – the 'real' voice of Māori culture compared to the 'inauthentic' voices of others (Pearson, 1984).

> A protestor flung a black T-shirt at the Queen just after she arrived at Waitangi and Mr Peters said if people could get close enough to throw objects then the security was not up to standard. The tradition of everyone being welcomed on to the marae had been abused for years by protestors and it was time for the elders to say 'enough is enough' . . . Māori tradition had been 'massively abused', he said. Elders were becoming 'too lenient'. (*The Hawkes' Bay Herald Tribune*, report of a speech by Winston Peters, National MP for Tauranga, February 1990)

Culture as heritage encourages, too, concerns about the dangers of 'culture contact' and the 'clash of cultures'. Culture can be so deeply equated with the traditional and the archaic that all modern Māoris become liable to damage, by definition. Any contact with a 'modern' society becomes viewed as disturbing for those formerly rooted in the 'ancient'. The experience of Western societies can be 'shocking' and some of those we interviewed thus found it 'surprising' how well some Māoris cope.

> Cord: . . . there should be some government effort in trying um to say well 'look, what is the problem here? Why is it that these people are unable to come up to a certain level? Is it something wrong with the education system? Is it some kind of culture shock we're facing?' . . . See it may be that there's an educational problem, it may be, or in a sense, culture shock; you've got er one generation removed who always lived in a relatively tight community coming into Auckland and the community's broken down.

This view of the modern world as distressing for Māoris appears in parliamentary discourse throughout the 1970s. 'Culture shock', however, was largely formulated within the old framework of assimilation and the eventual incorporation of the Māori into European culture. It was presented as a problem of welfare, the goal being to ensure that the Māori people remained 'well-adjusted and happy', and continued to be educated 'in the simple business of understanding the European system' (Mr MacIntyre, Minister for Māori Affairs, *Hansard*, 1971, vol. 736, 4453 and 1971, vol. 376, 4445).

As the discourse of culture developed, however, other possibilities besides 'adjustment' became apparent. Culture became transformed from a source of difficulty into part of the solution.

Culture as therapy

As culture shifts from 'heritage' to 'therapy', the focus changes from arts and crafts, rituals and traditions to identity, values, roots and pride. The portrait of the Māori in 'modern' society becomes more optimistic. Culture becomes not just a preservation order, but a psychological need and even a right.

> Reed: Well, I think the sort of Māori renaissance, the Māoritanga is important because hh like I was explaining about being at that party on Saturday night, I suddenly didn't know where I was (yes) I had lost my identity in some ways and, I was brought up with the people that were there, I'd known most of them all my life and I couldn't identify with them (yes) and I was completely lost (yes). Um so when I found my identity again by being able to talk about something that I was really into, then I became a person again . . . and that's what's happening with the Māoris . . . young Māoris were strapped if they spoke Māori at school and we almost succeeded in wiping out a culture, a way of life, an understanding and I don't think it is necessary to do that and I think it is necessary for the people to get it back because there's something deep-rooted inside you.

Using an analogy with her own experience, Reed develops a particular psychological account of Māori people, arguing that loss of culture equates with loss of identity which is defined as a disabling experience. To be able to 'find themselves' Māori people must become immersed again in a Māori way of life and become their own people once more. As social scientists began to talk about the 'search for identity' and the 'identity crisis' (Rorty, 1976), it became possible, too, for Pākehā New Zealanders to converse in this way.

Culture as therapy blends together humanistic psychology with a social analysis of anomie and alienation. Culture becomes offered as a form of treatment for delinquent and dispossessed individuals and communities. Modern urban Māoris are presented as lost and aimless, searching for meaning and structure for their lives, and, in the absence of these things, prone to crime and disorder.

In a curious way modern Māoris become positioned in this discourse as non-persons. If you 'carelessly' lose your culture and identity, really all you can become in this discourse is an empty vessel, waiting to be refilled. Māoris are no longer seen as deficient in relation to Pākehās, they are seen as deficient *as Māoris* (Nash, 1982, p. 20). The young Māori adrift on an urban sea, disinherited, can be contrasted with a 'proper' Māori embedded in culture and with a secure sense of identity. Again, therefore, the onus and the blame are largely passed to Māoris.

Anecdotes and stories abound in our material of young, usually male, Māoris 'redeemed' through the provision of a bit of 'structure' and 'purpose' to their lives.

Sargeant: There's a very beautiful open-air theatre in New Plymouth called er (.) anyway I've forgotten the name. . . . It was falling into disrepair. There was a lot of litter, a lot of rubbish, all it needed was labour. The New Plymouth City Council did not have the labour force or the money to tidy it up; all it needed was about twenty men for a couple of days (yes). The councillor, city councillor in charge of parks went up there on a Saturday and said, 'oh my God, what can I do about this, it's sad', then he went downtown on the Saturday afternoon and there was a gang of about a dozen louts most of them Māoris sitting astride their motor bikes, just looking for trouble and this brave man went up to them and said, 'Look, I badly need some help up at Brooklands just picking up rubbish, what about coming along?' (mmhmm) and they said, 'Okay, okay mate', or something like that and they went and they got stuck into it and they loved it . . . All it needed was someone to guide them into something constructive and they will respond . . . [the young Māori] he's craving for something constructive to do.

So, what is recommended for the dispossessed and the discontented? Māori people should be made to 'feel good about themselves' and in this way social discontent will be ameliorated. It is seen as good for the soul to be deeply embedded in one's traditional culture. It encourages pride in oneself and a self-esteem based on knowledge of difference. The following extracts take up this theme.

Broadman: . . . Uh, you know the rootless young Polynesian is perhaps a little more obvious than the rootless young European although there's quite a few of those, and for the same reasons surprisingly, is still very visible in the streets (mmhm). Um, and part of the recent upsurge in Māoritanga has been to encourage many of them to go back and find their roots, and that's exactly what they needed (yes).

Pinter: . . . I think the, you know, latest moves in part of part of some of the Māori activists to try and raise some social consciousness and so on about, you know, and pride in Māoridom are quite good actually (yes?) yeah. It's a pity I think we missed a great, a golden opportunity years and years ago when the urbanization of the Māoris started probably in the thirties (Wetherell: Yes, it was around that period when there was economic recession, yes).

> Right, when they started coming to the city that we didn't put in
> maraes and so on it's silly (yes) it's stupid. (Wetherell: Yeah, and
> it's just happenning now in fact). Yeah, it's a culture, you know,
> they're a family-orientated people and, um, you know, they come
> to a city and they get stuck in a rented house in some dingy
> suburb and what chance do they have? (yes). They lose their
> identity, they lose their will, they lose (Wetherell: their family
> connections?) exactly they're nothing. And their society's rooted
> in the land, and family, and elders, they lose that or they lost it
> and I think they're getting it back.

Government policy of the late 1970s reflected this emphasis on culture as a
cure and not just through the building of urban maraes and community
centres (a detailed description of state intervention in the last two decades can
be found in Spoonley, 1988). The Māori Affairs Department, for example,
introduced a policy of 'Tu Tangata' – the Māori people were encouraged to
'stand tall', to have pride in themselves and engage in self-help. Here is Ben
Couch, a Māori Affairs Minister who held office in the 1980s, reflecting back
on Tu Tangata in an interview we conducted with him in 1984.

> Couch: Well, when you say the initiative this was started politically by my
>   predecessor er er Duncan MacIntyre. He was a Scotsman, he had
>   pride in himself, pride in his own race and he used to keep telling
>   us (the Māori people) and this is all what it was about, Tu
>   Tangata, why don't you stand tall?

By the end of the 1970s the view had become established that cultural
differences should be worked as a national resource not seen as a stumbling
block to full-blown 'integration' (Barber, 1989).

The notion that Māoris were in need of an identity revival had in fact been
promoted earlier by Māori activists of the late 1960s and early 1970s. The
group Nga Tamatoa, for example, had called for the enculturation of young
urban Māori in *taha Māori*, or Māori ways (Greenland, 1984). This demand
for cultural resources, however, was tied to a demand for social and political
change and the resolution of land and sovereignty grievances. Loss of identity
was also interpreted as an effect of the social position of young Māori in
Pākehā society rather than as a deficiency in Māori socialisation.

In Pākehā hands, culture as therapy re-interprets the protest and grievances of the Māori people as, by and large, their difficulty and weakness.
Reactions and responses which could be understood as anger at loss of
sovereignty and as resistance to becoming the proletariat for a capitalist
economy can be translated into a psychological malaise. Remedies can be
divorced from social and political struggles and treated simply as a feature of
inter-cultural relations.

We will shortly try to summarize the ideological work done by culture
discourse; but, first, what subject positions does this discourse offer Pākehā

people? If culture positions the Māori people as alternately archaic and rootless, what identities are offered to Pākehā?

Pākehā positions

There are several possibilities here. The formulation of Māori as the 'cultural' group gives Pākehā an arena where new skills and abilities can be tried out and new talents shown off. Māori culture can become a site for Pākehā skill acquisition. Whereas for the Māori, culture is presented almost as a burden, a double-edged and unavoidable duty, for the Pākehā it can be a potential playground.

One can learn the Māori language like learning French or learning to ski. The strange is acquired and tamed and made one's own by an act of mastery. Acquisition for the Māori is, of course, not seen in the same light. Culture and identity are more ambiguous possessions for their 'proper' owners – somehow outside but also already there, deeply-rooted, seeded inside, waiting to flower. Acquisition is semi-mystical, a revelation of what is, at some basic level, already possessed, even if you are an urban Māori; but, for the Pākehā, Māori culture can be a rich extra dimension, like having a Constable painting to decorate a wall. Pākehā are free actively to choose this culture, Māori can reject it only at the risk of being found anomic.

Stones: My son can count to ten in Māori from the TV (really?), and he takes great pride in being able to do it. He likes the Māori language. He's he's (.) I'm not sure why, I haven't, I haven't really been able to work out why he's taken this interest, but for him to have actually sat down and learnt one to ten, and several other words, stomach and leg and, you know, he quite often comes out in, 'oh, it's the Māori word for such and such', well I wouldn't have a clue but he does. Um, I don't know . . .

M. Jones: I, I don't know, I think it's a pity for them to lose their heritage, but I think that's for the Māori people to promote it (right) and for the Māori people to want to to be able to speak and to gain a pride in it, in doing it themselves (right), but I don't know that I've got, I'm quite keen on it, my parents were keen on learning the Māori language (yes), just to be inquisitive I think, and I have Māori dictionaries at home, and I'm fascinated (yes), but I've not really done any more than that about it.

Culture brings other emotional possibilities in its wake. Culture discourse, unlike race, is, at this period of history, extremely 'user friendly'. It is about being 'sensitive', 'tolerant', being sufficiently magnanimous and enlightened to 'respect difference' and 'appreciate' others. A very different knowledge/ power axis operates here in comparison to race. The importance of the acceptance of diversity and the tolerance of difference ran through the bulk of the interviews we conducted.

Unlike the racist, the culture buff is understood as generous, progressive, committed to harmony and imbued with good-will. As Kalantzis (1988) points out, multiculturalism is about 'feeling good about difference' (p. 92). Everyone is beautiful in their own way, one can learn to listen, all differences are of equal value and racism is an unforgiveable moral lapse (p. 95).

> Waites: ... we uh we arranged a marae experience for about, uh, over six hundred people uh from uh parishes ... and it was really a very successful occasion, I thought. It got behind time of course, you know, there were a lot of speeches, time went on, um, and uh the marae people were embarrassed because they hadn't, uh they hadn't really thought that there would be as many coming as we said would be, and though, you know, we had timed things approximately through the evening, of course it got later and later, and I was really quite disappointed that out of all that experience where there was so much to learn and so much to understand and an opportunity to come alongside people, you know, and understand their way of thinking, so many people said to me, 'oh, it got late, you can't trust the Māoris, they'll always, you know time doesn't mean anything to them'. There was, among some people that I would hope for some understanding, there was a total lack of understanding.

The pleasures generated through cultural discourse are real enough. In analyzing these new identities and desires as 'subject positions', we are not attempting to question the sincerity of those, including ourselves, who are captivated, or make a contrast with some more 'authentic' realm of emotional experience.

> Williamson: Yeah it could be, yeah. Probably one of the greatest things, Margaret, that I, I've done, that I always enjoy doing is stopping on a marae. Have you ever done it? (Wetherell: Yes, I have, yes) What about it? (Wetherell: Great, isn't it?) Isn't it? All the Māoris come down and everyone talks to each other and (yeah) and everyone sort of shares. Ah? Working together, it's a great thing (yeah).

The issue is always: to what ends are these emotions harnessed and what other possibilities may be silenced in the process?

A further question remains. If Māori people have culture, what do Pākehā people have as the contrast? As with the Hunn Report, the implication is that Pākehā people simply possess society (Spoonley, 1988). The Pākehā have 'civilization', they have a mundane, technical and practical outlook. They have the attitudes of the modern world. These are presented not as culture, but as simple common sense.

In culture discourse, Māori people become exotic and the Pākehā majority become the normal mode. Pākehā are pervasive and Māoris represent an enclave of difference. This bestowal of normality and difference is ironic. Once it was the Māori who were 'normal'; the term 'Māori' means simply the people who live in this land. 'Pākeha' was the Māori term for foreigner or stranger.

If the Pākehā have a culture at all, it is the 'high' culture of operas, novels and art. Frequent complaints are heard that New Zealanders are 'uncultured', meaning not that Pākehā have no sense of their roots, or no sense of identity, but that they are a pack of philistines, neglecting the finer things of life in favour of 'rugby, racing, and beer'. Interestingly, however, there have been some attempts more recently among academic commentators to argue for a Pākehā ethnicity based on local popular culture rather than imported high culture (see Pearson, 1989, for a discussion of these moves).

The contrast between the exotic and the taken-for-granted is unfortunate to say the least for Māori people (see Awatere, 1984 for a discussion of its effects from a Māori perspective). If a Māori 'loses their cultural identity' they do not automatically become Pākehā or 'civilized' by default. They are seen as entering a no man's land of 'rootlessness'. They become not normal (like the Pākehā) but positioned as abnormal: the restless, urban discontented, crying out for heritage therapy which is presented as their due; for it is assumed in this discourse that Pākehā can get by very well without culture, whereas the Māori have a 'right' to this dubious commodity – dubious, that is, in some of the ways it has been packaged.

Culture also allows the old concept of the 'white man's burden' to be reworked afresh. Pākehā become the agents who can dole out cultural opportunities to the Māori. Wider Pākehā *society* surrounds narrower Māori *culture* and thus determines its boundaries. Whereas once colonists saw it as their task to smooth the pillow of the dying race, modern Pākehā see it as their duty to provide paternal leadership and guidance which will encourage the 'passive' Māori to revive themselves.

> Morrison (MP for Pakaranga): . . . I think it is a great idea, um, teaching Māori language and all of these – to give back pride and dignity to a lot of Māori people who have lost it, and they probably lost it because we killed off all of their leadership people uh at the, in the latter half of the last century (yes). And once a leadership uh situation has been destroyed it takes a very long time to rebuild it. Because they were the people who passed on the pride to the . next generation. So I think we um, (Wetherell: So there is good cause for actively fostering Māori culture, do you think?) Yeah, absolutely um and I accept the responsibility on, is on us to do it. I mean after all we eliminated all the leadership um um . . . and I I think it's up to us to replace it. (interview conducted 1984)

The Pākehā relationship to Māori culture is, in the end, ambiguous and ambivalent. It is possessed but not possessed. 'Ours' to control, own and guide, something 'we', Pākehā, can feel proud of and take responsibility for as 'New Zealanders', but 'deep-down' nothing to do with us.

Culture as ideology

> First they steal our land, and now they want to hold hands with us.
> (Greg Whakataka Brightwell, cited Channel One, Television New Zealand,
> Discussion Programme, Treaty of Waitangi, 28 December 1989)

We have tried to document some of the manifold ways talk about culture can become a legitimating ideological discourse (see also Nairn and McCreanor, 1990; McCreanor, 1991). Culture presents Māori people with a sphere of autonomy but we have seen that it is a space with an elastic perimeter. It is possible to shrink the boundaries so that culture becomes merely a matter of rituals and traditions, arts and crafts. As one person we interviewed (Smith) said: 'Māori culture is more a game thing, you know, it's not solid life, it is something you do on special days'. But culture can also be expanded to 'lifestyle' (Simon, 1989, p. 30), and then portrayed as a vital part of the life of a people, not just frills for special days.

In either case cultural discourse does not contradict the demands of capitalism. It is presented as a matter of relatively peripheral preferences, tastes and values. The 'rootless' Māori in metropolitan areas can still be a modern worker, as can the 'new' Māori, freshly rerooted in ethnicity. Culture provides a central identity but it is also ethereal. Culture is for spare time but the identity provided in this spare time is somehow supposed to diffuse through the personality in a powerful and useful way.

Culture discourse, therefore, takes over some of the same tasks as race. It becomes a naturally occurring difference, a simple fact of life, and a self-sufficient form of explanation. Culture also continues the doctrine of fatal impact and the white man's burden; but this time around the 'fatal flaws' in the Māori people do not lie in their genes but in their traditional practices, attitudes and values. Within the discourse of culture the ancient and archaic can be contrasted with the modern just as the 'primitive' is contrasted with the 'advanced' within racial discourse.

In addition, culture has this aura of niceness, of progressiveness and humanitarianism. It covers over the messy business of domination and uneven development through advocacy of respect and tolerance for differences. Colonial history can be reconstructed as a story of clashing values, the modern against the traditional, as opposed to a story of conflicting interests, power relations and exploitation. There is an inevitability and acceptability in the notion of 'culture contact' not found in the rhetoric of annexation, conquest and oppression.

Pākehā New Zealanders are confronted with some genuine dilemmas as they puzzle over their history, the pattern of Māori disadvantage and the problem of generating social reform. Culture discourse accounts for the disadvantage and suggests remedies which will not unduly disturb contemporary social structure and organization. Multiculturalism, says Kalantzis (1988), is all about singing in our community languages in the dole queue (p. 93).

Indeed, ideally, the notion of 'multi'-culturalism does not give precedence to any cultural group. All groups are equally able to realize their cultural ambitions defined as tastes and values. As many Māori have recently pointed out, the doctrine of multiculturalism denies the special indigenous status of Māori people, as the *tāngata whenua* of Aotearoa, the people of the land, and the sovereignty rights devolving from that status (Kia Mohio Kia Marama Trust, 1990). Under multiculturalism, Māori become just one cultural group among many potential groups. The nature of their specific grievance becomes blurred as the fault becomes defined as the general failure of Pākehā to be sufficiently tolerant and accommodating towards any difference. For this reason some Māori activists have opposed multiculturalism with the concept of biculturalism, with considerable success in undermining this implication of multiculturalist discourse (Simon, 1989).

Several social scientists (Castles *et al.*, 1988; Foster and Stockley, 1984; Jakubowicz, 1981; Yuval-Davis, 1986) have argued in relation to social policy in Australia that multiculturalism has become *the* preferred capitalist strategy for dealing with ethnic groups and for the 'servicing of diversity' (Kalantzis, 1988, p. 92). The same points are beginning to be made about multiculturalism in New Zealand (e.g. Barber, 1989; Simon, 1989).

This analysis argues that multiculturalism usefully re-presents inequality as a problem of backwardness and individual identity rather than a problem of resources, social class and the needs of capital. Multiculturalism allows for state intervention into class relations disguised as race relations policy (Jakubowicz, 1981). Thus, for instance, ethnic welfare becomes an acceptable way of attempting to circumvent some of the dangers for the state of entrenched class divisions, repackaging these as simple forms of cultural discontent. The politics of the dispossessed can be separated off into 'ethnic politics', thereby sanitizing struggles from the mainstream and limiting claims for justice by specializing them into claims for culture.

These analyses of ideological effects tend to privilege the discourse of social class over other forms of group description (see also Miles, 1987) and thus adopt a class-determinate view of ideology. From our perspective the formulation of groups as social classes could be explored in the same way that we have tried to explore formulations of race and culture in this chapter. However, we agree with the assessment of the general effects of multiculturalist discourse for power relations and with this description of the mobilization of culture as a justificatory strategy.

In the next section we will move on to examine the community of nation and how it operates, often in tandem with culture; but – as a final word on culture – it is worth stressing that we see culture as a discourse with mixed potential. We have strongly emphasized what we think are its oppressive forms but that is not to say that culture cannot also be a liberatory discourse, an important source of resistance for Māori people, and a profound way of articulating difference.

One theme which will recur again and again in Part II of this book is the flexibility of signification. Discourse is not, we shall argue, inherently ideological. It becomes ideological in argument, debate and application. Even race accounts, unlikely as it may seem, can be used in a counter-ideological manner. Some Māori groups have frequently employed the essentialist framing of race to advantage, arguing, for example, that Māoris have an inbuilt biological affinity with the land which justifies restitution. As we shall demonstrate, the discourse of nationalism also has this contradictory potential.

The premises of nation and nationalism

He iwi tahi tatou – We are one people.

This remark was attributed to Governor William Hobson as he shook hands with Māori chiefs after signing the Treaty of Waitangi. In 1840 the rhetorical value of unity was clearly appreciated. In modern times, the discourse of cultural difference, as we have tried to show, has submerged the theme of one people; and, indeed, difference does some useful ideological work. But having set up diversity, with all its dangers, how can Pākehā New Zealanders re-assert their particular interests as universal interests and present their agenda as applicable to all New Zealanders? How can Pākehā New Zealanders reconstitute 'one people' after their journey into difference?

The community re-presented as nation is one answer. New Zealanders can be two peoples but they are one nation. This phrase, which resonates through contemporary political discourse, attempts finally to set the bounds of Māori aspirations and autonomy. Cultural identity becomes presented as subordinate in the last analysis to nationality.

Nations are such a dominant feature of the modern political landscape that it seems almost eccentric to treat this form of belonging, not as a self-evident fact – a natural division of populations – but as a signifying system linked to certain material arrangements of territory and resources. Yet, like race and culture, the formulation of community as nation has a chartable history. People have not always described themselves in this way. Nations and nationalism are relatively modern phenomena.

A distinction is often made between the 'old' nations such as England, France, Scotland, Denmark, Poland, for instance, and the 'new' nations which emerged from self-conscious, nineteenth century, nationalist, independence movements; but even in the case of the 'old' nations, nationalism is part of recent, if not immediate, history. Seton-Watson (1977) argues that England, for instance, had developed into a coherent political entity by around 1600, with the mass of people recognizing themselves as English with allegiance to the Crown. However, the main body of doctrines associated with nationalism did not take hold until the late eighteenth century.

> During the stages of their history in which the national identity and self-consciousness of these 'old' nations were formed, the concepts of 'national consciousness' and the modern concept of the 'nation' did not exist. The leaders had no idea that they were forming nations. This is the basic difference between the 'old' nations and the post-1789 'new' nations: in the case of the latter, the leaders knew perfectly well what it was they were trying to do . . .
> (Seton-Watson, 1977, p. 11)

Keith Sinclair (1986) in his extensive history of nationalism in New Zealand suggests that the experience of Pākehā New Zealand, although typical of 'colonial nationalism', reverses the usual route to the nation state. In most countries the ideal of a nation, where people share the same history, the same language and possess power in their own country, leads to the fight to establish a particular form of government – usually democratic and republican. In New Zealand there was a government, established by the British, but no nation. Pākehā nationalism emerged from the existing forms of administration rather than creating them. New Zealand became a dominion in 1907, and fully independent in 1947 (considerably after other countries such as Canada, Australia and South Africa), but retains today a governor-general appointed by the British monarch.

Despite this paradoxical start, the themes of nationalism are strongly established in the discourse of contemporary Pākehā New Zealanders.

Wetherell:	Um if I said imagine say in twenty years' time that it was suggested that Australia and New Zealand become one country with economic and political union so that, like New Zealand becomes part of Australia, would you be in favour of this?
Acton:	Um, no I don't think so. I don't know um it would probably be good from the country's point of view, economically and everything, but I think it's nice that we're New Zealand by ourselves and we're a country and we make it in the world, but I mean look at us at the Olympic Games and everything, it's just amazing. I think we do really well. Um a lot of people I'd say would resent [union with Australia] because there's always the idea of Aussie people sort of some of them have got a bad name, and you know. Um I couldn't see it happening really. Maybe (.) we'll see in twenty years haha.
Owen:	Oh I think most New Zealanders tend to think uh of the uh 'average' quotation mark Aussie as being uh, uh, more brash more like Texans of the USA (yes, heh) sort of business. It's

probably a bit of a myth (yeah). There are more extremes, aren't there? In some parts of Australia they are definitely more snobby, uh, Melbourne definitely is, I've been in Melbourne a few times, and, uh, they're pretty hot on the right school and that sort of thing (yeah) and certainly all you have to do is make money (heh). But the average Australian is quite good . . . they're more, probably a little more, extrovert (mmhm) than the average New Zealander. New Zealanders? Well we think we're better than the Aussies (heh).

Wetherell:	. . . What do we share in common? (Barr: As New Zealanders?) Yes.
Barr:	Very open, and em, you know, compared say to English people, or uh we're very open and forthright, and we're um uh what shall we say, more inclined to do things (yes). Uh, we're probably at least as friendly as the Americans, (mmhm) but then we don't have generally the same (mmhm) material well-being as they have (mmhm). I think that stands out. Any time that I come home from overseas, it (heh, yes) stands out.
Burns:	Well, I have travelled overseas a lot for (.) on company business, uh to all sorts of parts of the world, and there's never any environment that's (.) Here it's just so tremendous and, you know, a person no matter who it is, whether he's on, you know, he's um a low standard of living, he can just go on his bike, in the main, and get to the beach, and uh the environment, the air itself and the rivers, and anybody can go fishing these days. You get a mate and you can go and get a boat and go out try and catch a fish out there, and you can play the sport, and you know just the whole environment is just so tremendous compared with those places I've been to.

The discourse of nation, as these extracts illustrate, articulates the sense of a 'we' travelling together through time, acting collectively in our own space, with a common fate (Anderson, 1983). It posits an idea of 'national character', a set of personality traits and attitudes which people share in common, distinct from others, such as the Australians and British, and it constructs a framework of rituals, icons, anthems and flags. National discourse, like culture, organizes the emotions. Patriotism and pride are the 'positive' face, and xenophobia and chauvinism the unacceptable face of nationalism.

Nationalist discourse takes the familiar things of the small-scale – landscape, family, home and hearth, institutions, habits, idiosyncrasies, a local sense of place – and writes them large as a global, 'corporate' identity for three million people (Said, 1990). Attachment to the local scene becomes allegiance to the great New Zealand firm. The accidental and the contingent are transformed into destiny. Heterogeneity, celebrated at other times, becomes restyled as different faces of an underlying homogeneity.

The advantages of nationalism for modern states are clear enough; but what has the discourse of nation achieved for Pākehā New Zealanders as they attempt to formulate and fix the pattern of Māori–Pākehā relations?

Mimicry and ambivalence

> Young, small and a long way from home life can be hard. On the other
> hand, there is no-one to tell you you can't do something.
>
> (James, 1990, p. 124)

James's statement nicely sums up Pākehā New Zealanders' ambivalence towards Britain, their 'mother' country. New Zealand's relationship with Britain has, since the beginning, shifted between slavish adoration and foot-dragging covert rebellion, mixed with affront when 'home' does not seem to want 'us' any more. The resulting confusion of discourse suggests some of the tensions which arise as, increasingly, the idea of the nation is used to try and cement Māori–Pākehā relations. Nation should cohere New Zealanders together, it should be able to present sectional interests as universal, but it continues to be defined in such a way that Māoris are both included and persistently excluded.

Homi Bhabha (1984) has argued that the ambivalence of colonial discourse can be related to a typical colonial strategy of 'mimicry'. The establishment of a colony, he suggests, requires a form of 'camouflage', as institutions and an infrastructure are imposed on other groups in imitation of home. There is an attempt to 'fade' into the society imitated, merge with 'Greater' Britain. But, says Bhabha, imitation and mimicry precisely reveal that difference and the lessons of difference are instructive in this case for the colonizer (Britain), the colonized (Māori people) and for those in the middle (contemporary Pākehā).

The Pākehā New Zealander gazes at Britain as though looking, narcissistically, in a mirror but is confounded when the returning gaze is sceptical, negligent and sometimes uncomplimentary about the provincial Antipodean with the dreadful accent. The mimicry offered by Pākehā New Zealand society is both welcomed and found amusing. The 'model' country, Britain, is empowered by this gaze but can chafe at the dependence and ties of obligation, as the British establishment have done many times, from the days of disputes with settlers and protest at fighting land wars on their behalf (Sinclair, 1986).

Meanwhile, the Pākehā New Zealander gazes at the Māori and bemoans the incompleteness of their imitation of British institutions and mores. If only the Māori would look more closely and learn their lessons more thoroughly, then all would be well. In a recent popular article in a New Zealand magazine John Gould, an Emeritus Professor of Economic History, argues just this line, for instance. Māori culture, he says, is its own worst enemy. He claims that what he identifies as central Māori traits – refusal to acquire good capitalist habits of saving and investment, intermittent work patterns, preferences for co-operation rather than competition, and the predominance of group over individual effort, reward and responsibility – ensure that Māori culture is not an advantageous springboard for success in the modern world (1990, p. 146). As Gould's article demonstrates, Pākehā New Zealanders become chiding, petulant and, finally, incomprehending in response to this apparently wilful refusal to mimic.

For Māori, there may be possibilities of black humour here – Bhaba notes the potential for the colonized to engage in perfect imitations of their colonizers which by their very excellence reveal parody; but, since most crucial state institutions – education, law, the civil service – have been thoroughly organized around the mimicry of equivalent British institutions, resistance is fraught and difficult. Refusal may be all that is possible. During the 1990 general election in New Zealand, several Māori groups campaigned for Māori people to boycott the election. Election night figures suggest that nearly half of eligible Māori voters stayed away from the polling booths (Jackson, 1990).

An alternative strategy which has been pursued simultaneously is to turn nationalist discourse against Pākehā ambitions and resurrect the concept of an independent Māori nation. Māoris become redefined not as subject people, part of someone else's nation, but as engaged in a nationalist struggle of their own for sovereignty (Awatere, 1984). In this way, then, nationalist discourse becomes split and contradictory and offers Māori a form of resistance, exploiting the ambiguous status of the Treaty of Waitangi, which can be read as guaranteeing Māori sovereignty and dominion over their lands in return for British administration. Much current Māori activity centres around efforts to have this treaty properly ratified and acknowledged.

Towards a South Pacific nation?

For most of its history Pākehā nationalism in New Zealand has thus been focused on Britain. At Gallipoli alone 2,700 New Zealanders died, fighting for Britain in the First World War, and 4,700 were injured, many others died in France. Similar losses were sustained in the European and Mediterranean theatres of the Second World War, and in 1943, commodities in short supply in Britain but not in New Zealand, such as butter and meat, were extensively rationed (McKinnon, 1990). For long periods patriotism in New Zealand was patriotism for British causes. The war efforts and sacrifices strongly cemented these ties.

The continuing focus on Britain is not surprising. The majority of settlers were British, and, unlike Australia, immigration policy, often unstated and sometimes covertly formulated, successfully ensured that British people, as opposed to other European, Asian or South Pacific groups, remained (and continue to remain) the dominant migrant intake (New Zealand Race Relations Office, 1986). Looking at Pākehā nationalist history as a whole there seem to have been three phases in the strategy *vis-à-vis* Māori people: an initial neglect, a partial incorporation and, more recently, as the ideological paucity of national discourse centred on Britain has become more evident, a refocusing of New Zealand as a South Pacific nation around Māori iconography. Hence the 'Huia Tuia, Tui Tuia' – unite together in the common bond of fellowship – which was the motto for the 1990 celebrations.

One episode vividly demonstrates the first phase of Pākehā nationalist strategy – the attempt to form, in the 1890s, 'New Zealand Natives' Associations' (Sinclair, 1986). The 'natives' were defined as male settlers, of British origin, who had been born in New Zealand. By 1890 there seemed to be sufficient numbers of white, first-generation New Zealanders to justify an organization. The aim was to set up a benefit society but principally to 'stimulate patriotism and national sentiment; to provide for social intercourse; and to unite all worthy sons of New Zealand in one harmonious body throughout the Colony' (quoted in Sinclair, 1986, p. 37).

The Natives' Associations represent some of the first faltering steps towards independence from Britain and towards a home-grown identity. A poem read at one of the inaugural meetings and reproduced in Sinclair's account (1986, p. 36) expresses the dominant sentiment:

> We greet you, stranger, to this land.
> Where slaves have never trod,
> The breeze which sweeps our mountains,
> Is the wreath of freedom's God.
> If you've a hand to keep us,
> In the work we've got to do –
> The building of a nation grand,
> Then friend we welcome you.

The example of the Natives' Associations indicates the pattern Pākehā nationalism followed for a considerable period thereafter – the automatic exclusion of Māori from the group of 'worthy sons', the seemingly non-ironic description of Pākehā as the 'natives' and the building of a national identity which associates the category New Zealander with Pākehā interests.

Pākehā New Zealanders later, in a second phase, became proud of the exploits of the Māori, particularly those of the Māori battalion who fought for Britain in the Second World War. Māori people (men) became partially incorporated into nationalist discourse and given an iconographic or emblematic status. The haka performed by the All Blacks, the New Zealand rugby team, before they yet again defeat the Welsh at rugby can be a source for swelling hearts and surreptitious tears of nationalism. However, this inclusion has always been patchy. Pākehā people were very slow, for example, to deplore the exclusion of Māoris in rugby teams touring South Africa, for instance, and slow to notice that Māori soldiers were confined to their ships during visits to South African ports (Awatere, 1984). Māori people became included symbolically as a proud possession: not one of 'us' so much but something 'we' confidently own and can display to the tourist and to visiting royals.

The story of Pākehā nationalism continues as we write. A South Pacific theme is becoming more dominant in political and lay discourse as the articulation of a 'multicultural nation', distinct from Britain, becomes established. New Zealand could be said to be resuming its actual geographical position in the southern hemisphere as opposed to its 'imagined position' in the English Channel. Only a few of those we interviewed in the mid-1980s, adopted nationality as a meta-categorization drowning the competing claims of race and culture. Among this set of interviews, the cultural and racial themes we have described were more prevalent, carrying the ideological burden.

By 1990, however, this minor theme in our interviews had become the major theme in public and political discourse surrounding the 150th anniversary celebrations. But, as the extracts below from our interviews and from the commemorative discourse of 1990 indicate, the 'discovery' of shared national imperatives generally reinforces, rather than questions, Pākehā hegemony. Increasingly, Māori people are presented as 'free' to set cultural agenda, but it is Pākehā 'society' which comes to define the economic structure and goals of the new 'two people' nation (see Kelsey, 1990, and Nairn, 1991 for a detailed description of how this combination develops in practical policy-making). From a Māori perspective, the danger of being part of a nation which is 'more than two cultures' (Stead, 1990, p. 52) lies in how that 'more' is defined.

Barr: I think everybody should be free to follow their culture as part of (mmhm) their heritage. But, uh, I think it's also important that we recognize that we are in fact all New Zealanders (mmhm). And we should be tending to become more one rather than separately developing (right, yeah). You see it in places like Melbourne, where, uh, there's many different ethnic, there's many different ethnic groups (mmhm) but they still regard themselves as Australians (mmhm). Whether they're Greek or Italian or whatever (mmhm). We're tending to push or not push, pull (mmhm) that part of our culture, to a uh almost a sense of importance (mmhm) that I don't think it really has (mmhm).

Simpson: I tend to think that we've really, it's gone the whole cycle, when I was in Māori Affairs assimilation's the answer and one was supposed to intermarry and become one New Zealand, um, which I suppose is not silly. And then, of course, over the last ten years or so, since I've been back in New Zealand, it's gone the other way and everybody wants a marae and this sort of thing, and the

> Māori culture's becoming quite an in thing. Um, I don't think
> that, I think it's good, I think they ought to keep their identity,
> but I think as long as they're New Zealanders first, (yes) I, you
> know, I think most Māoris are, quite honestly. Same as most
> Negros in America.

Most important of all, the Government and a new-generation Māori elite,
responding to a powerful revival of confidence among Māori, have smashed the
assumption that Māori must be British in thought, word and deed. Henceforth
Māori will be Māori.

The Anglo-Saxon homogeneity of culture has given way to diversity. The
cocoon of colony and the perpetual youth it granted is broken. New Zealand
and Aotearoa are passing into the painful and difficult process of becoming a
fully-fledged nation. Smallness doesn't help in that.

. . . There is consensus of sorts among the intimate business, political and
bureaucratic elite on the economy and contingent matters: economically New
Zealand must be freer, more open and more self-reliant.

(James, 1990, p. 126)

It remains to be seen whether this latest articulation of the nation will finally
silence the ambivalence in the discourse of the colonial and, from the Pākehā
perspective, prove to be effective ideology, reworking and subjugating the
competing voice and logic of Māori nationalism.

The practice of categorization

This chapter has focused on acts of social categorization and has tried to
specify their varying ideological force. Throughout we have remained
committed to the idea that there is nothing natural about 'national', 'racial',
and 'cultural' distinctions. These categorizations have been analyzed as
discursive orderings with traceable historical origins. Most importantly, we
have tried to show how categorization is constitutive as well as reflective – the
discursive act creates groups, interests, emotions, similarities and differences,
a social landscape, an anthropology, a psychology of identity and even a
geography.

Chapter 5 has thus taken up and illustrated theoretical points developed in
Part I. Our emphasis in this chapter on the productive nature of discourse can
be contrasted with the usual socio-psychological approach to group categorization which was the target of criticism in Part I. From a lay perspective, the
action of describing someone as a 'Māori' and someone else as a 'New
Zealander' often feels just that – a description of the person's essence. Some
social psychologists, too, have confused the descriptive with the ontological in
this way. Social categorizations become, particularly in experimental investigations, *a priori* givens, not the object of study.

It is now clearer why that is such a problematic move. As Miles (1982) has
pointed out for the sociology of race relations, and Billig (1985), Condor

(1988), Potter and Wetherell (1987) and Reicher (1986) for the social psychology of intergroup relations, the danger here is that contingent, historically specific, ideological solutions will be reified as science. When a social psychologist decides to use 'cultural group' as an independent variable in an analysis of competitive or co-operative behaviour, for example, relying on common knowledge to identify what counts as culturally different, it is important that someone else deconstructs the theory of groups which makes that move possible.

In this chapter we have looked at social categorization through the theoretical lens of the 'imagined community' (Anderson, 1983; Said, 1978). Before embracing this concept too fervently, however, it is important to point out some ambiguities and disadvantages. The idea of the 'imagined' undermines the seductive view that acts of categorization are simple descriptions of what is really out there. It questions the community rather than reproducing it as fact. The notion of the 'imagined community' also draws attention, in a way that is extremely pertinent for social psychology, to questions of subjectivity and the manipulation of identity. In articulating the community, one's own identity becomes interpreted. As Said (1978) notes, identity is often acquired negatively through a strong sense of what 'we' are not (see also Miles, 1989, Ch. 1). However, paradoxically, the term 'imagined community' also opens the possibility of the 'unimagined community'. It may suggest that whereas imagination is the province of lay members of society, critical social scientists are distinguished by their rationality, their sense of reality and their detachment from the imagined. It could imply that the only orderings of community which should be questioned are those produced by non-scientists enmeshed in fantasy and false consciousness and by those reactionary social psychologists who unreflectively reproduce this false consciousness.

Robert Miles (1987), for example, takes this sort of line. He argues that discourses of nationalism and racism obscure and distort the realities of economic production. That is, social class or categories based on production would be, for him, a non-fantastic and real basis for analysis compared to the imagined communities of nation and race. Is this our view too – that some accounts of community and some group categorizations have a privileged status as reflectors of the real? That with sufficient research and deliberation one can move behind the imaginary?

In arguing that a social psychology of categorization should pay attention to the productive role of language, we are suggesting that all acts of categorization should be investigated in the same way. We are not proposing to privilege some scientific accounts over others, or proposing to set scientific accounts over lay accounts, at least on epistemological grounds. It is possible, however, to contrast the ideological force and potential of different discursive acts of categorization and the scope they offer for resistance. If ideology is defined, as we proposed in Part I, as discourse linked to oppressive power relations, then it is possible to interrogate, as we have tried to do in this chapter, the ways in which different forms of categorization, either in social science or in lay discourse, become bound in with practices which sustain power relations.

Our investigation of categorization will thus be neutral in some respects – interested equally in class categorizations and race categorizations – but will also try to differentiate through an analysis of the empowering or disempowering force of certain forms of discourse. Given the centrality of these issues of social psychological practice, ideology and categorization, the remaining chapters in Part II will return again and again to these questions.

6

Accounting for 'the social': stories of social conflict and social influence

Ideology is frequently defined as discourse which re-presents social products as natural products or, even, as biological in origin (McClellan, 1986). Through 'naturalizing', as the previous chapter demonstrated for racial categorization, some social relations and some sets of interests can be made to appear universal, eternal and immutable. However, the natural is not the only available resource. Justification can work equally well through accounts which stress social dimensions and which construct narratives of what society is and how it operates. It is accounts of this kind, and their effects, which will form the focus of this chapter.

There were many points in our materials where those we interviewed began to develop accounts of 'the social body' or began to describe a social process. In one sense every account of Māori/Pākehā relations can be seen in this way – as an explication of social relations; but here we are interested in a more confined domain, in the versions of social processes found in stories about social conflict and social influence. We want to examine how Pākehā New Zealanders' narratives of social process and social influence are made 'interested', that is, how they become organized ideologically to discredit Māori groups, and maintain the status quo.

Our analysis follows a procedure recommended by Bowers and Iwi (1991). Conventionally, the social theorist and the social psychologist are concerned to establish ostensive definitions of society. We study people's accounts, we observe social reality, we conduct questionnaires, we perform experiments and then we describe the way society is, or how social influence works. Bowers and Iwi argue that discourse analysts should, in contrast, be concerned not with ostensive definitional work but with *performative* definitions of society. People's accounts of the social (in the classic ethnomethodological move) should become the *topic* for analysis rather than the resource through which the nature of the social is discovered.

It is more complex than this, however. As Bowers and Iwi argue, following the line developed by Bruno Latour and his colleagues (Latour, 1987; Latour and Strum, 1986) in studying how society is talked about we are also studying, in a very immediate way, what the social is. In other words, as we argued in Part I, discourse (along with other practices) is constitutive of social forms and has material consequences. Society comes into being partly through the act of description and definition. Varying methods of talk about the social, contestations and struggles around different versions instantiated in and linked to material practices, bring society into order (or sometimes into disorder) and make it work.

Our analytic procedure in this chapter, therefore, will parallel the line taken in Chapter 5 regarding social categories. There we were not interested in whether Māori and Pākehā are indeed 'racial groups'; we did not assume, as many social psychologists have done, that social categorizations such as race, culture and nation, simply reflect real divisions among people; we assumed that social categorizations are signifying practices with a history and with ideological import, and our aim was to study that practice and that import. Similarly here, in Chapter 6, we will be interested in how different descriptions and definitions of social process form part of a signifying practice and what they seem to accomplish and achieve for participants.

This focus on versions of the social encourages a closer examination of the potential areas of overlap between academic and lay discourse. Pākehā New Zealanders and social psychologists can be seen as engaged in the same basic intellectual activity – making sense of social influence and social conflict. We shall argue that the interpretative resources on which both draw are closely related. But what does it mean that a social psychologist working in North America in the 1950s should theorize social influence in pretty much the same way as a Pākehā New Zealander in the 1980s? Is this a conspiracy or a coincidence? And just who is ideologically motivated? Towards the end of this chapter we shall take up these questions and explore further the way in which academic and lay discourse can be counterposed within studies of ideology. First, however, we will lay out the main axes organizing Pākehā New Zealanders' accounts of social conflict and social influence.

Discrediting protest

In the interviews we conducted, Pākehā participants were asked about various continuing and past disputes between Māori and Pākehā which had resulted in Māori protest and, in some instances, the development of groups and social movements committed to change. In many cases these were disputes about land ownership (e.g. the Bastion Point and Raglan disputes) but also involved Māori mobilization around the Treaty of Waitangi celebrations and broader land and sovereignty issues (e.g. the Land Marches) (see Walker, 1986).

In discussing these topics, conversation would typically circle around the status and activities of 'Māori activists' and 'Māori protest movements'. Those we interviewed gave their version of the reasons for Māori protest and their version of the process by which individuals and minority groups become influential in a society and accomplish social change. These versions, of course, were always charged. With very few exceptions, the Pākehā New Zealanders we interviewed were concerned to discredit groups described as 'activists', 'stirrers', 'protestors', 'militants' and 'hard-liners', wished to denigrate their influence and were concerned to argue for the desirability of the status quo, and against the need for implementing change (see also McCreanor, 1989b; 1992; and Nairn and McCreanor, 1991, for similar findings).

We will examine, first, the standard rhetorical methods or argumentative practices found in these accounts, as a route into an analysis of the interpretative resources structuring these versions. Look, for example, at the following six extracts.

Sedge: Um, a lot of the racial prejudice is brought on, you know, by the Eva Rickards that stand up. I've been out time after time and played golf at Raglan (yes) and playing on the golf course there, and I've played with Māori people, and they've said, 'oh, you know, this is the old burial ground, hiya Trevor'. And, you know, nobody minds you playing golf across there, and I said, 'no, no, no, fine'. And it takes Eva Rickard to come down from somewhere else and to stir the whole blooming pot and er, you know, the [inaudible word] government gets in and buys the land. Well they've sorted it all out and given them all a brand new golf course and I mean they (.) I haven't tried the new one.

Shell: There's too big a demand (mmhm) being made on New Zealand society from Māoris which (.) who have, I guess they've been feeling deprived (yeah) in the past and now they're suddenly (yes) finding their feet and making themselves very vocal. It is starting to build a resentment (mmhm), there's no doubt about that (Wetherell: Among the Pākehā majority?), within the Pākehā majority. There's no doubt about that. And I think that people feel that we're getting almost a reverse apartheid situation.

Wood: I think we'll end up having Māori wars if they carry on the way they are. I mean no it'll be a Pākehā war (yes). Um (.) they're making New Zealand a racist country. Um but you know you usually feel, think, that racism is um (.) putting the, putting the darker people down but really they're doing it the other way around, I feel. Um, everything seems to be to help the Māori people, um, you know. I think at the moment sort of the Europeans sort of they're just sort of watching and putting up with it, but they'll only go so far. Um you know we've got Māori friends out here, uh who we have into the house, you know they're friends, um but when things happen when they suddenly say oh they're going to make Māori language compulsory, um it is, it's antagonizing and the Māori friends that we've got, they don't agree with it. OK you've got your extremists there too, the ones who feel, you know, that everyone should learn it but um I think the average Māori sort of perhaps is worried too.

Munman: You know, I, I'm all for them bringing their culture in as much as possible, it's a good culture. The Māori race is, is a very fine race, it's just a shame that they have lost a lot of their culture. Um I see one or two problems there, that you've once again got one or two people who are stirring. But they're not the majority, they're a very, very, small minority. Um you know they want their land back and this sort of thing; well that's all very nice, but it's happened everywhere in the world for years.

Maxwell: We had three Māori women out to speak at [inaudible] (Wetherell: Oh yes (.) that would be interesting.) And one of them, her name is [inaudible] and I always forget her surname, and she has, she's an extraordinarily intelligent young woman, three degrees or four degrees or something. And she was with the High Commissioner up in Canada, and she was sent home because she said that the Canadian American-Indians get far more freedoms than New Zealand Māoris and I'd always understood they lived in reservations and they were all sodden with drink but, you know, I may well be wrong. And anyway she came back and she sat there and, she's very beautiful, and she sat there with this scarf tied around her head, she had the most expensive beautiful jewellery on her fingers and she was sort of in this incredibly expensive outfit and French shoes and she was, she looked like something off the cover of Vogue (yeah). And somebody said to her, 'do you feel that Pākehā culture's given you anything?' And she said, 'NO ABSOLUTELY NOTHING AT ALL'. And I thought look lady, hahaha, you know, she was (.) and, but they were advocating violence (yeah). They wanted Māori clinics for their children, they wanted Māori schools, and they said if we don't get these things then they will fight, and they were meaning it.

Rock: That, that, kind of land march? You know, like the Bastion Point one? Uh, I think that that, uh, the Māoris involved there are really quite selfish and greedy that um (.), you know, that they're only for their own gain, um personal gain and very material gain.

These extracts refer either to the Māori people as a whole or to particular Māori defined as activists. Each offers a partial and, as in accounts of community, typically offensive characterization of either a particular dispute such as Bastion Point or events in Raglan, or attempts by Māori groups to influence events. Some of the extracts develop anecdotes and stories about those seen as key protagonists such as Eva Rickard in Sedge's anecdote about being invited to play golf at the Raglan course.

Discrediting, blaming and denigrating are achieved through several routes in these extracts, which are representative of the corpus more generally. The argumentative practice is as clear as if dictated from a recipe book of rhetorical strategies for discrediting opposing political groups. One strategy is to call into question the genuineness of the opponent's motives; another is to question the effectiveness of their tactics; a third to accuse those one disagrees with of violating norms of moderation; a fourth involves accusations of inconsistency, although consistency, too, can be made problematic. It is also possible to question the representativeness of the opponent's support, and to accuse them of infringing the rights of others.

In the extract above from Rock, for instance, Māori protest is attributed to some other, less noble, set of motives – selfishness and greed. Maxwell similarly questions the motives of Māori activists but this time through the accusation of inconsistency, dishonesty and hypocrisy (see also Potter and Wetherell, 1988b). Paradoxically, Māori activists were also accused in our interviews not only of this kind of inconsistency but of being *too* consistent, that is, of being the kind of people who consistently turn out for any demonstration or protest march, 'simply stirring for the sake of it', and thus once again become accused of protesting from questionable motives (see also McCreanor, 1989b; 1992; and Nairn and McCreanor, 1991, for similar findings).

It seems that both consistency of protest and inconsistency in Māori reactions to what is defined as Pākehā society can be interpreted as blameworthy behavioural traits. Either invalidates protest. Wood and Munman in the extracts above develop the argument that 'militant' Māoris are not representative of the majority or supported by 'average', 'ordinary' or 'normal' Māori groups. While Shell and Sedge follow the strategy of arguing that Māori groups adopt ineffective, naive or impractical tactics, pursuing forms of politics which will result in the opposite effects from those intended. In this case it is suggested that it is Māori protest which creates 'racial prejudice', division or resentment.

There are no instances in these particular extracts of the final argumentative form commonly used to discredit opponents in these kinds of debates – accusations of infringements of others' rights. In the interviews this was more usually deployed to describe the actions of those who protested against South African rugby tours of New Zealand. Typically these accusations adopted a 'concession/criticism' disclaimer format: a limited concession of the legitimacy of protest, followed by the postulation of the limits of legitimacy around the rights of others – for example, Sargeant: 'I'm all in favour of people marching but when it steps over into the destruction of property, denying me my rights, then it goes too far, and the police have to step in.'

The six extracts also indicate how Pākehā New Zealanders' attempts to develop persuasive arguments in this domain, as in other domains, are bolstered through the use of extreme case formulations, contrasts, evaluative terms, passive nominalizations and the usual paraphernalia of argumentation. Shell, for example, in his account carefully separates and thus contrasts Māori people with the rest of 'New Zealand society'. He weakens Māori claims through the description of Māori as 'feeling' deprived, as opposed, say, to being 'actually' deprived. Māori protest is then described as 'sudden'. Indeed, in general across the interviews, suddenness proved a favourite rhetorical tool. Wood also, for instance, refers to when 'they' (unspecified) 'suddenly' say that Māori language should be compulsory. Speakers attempted to stress the normality and habituality of the status quo and thus the contingency of Māori protest which, in contrast, is positioned as 'coming from nowhere'. Finally, Shell, through his choice of a passive grammatical form ('it is starting to build'), manages to characterize Māori people as active ('very vocal') in comparison to Pākehā people, who become merely reactive and responsive.

The argumentative and rhetorical work evident in the six extracts depends on a shared set of interpretative resources, not always clearly explicated, concerning the nature of social influence, the process and agents of social change and what society is in relation to this process. It is these interpretative resources, rather than the procedures involved in the construction of discredits, which will be our main focus in this analysis.

Shared interpretative resources structure what could be called the 'obviousness' of the rhetoric and determine the end-points of argumentative work. Those in our sample share a collective set of taken-for-granted procedures for bringing off arguments, and thus there also seems to be some practical working consensus about what is likely to count as a 'good argument' or a 'persuasive case'. In the extracts above, for example, it often seems sufficient to achieve a characterization of Māori activists as 'immoderate' or 'extreme' or 'not genuine'.

But why does rhetorical work stop here? Why is the attribution of extremism, or unrepresentativeness, or inconsistency (or consistency, for that matter), considered to be a 'clinching argument'? We will be mainly concerned with these questions and the implications for ideological practices.

Variable scenarios of influence

A second route into interpretative resources emerges if we examine the pattern of variation across the sample's accounts of influence. There were several striking inconsistencies in the identification and construction of the relevant groups and the characterization of their attributes. It is clear, for example, from the extracts, that the relevant groups, actors and the lines of force, power and influence are negotiable and variable.

Groups and actors enlarge in size and can be collapsed and telescoped.

Māori people in some form or other tend to be positioned as the main agents in these accounts, but, on some occasions, as in Shell's extract, and in parts of Wood's extract, it seems the Māori people as a whole act on some unspecified Pākehā majority, while, on other occasions, as in Sedge's account or in the extract from Munman, Māori people become divided into activists versus 'average', 'normal' or 'sensible' Māoris, and sometimes into activists versus followers.

The attributes ascribed to the main actors (Māori activists or the Māori people) also shift. On the one hand, there were many instances in the transcripts where these groups were presented as forceful, effective, persuasive and powerful; but at other moments, both across the interviews and within interviews, they were also positioned as ineffective, naive, not at all powerful or influential. Similarly, those described as 'activists', 'militants' and 'protestors' were frequently presented in contrasting ways – too emotional, 'stirring for the sake of it', lacking in proper commitment, inauthentic – but also as an elite, a highly committed group, leading the masses. Activists who in one context are described as not credible because they lack the support of the masses, are in other contexts described as clever demagogues – effective representatives of mass opinion.

These variations in the categorization of actors and ascription of traits seem to reflect shifts between three prevalent but contrasting scenarios or constructions of the influence process. In the first scenario we wish to pick out, the Māori people in general or Māori activists more specifically are presented as acting on the majority of New Zealanders. In this distribution of power and lines of force, the agents of influence are commonly positioned as powerful and threatening, capable of impinging on a 'peaceful and harmonious' society and capable of disturbing the 'placid' and 'tranquil lives' of 'the majority'.

Wood, for example, presents a strong account of this kind, where a menacing but vaguely sketched Māori lobby intimidates a concerned, 'watching' and presumably mainly Pākehā majority. In these accounts of the influence process, however, speakers usually also argued that all this force and effort to exert pressure was, in the end, ineffective. Typically, for instance, it was concluded, as in Shell and Wood's extracts, that the unspecified majority became alienated or resentful in response, in some way 'turned off', or provoked to violence in return.

In the second scenario we wish to identify, the relevant groups are categorized rather differently. The principal actors become the 'radical activists' versus 'sensible, normal and average Māoris'. In this case, influence agents, the 'radical activists', often lose their potency and forcefulness. They are no longer powerful and threatening but become an unrepresentative minority, an oddity or extrusion. The motives of influence agents are made even more questionable through this contrast with 'reasonable Māoris', and these agents become positioned as the 'emotional fringe'.

Munman, for example, refers to 'one or two people who are stirring', and describes this group as a 'very, very small minority'. Similarly, Sedge constructs a distinction between the 'reasonable', welcoming and presumably *local* Māoris who invite him on to the golf course – Māoris who are not worried about the anachronisms of the past, burial grounds and such like – and the protestors, the 'Eva Rickards' who 'stand up', and who 'come down from somewhere else'. Wood, too, towards the end of her account begins to construct distinctions between 'average' Māoris, who are 'friends', and Māoris who are 'extremists'. Although in this account the 'average Māoris' seem to be included, in a paternalistic manner, within the 'worried' and 'antagonized' majority through their characterization as 'friends' whom it is possible to 'have into the house'.

Finally, in the third scenario, the relevant groups become reconstructed as 'hard-core elites of radical Māori activists' influencing 'susceptible masses of Māori followers'. The influence agents tend to turn once again into forceful, committed and powerful advocates. And this time, unlike the other scenarios, the influence agents (the 'radical activists') become successful and effective – persuasive and charismatic – with a hold which sways their targets.

There are no examples of this type of account in the extracts above but take a look at the following characterizations of two influence processes from Irvine which do develop this construction. Irvine describes Māori activists in the first extract and develops a long account of those who protested at the South African Springbok rugby tour of New Zealand in the early 1980s.

Irvine: [Discussing disputes over the Treaty of Waitangi Day celebrations] Once again it's a minority group led by activists who have a a little say and they're given far too much media coverage (yes), and by doing that it brings the attention of all those who are, aren't even thinking about protesting and things like that – 'ah, but here's something to get on the bandwagon about' – and so they, and so they join in with it er. I believe that it should be played down, as far as Waitangi Day is concerned.

Irvine: [Discussing the protest over South African rugby tours of New Zealand] Why do I think there was <u>so much</u> violence? I think once again it was tied, er brought on by a small band of people (mm), and I think, from my teaching in Parnell I know that, um a number of Parnell people, for example, are radical in their ideas um, um, leftist to a a large degree. Some people I'm talking about, er, who will attend any demonstration because it's a <u>demonstration</u> (yes). Er, even pupils that are, that were at the school or, you know, just left, say third form, fourth form [inaudible] whom I recognized at the protest marches (ha). I did at, at, at, you know, at, um, Rugby Park (yes) and Eden Park, who would have no conception of what the hell it was all about (yes). But it was just that they wanted to get into the act of having the police on and, and, and, um, causing a kerfuffle. And I, I, look – that's [thumps the table] what it was all about [thumps the table] to a large extent for those young people. I'm talking about say the 15–16-year-olds, you know, who would have no conception of what it was all about but just wanted to get in on the act. (yes, yeah) And sure enough, you know, the Tim Shadbolt's are there, there are people like, like him, and others, who, who, led or can lead within this country, and people will pile they're like sheep, you know.

In the last extract, the reference to Parnell is to a suburb of Auckland with a reputation for 'trendiness', while Tim Shadbolt is a Pākehā New Zealander who became defined during the 1960s and 1970s as a 'professional protestor'. Irvine flits through several argumentative strategies here, suggesting that those who protest are an unrepresentative minority, and also that, as members of a category of 'stirrers', they protest from questionable motives; but he also characterizes the influence process as one where small organized groups act effectively on masses. The 'mass', in contrast to the small organizing group of activists, is described as not knowing what they are doing, as incapable of understanding the real issues, and as jumping on bandwagons. In some way they are rendered suggestible and 'sheep-like'; in these accounts the media are typically also seen as playing an important role in conveying the activists' message and in 'blowing issues out of proportion'.

The three scenarios summarized above were the most prevalent in our sample's accounts of protest and dispute. Each constructs and populates a social landscape with actors and groups and, most crucially, constructs modalities and lines of influence and distributes agency and power relations. Some of the actors in these dramas are no more than dupes, foils and ignorant scapegoats, others are sinister, machiavellian figures with immense power; and there are, too, the voices of reason, the inactive 'normal' majority who watches and waits, along with the calming influence of 'sensible Māoris'.

We have presented the scenarios as 'pure types' but, of course, as the extracts show, in any one account different distributions of power, actors and lines of influence may be mixed together. The main groups and protagonists may be drawn and redrawn in a variety of ways depending on the rhetorical work in hand. Key components may be developed in detail, merely alluded to or included with yet other ways of constructing relevant actors and modes of influence. Given the quite different contrasts and comparisons which seem possible – 'activists' versus 'sensible Māoris', 'activists' versus the 'conformist mass', 'the Māori people' or parts of the Māori people versus the 'placid Pākehā majority' – it is not surprising that the characterization is variable and sometimes contradictory.

In studying this pattern, we concluded that the tensions in these accounts could be interpreted and, indeed, could make sense if the Pākehā New Zealanders we interviewed were seen as engaged in two kinds of ideological struggle – where each struggle requires a contrasting account of the influence process. One of these struggles seems to concern 'proper' versus 'improper' influence. Rhetorical effort in this case is directed towards positioning oneself, those one agrees with and Pākehā politics in general within the realm of 'proper' influence with the stress on the 'reasonable', the 'rational' and the 'factual'; while Māori groups are positioned within the realm of 'improper' influence, within the 'emotional', the 'social' and the 'irrational'.

The second struggle is more obviously ideological: that is, it is a struggle to conceal and dissimulate power relations and the flow of power. To win this fight, Māori people and Māori groups must be positioned as powerful and forceful while Pākehā become inactive or merely reactive. These two struggles thus demand quite different constructions of Māori efficacy and force. Māori must be positioned both as powerful and as ineffectual, as potentially persuasive and as illegitimate – where illegitimacy and impotency are seen to derive from a failure to be powerful and influential in the *right* way.

Another way of viewing these struggles is to see Pākehā New Zealanders as engaged in theorizing both the 'social' and the 'psychological' dimensions of influence and social change. The psychological dimension involves some account of the 'pathology' of Māori protestors and thus some focus on human foibles, psychological and individual characteristics, while the social dimension involves some account of the relationship between protest groups and the social body in general. We now turn to examine each of these dimensions in more detail using, as a device to aid our reading of this material, a comparison with the ways in which central debates in the academic discourse of sociology and social psychology have been constructed.

Conflict or consensus: the organic society

As we have seen, in some accounts of the influence process Māori people become positioned as the active irritants while the Pākehā majority or 'New Zealand society' become the peaceful and quiescent body under attack. Over and over again we are told that it is Māori groups who initiate friction, division and disruption and who thus disturb the harmonious 'resting state' of New Zealand society. The society which is seen as responding to Māori activists thus appears, from one angle, curiously weightless and powerless. Most of the force, energy, impetus and dynamism, in Wood's or Shell's account for example, is attributed to those seeking change. Contrasting 'ordinary' social life is presented as relatively placid, harmonious, calm and unenergized. However, from another angle, it is clear that it is the unspecified majority who becomes empowered in this construction.

The imputation of passivity may make this majority seem weightless but it can also be made 'weighty' in these accounts through the ascriptions of normativeness, continuity, stability, cohesion and orderliness. Māori groups thus become like the bee who stings an elephant, the elephant may be slow to rouse, and not unduly bothered, but remains full of latent power, a force which is not applied or exerted. Through this means, then, an ideological trick is accomplished. Pākehā New Zealanders become inactive but legitimate, their power invisible and normative, while Māori groups become active and visibly energetic but, simultaneously, deviant.

The formulation of society here, or the formulation of the group or social body which contrasts with active Māori groups, parallels some constructions of the social which Bowers and Iwi (1991) identified in their study. They describe how society becomes constructed, in some discussions they analyzed, as uniform versus multiform, as totalizing versus partial and as an object rather than as an agent. Clearly, the rhetorical work of Pākehā New Zealanders also constructs a uniform social object and a nearly total social consensus which can then be positioned as under threat. But there is more to it than this.

There are some striking parallels with the 'consensus' versus 'conflict' models of social process found in sociological debates. The organic and functionalist formulation developed in some of the accounts of Pākehā New Zealanders would resonate with the likes of Durkheim, Parsons or Merton. For structuralist-functionalist writers within academic sociology, society becomes seen as an integrated entity, with modern societies distinguished by their 'organic solidarity', in Durkheim's words (Cuff and Payne, 1984; Giddens, 1979; 1989). In this tradition of thought, society becomes presented as a stable and interconnected whole with the parts of the system (such as institutions) functioning to maintain cohesion and stability. Societies are thought to develop and gradually change over time, adapting to new circumstances, but generally reaching new forms of equilibrium and integration.

For Merton, institutions, movements and groups which either intentionally or unintentionally produce 'disintegrative tendencies' are best described as 'dysfunctional'. These forms of social activity, in contrast to functional systems, threaten social order and challenge the social equilibrium (Giddens, 1989). Dysfunction becomes equated with disruption. According to Parsons, such 'deviance' (on the part of individuals and groups at least) could be traced to inadequate socialization and incorporation of conventional social roles, thus reinforcing the impression of pathology. As Cuff and Payne point out, within this school of thought it tended to be assumed, both explicitly and implicitly, that order and stability could be taken as the normal and natural conditions, with disorder as the unnatural condition.

The naturalness of order and integration and the negativity of antagonism, 'stirring' and friction emerges, too, as the dominant theme in Pākehā New

Zealanders' accounts. The emphasis is on the value of the habitual, 'normal' and repetitive actions which constitute ordinary and everyday social life. Given this weight of normality, it seems obvious the spotlight should turn onto the 'exceptional', to illuminate the deviant and the dissenter. Also, in this explanatory frame, accusations that Māori groups desire any form of 'separatism' (such as cultural autonomy or recognition of Māori sovereignty) acquire a particular rhetorical force. The organic account of society with its functionalist frame meshes with the calls for 'one nation' discussed in the previous chapter.

This account of social order and social change can be contrasted with conflict models in sociology linked to Marxist social theory. Here, obviously, the stress is different. Modern capitalist society is seen as structured around social divisions, inequalities and the conflicting interests of social classes. Society is held together through the coercive power of the state and through ideological systems which manufacture consent and maintain support for social order. From this point of view there can be no shared perspective on what is 'functional' for society or, indeed, 'dysfunctional', since the processes which support the position of one group will cost other non-privileged groups. Speaking for those non-privileged groups, Marx thus welcomed disruption, disorder and 'dysfunction'.

It is possible to imagine a formulation of society along these lines in Pākehā accounts. This might talk, for instance, of structured inequality and exploitation, of unequal power blocks which confront each other, and of social change emerging both from this confrontation and from the tensions and contradictions within New Zealand society. Very few accounts, however, worked in this way or, indeed, argued that conflict was *already* established in New Zealand society with Pākehā people as active generators and participators in this conflict. The dominant account stressed instead the before and after contrast. Society was harmonious and integrated *before* Māori groups ('inexplicably') generated conflict, and *now* society is divided, antagonized and full of friction.

On several occasions those we interviewed explicitly linked the before and after contrast to a 'golden age' in the recent past, to times, typically when the speaker was a child, when Māori–Pākehā lived in harmony, before the days of 'activism'. In these accounts the formulation of the organic society becomes linked into a common form of historical narrative described by Raymond Williams (1975) where an untroubled past is nostalgically compared with the barbarities of modern times.

Crucially, however, when the Pākehā New Zealanders we interviewed did move to more conflictual or 'them' versus 'us' formulations, it tended to be in the context of discussions of the relative positions and values of majorities and minorities. Within the frame of democratic politics it becomes 'ideologically safe' to talk of conflict between a majority of 'us' who are in dispute with a minority of 'them'. Majority rule has a justificatory value which places the outcome for majority–minority conflict beyond dispute, and indeed as the accounts above indicate, the very label 'minority' comes to serve in this context as an automatic discredit.

'Proper' and 'improper' influence

When we came to look at the struggle to establish legitimate and illegitimate forms of influence, what immediately struck us were the parallels with the construction of debates in areas of academic social psychology. Like Pākehā New Zealanders, social psychologists have also discriminated between those who are prey to 'proper' influence and those who are prey to 'improper' influence. Social psychological analyses have similarly circled around distinctions between the 'emotional' and the 'rational', and have similarly contrasted social action motivated by 'genuine beliefs' with actions based on 'inauthentic motives'.

The history of social psychology is replete, too, with accounts of suggestible masses swayed by hypnotic and charismatic leaders, with accounts of the pathology of extremism, and with stories where individual judgements are submerged and vitiated by the power of the crowd.

Since the 1950s a distinction between two main modalities of influence has been central to the study of social influence within social psychology (Turner, 1991). These modalities have been given a number of titles: 'task set' versus 'group set' (Thibaut and Strickland, 1956), 'information dependence' versus 'affect dependence' (Jones and Gerard, 1967) and 'inferential pressures' versus 'institutional pressures' (Moscovici, 1974); but the most commonly used description of the two modalities contrasts 'normative influence' with 'informational influence' (Deutsch and Gerard, 1955). Deutsch and Gerard's 1955 paper can be seen as the systematization of themes in Festinger's earlier (1950; 1954) work on informal social communication and social comparison and Kelley's (1952) work on reference groups.

Deutsch and Gerard develop the distinction as follows:

> We shall define a *normative social influence* as an influence to conform with the positive expectations of another. An *informational social influence* may be defined as an influence to accept information obtained from another as *evidence* about reality. Commonly these types of influence are found together. However, it is possible to conform behaviorally with the expectations of others and say things one disbelieves but which agree with the beliefs of others. Also it is possible that one will accept an opponent's beliefs as evidence about reality even though one has no motivation to agree with him [*sic*], *per se*. (1955, p. 629; emphasis in the original)

Deutsch and Gerard follow a relatively non-judgemental line in this definition but it became clear, particularly as the study of 'conformity' developed, that one of these forms of influence was seen as more acceptable and reasonable while the other became more shameful and inadmissible. Experimental investigators of social influence became concerned to discover whether the subjects who participated in their experiments had been subject to 'legitimate' or 'illegitimate' influence. Subjects themselves were more willing to admit to informational influence than normative influence in post-experimental briefings.

This reluctance, of course, stems from the link between these two ascriptions of influence and questions of authenticity, reasonableness, autonomy, independence, genuineness, credibility and facticity. Normative influence is signalled by public compliance rather than private agreement. That is, it is seen as involving agreement with another's opinions not because one is really persuaded that their version of the 'facts of the matter' is accurate but because the individual or group has some hold which exerts pressure and creates dependence. *Contra* Deutsch and Gerard, this hold has been seen in both negative and positive terms.

A group, for example, might have either real or imagined power to reward conformity and punish disobedience. Normative influence could also be generated through self-censorship or self-regulation. In this case it was thought to involve what was described as a 'socio-emotional process' – the expectations of others about how one should behave were thought to create tension within the individual, who is then motivated to fulfil those expectations and endorse whatever is the party line of the moment.

Informational influence was theorized to occur whenever there was uncertainty about the 'facts of the matter'. In cases of uncertainty, individuals would become willing to accept others' judgements about reality, and this was thought to be particularly so if those others expressed a consensus. In these cases, in contrast to cases of normative influence, the individual genuinely does not know the answer, becomes persuaded that others do know, and that s/he should thus conform to their view. Agreement, therefore, is more than token, the individual both privately and publicly comes to agree with others.

What seems to have happened here is that, as in other areas of social psychology (Edwards and Potter, 1992; Potter and Wetherell, 1987), forms of common sense have been reified as social science. One set of publicly available interpretative resources and collectively shared methods for accounting for social influence have been carefully reconstructed and represented through experiment and related theorizing. In textbooks the constructions of lay discourse become theoretical distinctions and analyses discovered as a result of the powerful intuitions and intellectual labour of skilled scientists. In this way, the public arena of everyday politics and the rhetorical skills of lay folk have been turned over to the private arena of psychology and the mysterious process of scientific discovery. A particular, indeed a partial and interested, communicative currency has been incorporated and transformed.

With this move the ideological charge of these discussions of influence so evident when groups of Pākehā New Zealanders, for example, address Māori protest, or when a social group is discredited by its political opponents, becomes obscured. Discussions of influence in the public arena are vivid, contested and real, sometimes highly consequential, a matter of establishing present credibility and future reputation and potency. In the laboratory, however, this materiality and urgency disappear in the framework of bland sets of choices over non-social stimuli.

The distinction between normative and informational influence in social psychology is particularly relevant to those moments in our interview transcripts where Pākehā New Zealanders were trying to accomplish the 'non-genuine' nature of Māori groups and Māori claims. As we saw, rhetorical work was orientated towards establishing the social and emotional basis of certain Māori actions. It was taken for granted that it would be sufficient to demonstrate that these actions were based not on the rational assessment of issues and genuine conviction but on mere conformity to others' questionable opinions, on base desires to make oneself look good, or on emotional needs.

Susceptible masses and hysterical extremists

Further aspects of the rhetorical work in the transcripts and the various scenarios of influence relate more closely to other developments in social psychology. The construction of followers who leap on band wagons and the depiction of impulses which sweep over protestors drawing them along, which is so clearly evident in Irvine's accounts above, relies upon the contrasts which underpin normative and informational influence but it also has a great deal in common with social psychological theories of behavioural contagion, of de-individuation and the atavistic instincts of crowds which have structured social psychological accounts of collective action more broadly (Reicher, 1982; 1987).

As Stephen Reicher has pointed out, the mainstream of conceptualizations of the crowd in social psychology have stressed the supposed psychological effects of the immersion of the individual in an anonymous mass, the subsequent 'loss' of identity and rationality, the 'primitive' and regressive nature of crowd action, the hypnotic effects of 'agitators' and 'ring-leaders', and the stripping away of socialization, logic, thought and civilization (Allport, 1924; LeBon, 1895; Zimbardo, 1969). LeBon's or Zimbardo's accounts of the susceptible mass may be more sophisticated than those presented by Irvine and others we interviewed but the theory of influence is markedly similar.

The particular value our sample placed on moderation, pragmatism, proportion and balance is clear, too, in the rhetorical procedures we have analyzed. It emerges in the assumption that 'extremist' can only be a term of abuse, and in the influence scenario we identified where 'stirrers' are discredited through a contrast with 'moderate Māori groups'. This assumption and contrast seem to depend on the alignment of moderation with facticity – the middle position is more likely to be the correct position. It also depends on the alignment of extremism with deviance, dogmatism and pathology. Moderation becomes synonymous with flexibility, a practical attitude and openness.

Again, as Michael Billig (1982) has demonstrated, this interpretative resource can be found constructing equivalent social psychological analyses; this time the focus is on the 'cognitive style' of totalitarians, comparing those with 'open and closed minds' (Rokeach, 1960), and on the connections between personality and political beliefs (Eysenck, 1954; Eysenck and Wilson, 1978). In these and other accounts (such as the authoritarian personality work of Adorno and his colleagues) it is frequently assumed that the healthy personality or the healthy political response involves finding a middle path between extremes, especially the extremes of left and right, although any position vulnerable to the characterization of extremity will also be vulnerable to the charge of dogmatism and cognitive rigidity.

Chapters 7 and 8 will return to this valuation of moderation in lay and academic discourse in the context of discussions of 'real politic' and prejudice respectively. Here we want to note the arguments of social psychological critics of normative and informational influence distinctions, contagion and de-individuation theories and cognitive and personality accounts of political beliefs, particularly the links these critics make between these connected bodies of work, theoretical trends in social psychology, liberal philosophies and the politics of individualism.

Formulations of the individual versus the social

The distinction between 'proper' and 'improper' influence can be made to work so efficiently as an attack on Māori groups because of the articulations of the social body and social process, and indeed, the formulation of the relationship between social and physical reality, which underpin this distinction. Individualism is indicated in the construction of a standard and ideal for judgement which privileges the individual, subordinates the social, and which makes individual observation of the facts the norm.

As Turner (1987c) and Moscovici (1976a) have noted, this privileging can be seen operating within social psychology if we deconstruct further the concept of uncertainty. Festinger's (1950) notion that uncertainty fuels social influence through making the individual dependent on more knowledgeable others rests on an underlying comparison between 'social reality' and 'physical reality'.

Festinger argued that most of the time in our dealing with the physical world, individuals are not dependent on others for information – certainty is readily available – everybody is competent to judge how things are through their own sensory apparatus. Sometimes, however, physical reality becomes ambiguous (is that colour best described as blue or green?), and in these cases of uncertainty, informational influence from those who appear more knowledgeable is possible. Festinger also argued that, whereas certainty is a common commodity in observations of the physical world, it is a rare commodity in judgements of social reality. Questions of values and politics, for instance, are uncheckable, always a matter of convention and consensus. There are, according to Festinger, no other benchmarks for the social. When it comes to social judgements, uncertainty is thus rife and individuals become especially 'vulnerable' to influence from others.

As Turner and Moscovici point out, in this account, 'social' influence is devalued and made a secondary form of knowledge. Individual perception is made sovereign. Just as, indeed, the texts of liberal economics, the work of Adam Smith, Hayek and Friedman, privilege the individual consumer and individual freedom within the market (Billig, 1982; Hall, 1986). Valid information becomes equated with asocial information, with social influence becoming a substitute for the 'real' knowledge which individuals can gain when they act independently.

The postulation of 'normative' influence as a contrast to informational influence merely extends this trend. Social influence and collective decision making become further marked as inadequate, blind, partial, interested and irrational forms of knowledge. The way is paved for the contrasts which run through the rhetorical work of Pākehā New Zealanders; or, rather, we should say that, in taking these contrasts for granted, the Pākehā New Zealanders we interviewed participate in formulations with a long intellectual history and join with some social psychologists in perpetuating and continuing this history.

In a similar vein, Reicher has noted how the predominant discourse of contagion and suggestibility in social psychological research on crowds and collective action 'magically' causes the social context – the outgroup and the history of conflict – to disappear, through its focus upon the submerged and irrational individual. This effect can be noted in lay discourse, too. To the extent, for instance, that Irvine focuses discussion on the irrational properties of those who join in protest, he obscures the social context of the dispute and particularly he blurs the actions of other groups involved – the police and pro-Springbok tour protestors in one of his examples and the organizers of the Treaty of Waitangi celebrations in his other example. Reicher's critique of the social psychology of the crowd applies equally to lay discourse. In both cases the method of analysis and the characteristic formulation of events erase intelligibility. The actions of those one disagrees with become meaningless, frenzied, inexplicable and we are left with, in Reicher's words, an impression of 'the rationality of the social isolate and the idiocy of social being' (1987, p. 174).

Billig's (1982) critique of the social psychology of moderation also points to the ideological effects of some formulations of the individual–social relation but is also more equivocal. On the one hand, he wishes to argue for a social psychology which is more sensitive to the balances, compromises, contradictions, inconsistencies and pluralisms which he sees as characteristic of the way ideology typically works in modern capitalist societies. In this sense he wants to encourage social psychological analysis of the ideological patterns and the confusion found in 'middle ways' and in the discourse of those who define themselves as moderates. He pre-figures here the emphasis in discourse analysis and rhetoric (Billig, 1987; Edwards and Potter, 1992; Potter and Wetherell, 1987) on developing theories and methods for studying variability, sense-making and ideological practice.

Billig also wants to place the valuation of moderation in a political context. He notes, for example, how the emphasis in contemporary political arguments on golden means, rational compromises and senses of proportion, the rhetorical techniques which distinguish the philosophy of the 'trimmer', are particularly suited to the justification of capitalist systems and mixed economies based on the contradictions between liberal economic policies and social reformist palliatives such as corrections introduced for free-market effects.

He notes how effective the diagnosis of extremism can become in this political context. If others (political opponents) can be successfully presented as inflexible extremists incapable of compromises then, by definition, one's own policies, claims and stances achieve the signature of moderation and realism. One peculiarity of 'moderate' political positions is that their moderation can only be discovered and identified through contrasts with 'extreme' positions. This dependence of the items in a dualism upon each other, and their need for each other, has been noted, too, by deconstructivists.

The intimate link between the construction of moderation and the construction of extremism allows, Billig argues, 'the moderate' to break with ethical and moral principles and justify this break as the flexible pursuit of workable compromises or through describing the violation as the exception which proves the importance of the rule or principle. In the same breath, the 'moderate' may reinforce their distance from 'extremism' through describing 'extremists' as those kinds of people who consistently break the ethical principle in question and fail to appreciate its importance and prescriptive power. Billig describes, for example, Margaret Thatcher's use of this technique in discussions of racism – simultaneously defining extremists as those, such as the National Front, who are consistently racist and who fail to appreciate the rights of others, while arguing that racist immigration policies are necessary in certain circumstances for practical reasons.

There are close parallels, too, between the construction of 'moderate' discourse and the use of argumentative procedures which we have described in other contexts, such as the *practical/principle* rhetorical device (Wetherell *et al.*, 1987) or the *de jure/de facto* device (Potter and Wetherell, 1989). In this rhetorical construction a human right or ethical principle is presented but then immediately undercut by the presentation of practical difficulties. The speaker lays out an important principle but immediately 'discovers' an objection which renders the principle unworkable in this circumstance. Sometimes one moral principle is undercut by another principle within the concession/criticism format as, for example, in the short extract from Sargeant quoted earlier, where Sargeant first endorses the right to protest and then argues protestors go too far infringing his rights.

It would be a mistake, however, to reify 'the moderate' here and see moderation or extremism as an attribute of individuals. We do not want to argue that 'moderate individuals' are those who use these rhetorical styles while 'extremists' adopt other styles. We are not suggesting a modified version of Rokeach's (1960) distinction between individuals with open minds versus those with closed minds, an alternative formulation of the distinction between the cognitive styles of dogmatism and tolerance, or another version of Eysenck's tough-minded and tender-minded individuals. Rather, our argument is that 'moderation' and 'extremism' are best studied as discursive constructions and achieved categorizations.

The rhetorical procedures for constructing the effect of moderation, or, indeed, the effect of extremism are publicly available and collectively shared resources which structure political discussion and dispute. The formulation and deployment of these resources is sustained by broader recognizable discourses or philosophies of liberalism and individualism which in turn have structured and helped set in place the political environment of modern capitalism. We have here an example of Gramsci's observation of the close connections between intellectuals and the common sense of ordinary life.

We can see in liberal social psychology, philosophy and economics the systematization of themes which structure the discourse and debate of non-intellectuals. The social psychologist of social influence talks of 'public compliance' and 'private agreement', the Pākehā New Zealander chooses to call foul in other ways but both sustain a framing of debate which reflects social circumstances and a broader discursive context and which also instantiates and reproduces those circumstances and that context. But what are the lines of influence here? And on what basis can social psychological discourse be described as ideological?

Trickling down or trickling up, conspiracies or coincidences?

One possibility is to see lay discourse as basically parasitic on academic discourse – the trickle-down approach. Moscovici (1976b), for example, in his account of the interplay between academic psychoanalysis and lay psychological analysis notes how technical terms (projection, the unconscious, rationalization), originating within social science, become reworked into popular social representations of mental health. Social science in this narrative becomes a resource plundered by common sense.

Gramsci's account, mentioned above, of the role of intellectuals similarly contrasts the self-conscious systematizations of philosophers and theorists with the more organic, often contradictory, ideologies of the masses. Again Gramsci sees the latter as principally dependent on the former, with common sense as the repository of past intellectual movements.

> Every social stratum has its own 'common sense' and its own 'good sense', which are basically the most widespread conception of life and of man [sic]. Every philosophical current leaves behind a sedimentation of 'common sense': this is the document of historical effectiveness. Common sense is not something rigid and immobile, but is continually transforming itself, enriching itself with scientific ideas and with philosophical options which have entered ordinary life. 'Common sense' is the folklore of philosophy, and is always half-way between folklore properly speaking and the philosophy, science, and economics of the specialists. (1971, p. 326)

For other writers, what has been more evident is the way lay distinctions trickle upwards to become codified and glossed as science. As Mike Gane (1991) points out, this seems to be Baudrillard's view, for example. When interviewed in 1984/5 Baudrillard argued that intellectuals who believe they are the origin points of their ideas are under an illusion. In actuality, academic theories and intellectual labour always feed off the currency of ideas *already* available in a society. Academic work, including radical and critical work, can only become effective when elaborating and 'speaking' what is already present in alternative social movements or in common sense.

Sartre, too, wanted to emphasize the dependence of the intellectual, especially this time the 'bourgeois intellectual', on her/his culture, acting not just as the midwife for this culture, but with intellectual horizons set by the limits of contemporary common sense.

> The bourgeoisie has always been worried about its intellectuals, as well it should. But it looks upon them with a wary eye, as though they were some strange creatures to which the bourgeoisie had somehow given birth. Which in fact it had, for most intellectuals are born into the middle class and grow up imbued with middle class values. They come on as the guardians and custodians of that culture, and their role is to pass that culture on to the next generation. As a result, a certain number of technicians of practical knowledge have, sooner or later, played the role of watchdog, as Paul Nizan used to say. The others, having been carefully screened, remain elitist even when they profess revolutionary ideas. (Sartre with Astruc and Contat, 1978, p. 3)

Within social psychology, Kenneth Gergen (1989) has argued in a similar fashion for a symbiotic relationship between lay accounts of personality and selfhood and the 'self-disciplines' such as psychology and the philosophy of mind. 'Ordinary people', he maintains, create and elaborate new stories of self, and recirculate old narratives under the pressure of warranting. He notes how 'voice', or the power to speak and be attended to, depends on being able skilfully and persuasively to warrant and account for one's actions. Warrants (the need to account, justify and explain oneself) provide, in this way, the impetus for self-narration in lay discourse.

The 'self disciplines' of social science, Gergen argues, simply record and reify these discursive strategies. Furthermore, social scientists, too, face the same pressures to warrant and defend their theories. 'Voice' in the scientific community similarly depends on accounting skills. A second-order process is thus set in motion whereby psychologists and philosophers produce richer and more complex academic theories of the self prompted by their own need for successful self-presentation in academic competition.

We are not proposing to choose between these trickle-up and trickle-down accounts of the relationship between academic and lay discourse. Both are illuminating. We can see social psychologists and sociologists as the technicians and watchdogs of practical knowledge, legitimating through notions of normative and informational influence, for example, the 'good sense' of bourgeois culture. Equally, it is useful to examine how contemporary social science and lay discourse both re-instantiate in their different ways a 'sediment' of ideas elaborated by the liberal philosophers of the past. Whatever the lines of action and reaction, what is more crucial here are the implications of overlap for the analysis of ideology.

We have argued elsewhere (Potter and Wetherell, 1987) that one of the difficulties with Gergen's account of warranting is the weight given to self-presentation as a motive force in the history and sociology of knowledge. The frame of ideology, in contrast, would connect correspondences in lay and academic knowledge to the articulation of power relations in society. There are two main ways in which this argument might go. To construct an opposition once more, it is possible to distinguish between 'conspiracy' and 'autonomy' accounts.

A 'conspiracy' account would pay most attention to explaining the similarities between academic and lay discourse. This similarity would be understood as indicative of a dominant ideology, hegemonic culture or set of ruling ideas. In many important respects, social scientists and middle-class Pākehā New Zealanders can be seen as sharing the same social position. Both groups have acted as apologists for capitalist social formations. In both cases – the 'conspiracy' account would argue – representations of social reality serve essentially similar real interests and thus overlap in these representations is not surprising.

Stewart Clegg (1989) in his account of the 'dominant ideology thesis' (originally outlined by Abercrombie and Turner, 1978) notes Engel's claim that the bourgeoisie across countries such as the United Kingdom, the United

States, New Zealand and Australia and across Europe will have more in common with each other than they will with the working class in their own country. And it is this notion of 'common interests' which could be applied to make sense of the parallels we have noted between some forms of academic theorizing and lay discourse.

This is not to suggest that the 'conspiracy' between the academic and lay person is intended, pre-mediated or co-ordinated. Commonality of interests constructs a shared representation of the world and these shared perspectives become a 'powerful similarity'. Sometimes, among social scientists, the connections between class allegiances and ideas may be overt; on other occasions connections need to be hypothesized and discovered. Stephen Reicher, for example, notes how the class allegiances of the early social psychologists of the crowd were, by and large, explicit. LeBon saw the revolutionary potential of the crowd, and socialist movements in general, as threats which must be understood and contained. In the case of the normative and informational influence distinction, however, no one is suggesting a conscious strategy on the part of Deutsch and Gerard to discredit forms of social solidarity.

What is crucial here from our point of view is the theory of meaning and discursive action which underlies this explanation of the overlap between academic and lay discourse. In 'conspiracy' accounts of ideology, as we argued in Part I, certain arguments become seen as *inherently* ideological, because they reflect a ruling group's understanding of reality based on their interests and experience of that reality. It makes sense, therefore, to talk of 'ideologies', that is, bodies of argument and discourse which 'belong to' certain groups and which thus possess fixed effects. The social psychologist and the Pākehā New Zealander could thus be said to draw on the same ideology.

This ideology or 'ruling representation' may or may not be persuasive and successful in recruiting those with opposing interests, in this case many Māori New Zealanders; but in those cases where it does become a form of 'social cement', and does effectively incorporate and set the intellectual horizon for an entire culture, then it becomes sensible to talk of some groups as possessing a false consciousness, or misrecognizing their real position. Some groups (women, the working class, the Māori people) have thus taken over representations of reality which do not express their position and interests.

For those who study the sociology of knowledge from this perspective investigation becomes organized around the identification of the interests which structure forms of scientific and lay knowledge (e.g. Barnes 1977). The really difficult problem, in this account, becomes the theorization of 'alternative intellectuals' and the status of their knowledge. How can the representations of critical (non-bourgeois) intellectuals be legitimated as real as opposed to 'interested' knowledge? It is at this point that a theorist such as Althusser begins to differentiate between science and ideology.

The alternative 'autonomy' account of ideology we wish to identify is more sensitive to the potential differences between academic and lay discourse. Here it is more appropriate to talk of ideological practice and ideological effects rather than ideologies or ideological arguments. Emphasis is placed on the flexibility of meaning, and the construction rather than the recognition of interests.

In this account, no argument is inherently ideological by virtue of the characteristics of its speakers, their interests or their perceptions and experiences. Rather, an argument becomes ideological (linked to oppressive forms of power) through its use, construction and form of mobilization. The possibility is there that the 'same' interpretative resources may be put to work for both radical and reactionary ends – to both sustain and subvert existing power relations.

A distinction, for instance, between the rational and the social, or between proper knowledge based on direct individual apprehension and improper knowledge acquired through secondary collective understanding, could be made to work in many ways. It should not be treated as ideological *per se*. As those within the post-structuralist tradition have argued, the meaning of any piece of discourse is not guaranteed through the correspondence between its relational terms and the way the world is or appears to the author of the discourse. Rather, meaning emerges through the pattern of *differences* established between these relational terms, and through the differences, too, between discursive versions.

Terry Eagleton elegantly develops a similar claim in his description of Bakhtin's critique of structuralist linguistics.

> Language was to be seen as inherently 'dialogic': it could be grasped only in terms of its inevitable orientation towards another. The sign was to be seen less as a fixed unit (like a signal) than as an active component of speech, modified and transformed in meaning by the variable social tones, valuations and connotations it condensed within itself in specific social conditions. Since such valuations and connotations were constantly shifting, since the 'linguistic community' was in fact a *heterogeneous* society composed of many conflicting interests, the sign for Bakhtin was less a neutral element in a given structure than a focus of struggle and contradiction. . . . Bakhtin respected what might be called the 'relative autonomy' of language, the fact that it could not be reduced to a mere reflex of social interests; but he insisted that there was no language which was not caught up in definite social relationships, and that these social relationships were in turn part of broader political, ideological and economic systems. Words were 'multi-accentual' rather than frozen in meaning: they were always the words of one particular human subject for another, and this practical context would shape and shift their meaning. (Eagleton, 1983, p. 117; emphasis in the original)

There are, of course, possible tensions here with the perspective of a post-structuralist theorist such as Foucault. Foucault would argue for the importance of looking not just at how different social groups deploy language, in Eagleton/Bakhtin's terms, but at how power operates through the discursive construction of those very social subjects and groups engaged in struggle. None the less, the implications for the overlaps between academic and lay discourse are similar. What we have called the 'autonomy' account leads to a more localized examination of discursive practice.

We cannot assume that any overlap between academic and lay discourse is due to common interests or shared social position. It becomes necessary to investigate separately the field of discursive operation in each case. We could study what Stuart Hall (1988d) has called the 'machineries of representation' involved in the production of lay and academic discourse. These 'machineries' or intertwinings of discursive, institutional and material forces may be very different in each case, and it is this difference which opens up, at the most extreme, the possibility that any parallels between the Pākehā New Zealander and the social psychologist are best seen as a 'coincidence' of the play of meaning in local contexts as opposed, that is, to the global strategy of hegemonic groups.

The description 'coincidence', like 'conspiracy', is too strong, however. The post-structuralist-inspired account of ideological practice stresses both the flexibility of meaning, the shifting and unstable nature of framings of the world, the local intersections of discourse, power and other material and social practices and, also, the fixity of meaning. At a similar point in his working through of the implications of post-structuralist theory Stewart Clegg comes to this conclusion, having followed to this point Laclau's (1983) line on the 'infinitude of the social': 'Of course the matter cannot rest here because the social, as an infinite play of differences, is subject to hegemonic principles in which the discursive elements are forever articulated in determinate, albeit unstable and transitory, ways' (1989, pp. 178–9). We return, therefore, to hegemony and the correspondence between academic and lay discourse but this time through a different route. Clegg goes on to note and adopt, in a revised form, Laclau and Mouffe's (1985) very useful notion of 'nodal points'. He argues that patterns of meaning become fixed in clumps or 'articulations' of practices and discourses which specify agents and their social interests. These nodal points acquire stability and solidity, creating power through the forms of knowledge and 'truth', the types of actors and forms of subjectivity constituted. The legal system, for example, can be seen as just this kind of articulation which stabilizes patterns of meaning, forms of social being, groups and interests.

The field is open, therefore, for a similar investigation of sociology and social psychology, particularly the social science of the 1950s, in order to clarify how specific conceptions of the social body and the individual–social relationship became fixed and stable. Some work along these lines is already available in histories of psychology (Henriques *et al.*, 1984; Rose, 1985) and in the sociology of science (see Haraway, 1989; McCloskey, 1985).

We are not proposing to analyze the 'machineries of representation' or 'articulations of practice' involved in the examples we have been concerned with – that project is beyond our aims in this book. There are, however, some general principles we wish to reinforce from this discussion.

First, we want to adhere to the point concerning the flexibility of signification. It seems important to substitute the concept of ideological practice for that of ideologies. It is undeniably the case that the ideological potential of arguments emerges in practice. This point will be illustrated in an even more concrete fashion in Chapters 7 and 8, where we describe varying mobilizations of notions of human rights and equality, along with critiques of prejudice. We will try to demonstrate how the discursive material usually expressive of progressive liberalism has been turned within New Zealand into a rhetoric for racism.

On the other hand, it seems important, as Clegg notes, not to overdo difference, flexibility and variability. We want, therefore, to acknowledge areas of fixity and hegemony which make it, in the end, no coincidence that certain forms of social psychological discourse overlap with certain forms of lay discourse. We want to investigate why some arguments are difficult for some groups positioned in certain ways to formulate, so that, when they are adopted, predictable rhetorical cul-de-sacs result. Indeed, the history of racism precisely demonstrates the fixity and stability of certain patterns of meaning and practice.

Due to historical precedent, some practices of argumentation and some interpretative resources do seem inexorably directed to some agendas, and in that sense become almost (but not quite) inherently ideological. As we noted in Chapter 5, on a more immediate level, it is the case that some Māori groups (and some feminist groups) have used biologically essentialist arguments sometimes to persuasive effect. But what are the constraints and consequences here? These also need investigation.

Finally, it seems clear that just as the 'conspiracy' account creates areas of explanatory ease and areas of very difficult problems, the 'autonomy' account also has its lapses and absences. For the 'conspiracy' account these seem to revolve around the epistemological status of critical social science and 'revolutionary knowledge'. For the 'autonomy' account, the problem lies in being specific about power – power for whom and for what, and why these ends? In studying racism this doubt about power becomes negligible to the extent that the upshots of power relations are obvious but perhaps only because in our text Māori and Pākehā become simultaneously positioned inside and outside discourse?

7
Practical politics and ideological dilemmas

This chapter focuses on Pākehā New Zealanders' accounts of three controversial areas of intergroup relations; the question of land ownership and compensation for past injustice; the teaching and status of Māori language; and the development of affirmative action programmes for ethnic minorities. In all three cases there have been recent initiatives from Māori groups with considerable public discussion and furore. Māori communities, for example, have encouraged the development of 'language nests' for their children (the Te Kohanga Reo programme) to compensate for the monolingual state system, and have raised the question of a Māori curriculum in schools. Conflicts over land have, of course, a long history but the setting up of a tribunal in 1975 to investigate claims, and the subsequent extension of the tribunal's power in 1984, allowing the examination of claims pre-dating 1975, has prompted fierce reactions among Pākehā New Zealanders.

As in other chapters in Part II we also wish to push forward in this chapter some theoretical and methodological concerns. One of the most surprising features of Pākehā New Zealanders' discourse in the areas we shall examine is that it mobilizes classic liberal and social reformist principles of freedom, individual rights, equality and instrumental rationality, along with an idea of progress, to argue for racist policies. New Zealand has a reputation for being the 'Sweden of the South Pacific', reflecting early radicalism in social welfare, social policy and women's suffrage (Castles, 1985). It is to be expected that egalitarian and liberal concepts will structure practical politics. But how do apparently 'benign' forms of political rhetoric become regrouped into arguments opposing affirmative action, opposing Māori language teaching, opposing equal outcomes and so on?

Our interest lies in developing techniques for studying and making sense of some of the contradictions and shifts in the ideological battlefields which constitute and sustain racism. This, of course, is a path that others have explored before. Several groups of American social psychologists, for example, have recently promulgated the thesis that racism, and racists, have changed their shape and now display a 'modern' and conflicted face in contrast to 'old-fashioned' versions (McConahay, 1986; Sears, 1988). The 'modern' face of racism they identify is precisely distinguished by this mixture of egalitarian sentiments, liberalism and prejudice.

Racial attitudes among contemporary white Americans have been described as ambivalent, contradictory and inconsistent in comparison to the 'straightforward' bigotry of the past (Gaertner and Dovidio, 1986; Katz *et al.*, 1986). Researchers disagree about the precise nature of the ambivalence, whether it emerges from the combination of positive and negative belief systems or results from a clash of values and feelings (see Dovidio and Gaertner, 1986, for a summary of the differences). None the less these social psychologists agree that the conflict concerns the continued expression of anti-black sentiments in an ideological climate which supports egalitarianism, is opposed to discrimination and to blatant expressions of biological racism. McConahay (1986) suggests that white Americans tend to resolve their dilemma by disowning individual prejudice, attributing their own racist actions to non-racial motivations and by only endorsing items on racial attitude scales which present racist conclusions in a coded or veiled form.

Frank Reeves (1983) has similarly argued that racism in British political and parliamentary discourse has recently become disguised and covered over through a careful process of 'sanitary coding'. This process, he argues, leaves the racism still present, to be read by those inclined to do so, but also renders it deniable. Again the general impression is of a more mixed and contradictory discourse, which is more difficult to challenge directly as racist, but which, none the less, can be read in this way by supporters who wish to discover a racist message.

It seems clear, too, as we saw in Chapter 5, that expressions of 'old-fashioned' biological racism have recently become more pervasively intertwined with discourses of national belonging. Nation, rather than race, has taken over some of the ideological tasks of legitimating racism. There are parallels here between the New Zealand and UK experience. In the UK also the idea of the nation has been mobilized in recent years to exclude and marginalize black groups (Gilroy, 1987). Barker (1981) suggests that the 'new racism' in the United Kingdom has also developed more sophisticated sociobiological lines of argument about the naturalness of territorial defensiveness, the desire for ethnic separateness and cultural 'preservation'. While van Dijk (1984) has documented similar shifts in the Netherlands. In brief, crude expressions of racial hierarchies and innate inferiorities seem to have become suspect in New Zealand, the United States, the United Kingdom and in other Western democracies.

Whether the outcome is described as 'modern racism', 'new racism' or as 'sanitary coding', it is obvious that racism is flexible; its manifestations change as material conditions shift and as the agenda for debate become successfully redefined through various forms of struggle. Indeed, it is probably the case that the effectiveness and persuasiveness of ideological discourse, its resilience, and its potential for continued legitimation, depend precisely on qualities of fluidity, pluralism and variability.

The analysis we wish to develop in this chapter of 'modern' forms of racist discourse and some of the surprising shifts displayed in the New Zealand context has been strongly influenced by the concept of ideological dilemmas developed by Billig *et al.* (1988). They introduced this notion as part of a more general claim about the nature of common-sense reasoning. They argue that common sense is normally organized through contrary themes and is frankly dilemmatic in character. Argument, conflict and the articulation of contradictory positions, whether in racist discourse or in other arenas, are proposed as the standard stuff of everyday talk.

Billig *et al.* are critical of the impression of common sense given in both cognitive psychology and social theory. They accuse cognitive psychologists of ignoring the social and historical, that is to say, the ideological nature of the resources and material people use to think with when resolving dilemmas and making decisions. Cognitive psychologists are criticized for presenting an illusory picture of the individual thinker as a cognitive machine calculating away in a social vacuum. Social theorists, on the other hand, are accused of mistakenly assuming that lived ideology and common sense merely reproduce a unified dominant system of integrated beliefs and attitudes. Common sense, Billig *et al.* suggest, is a composite of egalitarian and authoritarian strands, of individualism and collectivism, and emphasizes both special expertise and shared knowledge, both prejudice and tolerance.

Our analysis follows up this point. We shall argue that Pākehā New Zealanders' discourse concerning land, language and affirmative action reveals a particular set of ideological dilemmas played out in the commonplaces of political argument. These dilemmas are genuine conundrums both in common sense and in Western democratic philosophy. They are difficult to resolve, and indeed could be pushed in many directions, but what interests us is how the various formulations of these dilemmas seem to lead, to an overwhelming extent in our sample, to the maintenance of racist rather than anti-racist practices. In essence, our goal in this chapter is to study 'bricolage' in action as people draw on contradictory resources in a flexible and variable fashion to construct their accounts.

Although our analysis is concerned with argumentative inconsistency and clashing political means and ends, it will become clear that we do not see this conflict from the standpoint of experimental social psychology, as motivated by psychological ambivalence. We see conflict, not as a new phenomenon, but as a normal discursive process. Thus towards the end of this chapter we wish to develop a critique of the American work on 'modern racism' and suggest, through the example of our own analysis, an alternative framework for the social psychologist interested in investigating ideological change.

Some commonplaces of political discourse

The following list of some of the tropes and commonplaces characteristic of practical politics in New Zealand has been constructed from our interviews and from examples of political debate and discussion. These or similar phrases recur throughout the interview transcripts, newspaper articles and extracts from *Hansard* we have analyzed. Each is normally presented in argument as 'rhetorically self-sufficient'. That is, as a clinching argument, or as a principle which should be beyond question.

1. Resources should be used productively and in a cost-effective manner.
2. Nobody should be compelled.
3. Everybody should be treated equally.
4. You cannot turn the clock backwards.
5. Present generations cannot be blamed for the mistakes of past generations.
6. Injustices should be righted.
7. Everybody can succeed if they try hard enough.
8. Minority opinion should not carry more weight than majority opinion.
9. We have to live in the twentieth century.
10. You have to be practical.

The ten statements above are unexceptional and familiar in form – they display the solidity and taken-for-granted feel characteristic of mundane politics. Taking each statement individually, who could disagree that it is important to be practical, that history moves forward, that injustice and inequality are wrong?

Commonplaces of this kind constitute a type of folk wisdom and summarize, in Billig *et al.*'s terminology, some of the tools of argument available to our sample as they struggled with the controversial issues of Māori–Pākehā relations. There are three claims we wish to make about these commonplaces in the following sections.

First, following Billig *et al.*, we wish to argue that the dilemmatic potential of these maxims and the contradictory nature of ideological discourse permits considerable rhetorical flexibility and argumentative power. Some possible ideological dilemmas are obvious already – individual rights conflict in our list with practical considerations; the particular injustices of colonialism cannot be righted if history is irrelevant. We wish to show how these dilemmas are actually constituted in practice.

Secondly, we wish to demonstrate that commonplaces and the broader interpretative resources of political discussion are best seen as a kitbag or patchwork of argumentative and rhetorical forms and should not be seen as rigidly applied templates or cognitive schema (Potter and Wetherell, 1989). In any particular context, Pākehā New Zealanders artfully fashion their justifications and accounts from these resources.

Finally, we wish to indicate the social and collective nature of these maxims and discuss their history in relation to competing traditions of political discourse. The patchwork of interpretative resources from which these commonplaces emerge connects individual speakers with their political culture but it also connects ideological developments in the South Pacific with the broader currents of European philosophy and politics. The Pākehā New Zealander arguing passionately for equal rights and for the primacy of rationality echoes, consciously or unconsciously, voices from the Enlightenment and restates, in a local political context which has its own particular inflection, the global discourses of modernity.

We shall begin with this last task of contextualizing commonplaces and ideological dilemmas within a 'history of ideas' before going on to look at practice and the mobilization of resources in actual accounts and arguments.

The patchwork of resources

In the commentaries which attempt to define the climate of political opinion in New Zealand various terms recur. New Zealand is described as having a populist rather than a socialist history, as a country with a petit bourgeois outlook (Castles, 1985), as a society dominated by a myth of egalitarianism (Consedine, 1989), as a colonial culture parasitic upon the social attitudes and cultural values of lower middle-class Britain (Gibbons, 1981) and as a country imbued with an ideology of welfarism (Bedggood, 1975).

Initially, however, New Zealand simply appeared to be a 'glorious country for a working man' (Steven, 1989). British immigrants came principally from the lower middle class and working class; many of the working-class migrants held radical Chartist views and saw themselves as escaping the stratification of British society (Castles, 1985). And, the conditions they first encountered in New Zealand were superior to those experienced at home. New Zealand employers were able to pay high wages, particularly in the agricultural sector, since land, taken from Māoris, was producing large profits (Steven, 1989). Also, employers found it necessary to pay these high wages since labour was in scarce supply, given the relative ease with which most agricultural workers could acquire their own land.

In the muddle of material conditions, practices and policies which form a political climate, it seems almost impossible to agree on the decisive factors but this material advantage, the relative absence of concepts of aristocratic privilege, and the initial low differentials between social groups seem likely to have given a distinctive twist to political discourse in New Zealand.

A consensus for social democratic welfare policies, as a strategy for ameliorating the effects of capitalism, developed early in New Zealand. A reputation as the 'social laboratory of the world' grew from innovations of the 1890s when radical pensions and fair-wage policies were introduced along with votes for women. As Keith Sinclair comments, 'by 1893 [New Zealand] was the most democratic state in the world, or that had ever existed' (1990, p. vii). In the 1930s–40s, New Zealand again became viewed as an example of progressive and socially enlightened policies when fourteen years of uninterrupted Labour government laid down comprehensive foundations for the first welfare state (Castles, 1985).

Yet, as Castles argues, this social reformism was not, as in other countries, linked to socialist policies or the result of working-class struggle and strategy. Several things seemed to have combined to bring about early radical social reformism with crucial effects for New Zealanders' continuing sense of how political life should be organized.

First, the Pākehā working class in New Zealand were able to join forces with the middle class around a shared political culture and set of interests. Intervention and the state in general were viewed positively, and the majority were happy to look to the state for security. Gibbons (1981) argues that lower middle-class values taken over from nineteenth-century Britain with an emphasis on respectability, hard work, thrift and the benefits of capitalism became fixed, largely uncontested and reinforced in each small town through cultural, recreational, social and sectarian organizations. According to Castles, the aim of the working class was not to question the system but to demand specific improvements, and their power to achieve this goal was strengthened by the scarcity of labour at these times. Those groups which might have resisted were, argues Castles, in disarray, split between urban and rural economic interests, with no customs of deference and privilege to fall back on.

New Zealand is probably still best described as a welfare state based on social democratic principles, although many of these principles have been questioned in recent years with the revival of new right economic policies (Jesson *et al.*, 1988). All the same, the prevalent themes of political discourse expressed in the commonplaces above still seem to reflect this early reformist orientation.

The importance of being practical

> Here we are, at the bottom of the habitable world. The very act of getting here made heroes and heroines of our forbears, brown and white. In challenging and conquering those unknown seas we earned the right to

think of ourselves as brave, resourceful, versatile. And so, by and large, we
have proved.

(Cole Catley, 1990, p. 56)

A strong theme of self-congratulation runs through New Zealand popular
literature based on an image of New Zealanders as eminently resourceful and
down-to-earth folk, who get on with the job, do not moan and who can be
relied upon in an emergency. This supposed national characteristic is found
particularly strongly in images of the New Zealand soldier (Phillips, 1989).

> Yet, as a whole, the picture that emerges of the New Zealand soldier
> corresponds to the Kiwi's rather flattering image of himself [*sic*] – tough,
> laconic, good-natured, self-reliant (unlike those Poms who always have to be
> told what to do!), always ready for a fight yet not provoking one. In essence, he
> is serious-minded under his easy-going exterior. He doesn't like war; but only
> Davin and Lee get really upset about it. For the others it is a dirty job to be
> done, which the Kiwi prides himself he does as well as anyone, even if he'd
> rather be in the boozer. (John Cowie Reid, cited in Orsman and Moore, 1988,
> p. 541)

It is a romantic picture which no doubt could be seen as fuelled by some of the
very real qualities required in a pioneering environment; but as a social
philosophy, a practical and rational stance clearly has other origins and is
articulated not just in colonial contexts.

Many social theorists, including Weber and Habermas, have argued that
one of the characteristic features of modernism and the period since the
Enlightenment is the increasing development of instrumental rationality as a
form of being in the world (Giddens, 1979; Harvey, 1989). The idea, they
claim, took hold that human societies can progress through the application of
reason and technical know-how and, with enough thought and investigation,
practical solutions will emerge to intractable problems. This modern attitude
replaces spiritual doubt and unknowable mysteries with the attentive gaze of
the expert technician, who, instruction manual at hand, is always ready to
intervene and tinker. As many feminists have pointed out, it is, *par
excellence*, a masculine stance delivering domination and power. Above all, it
involves the fantasy of the reasonable individual in perfect control of their
behaviour – cognitive omniscience replacing ambivalence and mixed motives.

Weber argued that the utopian goals of modernism are in fact seriously
undermined by the increasing rationalization of modern societies and the
bureaucratization of social life which they spawn.

> Here for Weber was the modern paradox eating away at the optimism of early
> liberalism and at the certainties of marxism; that modern men and women
> possessed an enhanced technical capacity to achieve ends that were no longer
> clear to them, that they were armed with a knowledge-based culture in a world
> that was now too complex to know. (Coates, 1990, p. 277)

Other critics, such as Adorno and Horkheimer (1979), have argued that there is a vicious 'dialectic of the enlightenment' such that the striving for freedom and mastery over nature, and the 'practical attitude', produces in turn the regulation and mastery of men and women along with effective forms of domination and stultification. While, more recently, postmodern critics have sought to oppose totalizing narratives of progress and design and embrace instead indeterminacy, fragmentation and open-endedness (Harvey, 1989).

None the less, the appeal to the practical and the rational remains a powerful argumentative and interpretative resource and, along with social reformist and social democratic discourse, is one pole in the ideological dilemmas structuring political discourse in New Zealand. Its influence is evident in the commonplaces reproduced above. Shortly, we will show the argumentative power of the practical when it is invoked dilemmatically but, first, we need to consider two other important nodules around which Pākehā New Zealanders' discourse oscillates.

Equality, freedom and individual rights

Political discourse in New Zealand has been deeply infused with traditions of liberal thought as well as by social democratic politics – with the liberalism, that is, defined by such exemplars as Locke, Hume and Adam Smith rather than the liberalism of David Steele and Paddy Ashdown and contemporary liberal democratic political parties in the United Kingdom. Liberalism emerged as a coherent political ideology or philosophy around the end of the eighteenth century and is thought to mark the transition from traditional feudal societies to modern capitalism. It is associated with the British Liberal party of the nineteenth century and in its economic guise, more recently, with the *laissez-faire*, market-orientated policies of UK Conservative and New Zealand Labour governments of the 1980s (Coates, 1990; Hall, 1986; Jesson *et al.*, 1988).

In contrast to the political philosophy which justified the social formations existing prior to the upheavals of the seventeenth and eighteenth centuries, liberalism can be seen as a progressive and even radical counter-ideology. Hall (1986) describes it as the ideology of the modern world – 'for decades the idea of "modernity" was "thought" essentially, within its categories' (p. 45). If not endorsing democracy and universal suffrage, it set in place some of the pre-conditions for the modern, democratic, capitalist state.

Not surprisingly, the traces linger in the common-sense and interpretative resources of Pākehā New Zealanders. The clearest signs of this influence concern not the push to 'free enterprise', although that is important in contemporary economic debate, but the persistence of particular notions of individual rights and freedoms and the importance of contracts and equality which were taken for granted by those we interviewed. These principles were summed up in pithy phrases – 'everybody should have a fair go', 'we don't want any unequal opportunities here', 'people must procure what they want from life through their own efforts' – and appealed to in more complex arguments about the concepts of natural justice and meritocracy (Potter and Wetherell, 1989).

One of the most striking features of liberal discourse, as Chapter 6 noted, is the way rights are assumed as a property of individuals: possessed in the way that humans own their bodies, arms and legs – natural characteristics which cannot easily be alienated. The general assumption is individualistic and the impression is of self-sufficient agents formed outside society who enter into social relations with their rights and freedoms intact. The role of the state is to protect these freedoms and rights and, as Hall (1986) notes, the individual can be seen as entering, on this basis, into a social contract with the state.

Equality is a particularly crucial concept within the political framework of liberalism, defined with a distinctive spin. It becomes a form of equality understood through meritocracy:

James: Yeah, that's sort of, sort of like the argument about the Ministry of Women's Affairs (yes) uh it's an unequal thing having a Ministry of Women's Affairs, why don't we have a Ministry of Men's Affairs? Um and I think to a certain extent the same applies, we have we have a Māori land courts, we have um Māoris can get uh loans from the Department of Māori Affairs, that sort of thing. Well I don't see why they can't just go to the housing court like everyone else?

Equality allows for passionate argument and forceful indignation at its supposed violation because the ethical grounds of argument seem so well established. Liberal principles are so firmly entrenched as common sense.

From an alternative perspective the partial nature of this type of analysis of equality becomes manifest. Liberal equality is premised on the claim that all begin from the same starting point. It is thus very different from socialist conceptions of equal outcomes. Society, in the liberal meritocratic view, merely supplies the conditions within which individuals, differentially endowed, can make their mark. The outcome is fair because all are assumed to have begun with equal chance and equal opportunity; all were assumed to be free initially and to have the same rights.

The resistance to compulsion and the strongly held principle that nobody should be forced to do what they do not want to do similarly derives from the liberal emphasis on the superior value of freedom; but it is a freedom tempered in liberal philosophy with two other core concepts. One is the constraint of property rights and the right to have contracts respected – leading to the notion that land taken away illegally creates a natural injustice – while the second concept concerns human nature. Individuals are free but, following the speculative line of Thomas Hobbes, and more conservative strands of thought, they are also assumed to be occasionally brutish, violent and selfish (Coates, 1990). Human nature, therefore, in this pessimistic analysis, can require a lot of 'forgiveness'. Liberals noted that individuals can choose to exercise their rights and freedoms in unfortunate ways.

Imperial history

In a colonial society such as New Zealand, discussions of contemporary Māori–Pākehā relations are inseparable, not just from philosophies of rationality, equality and rights, from modernist currents more generally and from social reformist discourse, but also from accounts of history. There is a particular concern with how much of the past should be carried into the future. One significant trope recurred again and again in the discourse of the Pākehā New Zealanders we interviewed: 'you can't turn the clock backwards' or 'what's done is done'. This repetitive theme in common sense was part of a broader consensual set of interpretative resources for making sense of history and its flow.

History seemed to be articulated in two forms either as continuity or as discontinuity. These formulations appear oppositional but they feed off each other and both could be characterized as part of the 'whig' view found in the conventional histories of New Zealand which describe, for example:

> How New Zealand rose from the depths of the sea. How it became inhabited by strange creatures and plants. How, after enduring unthinkable cold and heat, it became clothed with verdure, the home of numberless living creatures, and well watered everywhere, fit at last for man's abode. (Reed, 1946, p. 5)

These histories also tell us about 'the coming of the brown man', about Abel Tasman's journeys and map-making and how his

> perplexing zigzag line staggering across the South Pacific represented all that was known of our country from the days of Charles I to George III. Dust gathered on Tasman's journal: the land lay sleeping under the southern sun until awakened by the touch of our own Captain Cook. (Reed, 1946, p. 1)

Reed's *Story of New Zealand* was immensely popular in the 1940s and 1950s and became a standard school edition in that period. It is, of course, a particularly florid example of what Paul Carter (1987) has called 'imperial history' but its form as a particular type of cultural discourse lingers in contemporary Pākehā story-telling about the past.

Carter argues in his analysis of accounts of Australian history that this general form of history-making adopts the frame of theatre or the diorama. The historian becomes the playwright, moving events about, constructing historical spaces and a geographical stage. Botany Bay or Cape Kidnappers, for instance, and other central sites in Australasian history, become detached from the hurly burly of time, travellers and activities, and turned into 'places' and waiting rooms for history. Similarly, the narrative demands an omniscient, all-seeing eye, who can already foretell the future. In describing 'this land under the southern sun', Reed, like various Australian historians, can give the 'illusion of growing purpose', and the impression of 'diverse activities converging towards the single goal of settlement' (Carter, 1987, pp. xiv–xv).

This type of history-making is both continuous and disjointed. Continuous because our past history is seen as previewing and leading up to the present and disjointed because contemporary time, our present actions, have not yet become history and had the illusion of unfolding purpose placed on them. The past is organized, the present is not, yet the organization of the past produces the present. So sometimes the past appears as another land, a mythic place, separated from the present.

Those we interviewed rarely gave detailed accounts of particular historical events but their accounting for and justification of the present constructed some of the crucial features of continuity and discontinuity. In general, their accounts agreed with Reed that events unfolded in a pre-ordained fashion; history marches forward towards the progressive and desirable end which is modern New Zealand society. One could say that the predominant assumption was that 'everyday and in everyway we get bigger and better.'

As Chapter 6 noted, those we interviewed sometimes expressed nostalgia for the past which was imagined as a golden time of harmony and order (Williams, 1975). This nostalgia for a golden past, in this context, a past of ideal race relations where Māoris 'knew their place', was relatively frequent but this form of nostalgia is also difficult to carry off in a colonial context, and what was much more prevalent in our interviews was the image of a golden future.

The future becomes golden to the extent that history becomes a story of continual improvement. As time goes on it is assumed people become more advanced, more rational, more civilized, able to do more things, able to construct even more impressive solutions to social problems and so on. Interestingly, the society of the near future becomes imagined as a more liberal, just and ethically superior place.

This imagining, then, constitutes part of the ludicrousness of attempting to 'turn the clock backwards'. The phrase principally serves to mock the impracticality and lack of 'real politic' of those who seek to remind Pākehā New Zealand of colonial injustices but it also takes for granted the obvious desirability of the present.

Pākehā New Zealanders also have access, of course, to the other possible version of the future and will outline pessimistic and apocalyptic accounts of inevitable doom, chaos, failure and the barbaric times to come. What seems to be significant, however, is the different discursive contexts in which these two versions are utilized. Thus, as Chapter 6 argued, when considering Māori protest and activism over land and other issues, some of our sample were concerned at how increasing tensions and disruption might mar the future, yet when justifying the pattern of New Zealand history and current social organization, the future once again became golden and the present became ratified by its ongoing progressive nature in comparison to the past.

The continuous view of history and the golden future are powerful argumentative resources not least because it becomes irrational from this perspective to question the current form of society. Most crucially, race and history become elided together because the characteristics which make the future golden are presented as those of Western white civilization – increasing technological benefits, rational administration, civilized values, charitable good-will and the desire to make things better for the 'less fortunate' groups. This is the way the world is seen as going and resistance thus becomes quixotic. The critic is skilfully caught in a dilemma – how can one argue against such 'obvious' good things and such optimism, without appearing to advocate a return to the 'bad old days'? Another form of utopianism seems the only counter. It is the old conundrum: how can taken-for-granted 'progress' be made to appear undesirable?

The discontinuous formulation of history, its appearance as an alien and mythic place separated from the present, is also an extremely powerful resource for justification. The discontinuous accounts similarly view history as unfolding theatre but emphasize the distance of history. Key events of colonial history become with this distance faintly incomprehensible and mysterious to modern eyes. Because the world has 'moved on so much', the past becomes seen as a foreign country, peopled with exotic characters with inexplicable motives, displaying the unfortunate side of human nature.

The past becomes in these versions violent, brutal and primitive, full of those kinds of incidents, injustices and atrocities which are presented as 'characteristic' of history. However, injustice is also contained in the past. It is not possible to imagine these incidents happening in the present because, in comparison, the present is seen as such a new improved version of the past. Time has moved on and it is assumed the world has got better. The violence of colonial times can be firmly and safely placed in history and disconnected from the present. Again the critic is silenced. Why in this case should people take responsibility for the events of the past which are so different from the way that people would behave now? Simply put, accounts which most effectively justify the status quo flexibly stress the continuity of good and the discontinuity of evil.

Mobilizing arguments

In the previous sections we have tried to outline the main interpretative resources which contribute to the ideological dilemmas structuring practical politics in New Zealand. Through this brief and somewhat sketchy account of liberal philosophy, New Zealand's social reformist history, the emergence of the modernist technical attitude and imperial history, we have tried to show how the tropes and commonplaces of everyday politics have origins which extend beyond the shores of New Zealand. The tropes of practical politics may appear as spontaneous self-generated reflections on experience and 'life', and in one sense they are, but they are also structured by intellectual resources which indicate the broader discursive context in which Western democracies operate.

The issue now is, given these resources and some of their typical ideological effects, which we also examined in passing, how are arguments developed *in situ*? How are these resources put to work in particular rhetorical contexts, specifically in relation to the three controversial topics we identified in the Introduction: the issue of Māori grievances over land and the question of compensation; the issue of affirmative action such as the availability of places in medical school, Māori seats in parliament, special provisions in relation to loans and so on; and the question and status of Māori language teaching?

The available interpretative resources are liberal in two senses: they partly reconstitute the particular philosophical and political tradition we have identified; but they are liberal, too, in the everyday meaning of the term, seemingly genial, relatively positive, apparently supportive of some of the good things associated with democracies – freedom, equality and a progressive movement towards a more harmonious and just society. Does this 'liberality' pose a constraint on the argumentative possibilities?

The majority of Pākehā New Zealanders we interviewed used the resources of individual rights, egalitarianism, practical rationality, history as progress and so on to argue for outcomes which we would describe, taking up our own stance within the argumentative battlefield, as actually 'illiberal', as designed to maintain unequal power relations and the dominance of a particular group of Pākehā New Zealanders. The majority of our sample wanted to justify colonial land practices, argue against land compensation, fight against the implementation of affirmative action and prevent Māori language acquiring any significant status in schools or public life.

This argumentative direction is not inevitable, however. Perhaps less unexpectedly, the same patchwork of resources can be mobilized to argue for changing patterns of disadvantage. This point reinforces our argument in Chapter 6 that discourse can only usefully be characterized as ideological in practice. Discourse and argument become ideological at the moment of mobilization. It does not seem particularly useful, in this context, as in other contexts, to describe particular types of arguments as inherently ideological, that is, as inherently orientated towards the maintenance of unequal power relations.

The situated nature of ideology can be seen in the following two extracts:

Andrews: I think that [the introduction of Māori language as a core subject in schools] would be very sensible. It would make far more sense to me to have gone through my schooling and have learned Māori instead of learning Latin and French, you know. That would make a lot more sense as a New Zealander, sure Latin and French might have been useful to help me with my English (mmm) but it didn't help me with my Māori.

Bradman: . . . That's why I actually object to um them bringing um massive Māori culture curricula into schools etc. (yeah?).

> To a certain extent, um because I do feel that this doesn't equip them for the modern world at all (mmhm). Because what's the use of being able to speak Māori if you can only speak it to a limited number of people (yeah) um in a limited area and it has no use at all in the actual, you know, in the real world as it were, if you'll pardon the expression.

Here an argument based on practical considerations and instrumental rationality is used to make two opposing cases. Andrews argues that introducing Māori language into schools makes sense and is a more practical scheme than learning European languages, while Bradman argues that Māori language is impractical in the modern world.

Exactly the same pattern could be found with other argumentative resources. Thus individual rights, freedom and equality led in our interviews to a determined case for the assimilation of Māori people into the Pākehā system. However, these principles have also frequently proved to be a useful starting point for anti-racist campaigns and on some rare occasions were formulated by some of those we interviewed for that end too.

Flexibility of this kind is sustained by the dilemmatic nature of the combination of resources we have identified which permit selective debate and the skilful and judicious blending of claims and counter-claims. So, how are 'liberal' principles used for 'illiberal' ends? In practice, it seems to be simple. When appropriate, participants let the ethical principles of liberal philosophy do the rhetorical work, but when ethics raise embarrassing issues, practical considerations are mobilized to take over the argumentative slog. The dilemmatic possibilities are frequently obscured if responses to just one controversial issue are considered but they become apparent, as we shall now try to demonstrate, across responses to contrasting issues.

For the contentious issue of Māori language teaching, a typical and prevalent pattern was to argue, on the grounds of principle, against the compulsory learning of Māori, to acknowledge that Māori could be an optional extra, but to express scepticism about the practical value of Māori language given the 'characteristics of the modern world'.

> Irvine:
>
> I'll tell you something else, excuse me, that I'm dead against and that is the complete bringing in of the Māori language (mmhmm?) 'cos that's got tremendous support now hasn't it? (mmhmm) I've taught in Māori schools a lot of, up on the east coast way up in North Auckland, I've also taught in many er a number of schools which have er got a 1 per cent or 2 per cent of Māori population. Now therefore I've got nothing against the Māori people they're a, they are a, I've got many friends that are good Māori people, but I find the Māori language er of no use really, now it may be part of their heritage but I'm not buying that (yes) because in say the year 2020 or whatever we

won't be worried about speaking the Māori language. We'll be worried about speaking if if anything we'll be speaking um French or German or Japanese or something else because they are the people they are the countries we are trading with (yes) and to and to trade successfully we must be able to speak the language.

Wetherell: Yes, I was particularly interested er this was something I wanted to ask you about because of your you know position and that must be an issue that's being debated in the teaching profession a lot //

Irvine: // it is being debated quite a lot

Wetherell: er discussion about whether it should be brought into primary schools as a compulsory . . . ?

Irvine: No I haven't, it's never brought in as a compulsory language, sure if you if there are people who want to learn it, right, learn it, but as a compulsory language no I don't think it should be brought in. My staff here would go through the ceiling (huh) in the classrooms if you brought it in as a compulsory language (yes). And it's surprising as you move from school to school that the attitude of staffs do change (yes) and at this particular school they are not impressed with the Māori language in the slightest (yes) out at other schools of course oh yes good thing let's go and learn the Māori language (yes) so it's a pretty divided subject in New Zealand.

Wetherell: Yes I gathered that, I in some ways wish I could have gone along to the recent conference, teachers' conference 'cos er that seemed you know one of those sorts of discussions going on there and that's something that er . . .

Irvine: It's an experience going on to a marae, and I've done it many times, um it's an experience their way of life and we should know probably the basics of how to do that sort of thing but to you know to to to talk Māori fully as a language I would get no I would get no joy I would get no help out of that.

Wetherell: . . . this Taha Māori programme, is it? What is it actually?

R. Kenwood: Ah well you know I hope when I retire that I will learn the Māori language, I think it (.) I want to learn it you know because I think I have to learn it, but I'd like to, but I think it's they (.) unfortunate with these Te Kohanga Reo situations, is that, you know, they're sort of forcing Māoris and peop (.) forcing Māori children to learn Māori language, well I can see it has no value in our education system. Now they'll straight away say that our system is wrong. But um er er you know as far as the Māori language is concerned, singing and that sort of thing and

	on the marae, it has its place. But in a Western world it has no place at all.
Wetherell:	Right, so it's just um . . . you wouldn't think it should be taught in primary schools, say as // a core subject?
R. Kenwood:	// Oh (.) Oh (.) It, it could be an optional (.) but er what they're going to do I think, in time, you'll find that they'll they'll appoint more and more bilingual er people and with the ultimate aim of teaching Māori and just where it's going to get them I don't know . . .
Wetherell:	Yeah, yes, I mean what what do you feel about this issue of um learning Māori? Do you think um say given a choice between school-kids learning French or a European language and Māori, er that er which one should there be more emphasis on do you think?
Acton:	Well I think um there (.) I think, you know, Te Kohanga Reo, the children's learning?, um I think that's really good. Um for the Māoris, I, I wouldn't be interested in learning Māori because it's not my culture, um I think it's important for them to have (.) that's what's half the problem, because they haven't actually, there's no emphasis on their own culture. They've got nothing to be proud of, 'cause I'd say they're very proud people. Um I, yeah, I think it should be well not um compulsory, but there should be an emphasis on people learning Māori. But also European I think, there should be more languages offered, like Japanese, we've got to think what jobs you know, economically they're, you know, trading with Japan and things like that. Um maybe not so much French and German because, unless it's just for an interest point of view 'cause I do French and I enjoy it, sort of it's noth (.) I'm not really looking at it for a job or something like that.

To define something as compulsory is, in terms of the liberal discourse of freedom and human rights, to define it negatively. Compulsion is automatically rhetorically bad. However, there is a second strand of argument here. Māori language teaching, exemplified in the programme of Te Kohanga Reo, is seen as a nice idea, for the Māori people at least, but as also conflicting with the 'real politic' of the modern world and the economic interests of the nation. There is a powerful contradiction here, of course, which describes the compulsion for Māoris to learn the dominant language as only sensible in a progressive society but any pressure on Pākehā people to learn Māori as wrong precisely when it is compulsory.

Acton in the extracts above comes closest to the image Billig *et al.* (1988) propose of the individual thoughtfully puzzling over the ideological dilemmas of common sense as they attempt to sort out their position. Acton rehearses the dilemma of the right of a group of people to maintain their culture against the problem of compulsion. She notes the utility account, which values European languages and Japanese, but then worries over this claim since French is a central subject in schools but seems to be quite difficult to justify in these terms except as an interest.

This type of thoughtful puzzling which expressed the dilemmas as part of developing a response to a question was common in the interviews. However, it was equally clear that the functional requirement of mounting an effective argument produces consistency, as dilemmas become repressed and temporarily resolved to put a point across. It is for this reason that, analytically, the dilemmatic possibilities sometimes only become evident when looking across responses to different issues. The extracts from Irvine and Raymond Kenwood above, both primary-school teachers, are typical of this pattern in which relatively consistent claims are expressed.

Consistency disappears as the topic of conversation and the discursive activity requires change. Thus, while it seems reasonable to argue on ethical grounds against the teaching of Māori language (there should be no compulsion in a just society), when justifying the sharp practices of colonialism, ethical principles become subdued to human nature and the vagaries of that primitive time – past history.

Wetherell:	What do you, there's a lot of discussion and dispute about Waitangi day and whether that's a suitable day for New Zealand's national holiday because of the sort of land question. Um do you feel that there was a case there, for there was a grievance there about land, or that really it's . . .
Scarfe:	Um I think it's wrong for the Māori people of today to be anti the Pākehā today because of what happened two hundred years ago (yes). I don't think that's there's the same bolshiness [inaudible] of Waitangi week, they were so anti Pākehā but there's no way that Pākehās of today get at Māoris of today like that. So you've really just got to say well they were people, a couple of hundred years ago, whether they were Māori or Pākehā or whatever, they didn't get on (yes). Um but I think it was typical of those days that when you conquer a land you conquer it, you don't share, you conquer, and just like the Spaniards did in the 1600s and everybody else did. You go and you take over. And because the Māori was, um, unaware of Pākehā ways of doing things, they got sucked in I guess. But then they got a few things out of it, they decided that their muskets, that the Pākehā muskets were pretty good to have as well. I mean they made the deal, it wasn't taken. But um, (0.2) what was I going to say, it's (0.2) it was a bad deal. I mean so much land for a few muskets, on today's prices because land is so much more valuable, and I think now they're realizing that what their ancestors

did was a bad deal but two hundred years ago it was quite fair because there was so much land. And the muskets were valuable. So OK it was a deal that was made and you've got to live by it, really. There is still a lot of Māori land around. Uh a lot of it is inaccessible, um but I don't think there should be Māori land and Pākehā land, it's just land, I mean we're all going to live on it aren't we? (yes, right, yeah) Um, and if they want to have Bastion Point for a Māori landmark well it's just a landmark really, it doesn't have to be one person's, does it?

Benton:	The ridiculous thing is if you really want to be nasty about it and go back (.) um the Europeans really did take over New Zealand's shore, and I mean the Māoris killed off all the Morioris beforehand, I mean it wasn't exactly their land to start with (yes), I mean it's a bit ridiculous.
Wetherell:	So it's just a sort of //
Benton:	// I think we bend over backwards a bit too much.
James:	Yeah, and one of the arguments I hear continually is that that when the Māoris sold their land to the colonists, they sold it at the going rate, at the time. OK it might be worth millions now, but that's not a hundred and fifty years ago. They were quite happy to have a couple of barrels of whisky and a few blankets and beds for it, that was good pri (.) or or guns (yes). You know? I think of course they were exploited, I mean people like Samuel Marsden it's just like the the rum runners in in Australia. I mean we're just as bad, I mean Samuel Marsden's got to be one of the evilest men that ever lived, he was wicked! He used to fill them up with booze and then buy their land off them! But you know that sort of exploitation has (.) it's a part of human, I mean it's gone on for thousands of years (yeah) and OK you've got to try and right it to a certain extent and and if you realize that it was exploitation and don't sort of whitewash it over then I think you've learnt something from it.

In these extracts the discontinuous version of history is mobilized, the colonial past becomes another world – a world of violence, brutality and machiavellian motives where different standards of ethics apply. None the less, some liberal principles are presented as continuous. Emphasis is placed, for instance, on contracts and the rights of ownership and property. The 'magical' rhetorical force attached to the concept of 'rights' can even be extended to the 'rights of conquest' to develop an ethical justification. These 'discontinuous' and 'continuous' versions of history permit enormous rhetorical flexibility. It can be argued that contracts made in the past should continue today, it would be unjust to overturn them or not respect their terms; yet other injustices, those attributed to the evil side of human nature or to the oppressiveness seemingly inherent in the march of history, should be forgiven and forgotten.

Predominantly, our sample interpreted questions about land issues as demanding a justification of past actions. To engage in justification involves accepting a wrong has been done for which one needs to account. The majority of those we interviewed agreed that the past was indeed a rotten place but none the less wanted to temper the conclusions drawn from the awareness of historical injustice. The ideological dilemma between principles and practical considerations thus bites particularly deeply here and many arguments were structured around the *principle/practice* dichotomy (see also Wetherell *et al.*, 1987). Some things are alright in principle, but one needs to be realistic and look for the most effective forms of land use which, perhaps not surprisingly, are seen as occurring when Europeans productively farm the land and it remains firmly in European hands.

Wetherell:	What do you feel about the sort of land protest generally, things like the Bastion Point issue and eh em Māori land marches and so on? Do you think there's a case there or . . . ?
Ackland:	I can't um I don't think I don't really know what they're protesting about (mm). I think it seems to be uh some of the land they're protesting over is farm land, and other land is land that's been sold years and years ago (mmhm). You can't turn the clock back really (yes) but they're, historically or even today uh a lot of the Māori-held land isn't utilized to its best, anyway (yes). A lot of them are very indifferent users of the land (Wetherell: Mmhm, and so it's just, it should be more productively?) Yes, I think it's, it would be better if uh if it's productively um used by Europeans that it shouldn't be taken away from them to be given to back to the tribe to just say divide like among many people (mm) and let it deteriorate.
Davison:	It's land. For anybody to buy and for anybody to sell (yes). Whoever owns it can sell it but you look at the Māori land now that's invested in a multitude of people (yes) and nobody can do anything with it, it's covered in eh gorse and not being properly used (yeah) and the land is for the people the total people of the country. I don't believe anybody owns the land (yes) they're only leasing it during their lifetime. (Wetherell: They haven't got inherent rights to it? Yes) They're only leasing it during their lifetime, it's the land belongs to the country and uh we should be using that land for the best for the benefit of the country as a whole. And, although this would be very much against the total Māori thinking, because land is

> their whole foundation of their culture really, isn't it?
> (Mmhm) It's the owning of the land (mmhm).
> Unfortunately, they're not doing anything with the land in
> most cases. You just need to look around some of the
> Māori farms, they're shocking!

It helps here to re-present history as a movement from the imperfect to the perfect. If history and society are described as getting better and better, more and more rational, more and more developed, then injustice must be a thing of the past and it does seem incomprehensible to want to refer back to those 'barbarous' times. The sheer movement of history itself, from negative to positive, is presented as a guarantee that Māori can trust Pākehā to work for the best interests of all. Injustice, in the end, becomes a phenomenon which has nothing in common with the modern.

The same kinds of patterns and tensions between liberal rights and practical considerations form the background to discussions of affirmative action. However, unlike the responses to the issue of land grievances, arguments on this topic did not tend to be in the form of a justification, no wrong was first admitted; they took the form of establishing points and making claims. The dilemmatic aspects were accordingly more repressed to the rhetorical end of apparent consistency.

As we have demonstrated elsewhere (Potter and Wetherell, 1989), responses on affirmative action drew mainly on a discourse of equality and rights, but this was a form of equality understood, as we noted earlier, within a meritocratic context. Debate circled around and around a narrow track, backwards and forwards between fairness and favouritism. Thus attempts to recognize and compensate for Māori disadvantage educationally, politically and economically were ubiquitously characterized as 'discrimination', or, even, as a form of 'apartheid'. Māoris should 'take their chance the same as everyone else' and it was presented as only obvious that a rational society would want the best possible doctors, lawyers, politicians and teachers selected on their merits. Anything else could be characterized as acts of favouritism giving Māori, not equal opportunities, but unfair opportunities, handicapping Pākehā New Zealanders, since all were presumed to start with the same chances in life.

Johnston: Oh yes, well I mean that makes me angry (yes) because I think that we should have the equal, they've got equal rights for getting in there with their bursaries and everything else and their scholarships and their university entrance, like we have, why is it necessary to make them special and put them up with a scholarship? Or a special place, like there's four special places in medical school just for Māoris?

Knight: . . . if you've got your Māori and your Pākehā and the Māori Affairs Department, it can you can get really cheap

> loans if you've got a sixteenth or even a thirty-second
> Māori blood (mmhm), you can get extra grants for tertiary
> education, you can get this, you can get that, if you're
> Māori (mmhm). I mean I remember when I was in
> primary school being in an essay competition, I always
> loved writing essays (heh-heh). So I went along and they
> said, 'Have you got any Māori blood in you?' I said, 'No.'
> 'Oh, I'm sorry you can't enter.' I thought 'Good grief!'
> (mmhm). But nobody seems to say anything about it, they
> seem to accept that it's normal.

Because ethical principles could be applied so unequivocally in this debate, and the consensus against 'discrimination', 'favouritism' and 'unfairness' can so totally be taken for granted, a moral fervour and indignation entered the argument and is apparent in these extracts.

All of these controversial issues not only suggest the ideological dilemmas fuelling argument, and the way they are mobilized in practice, but also suggest some of the problems dilemmatic patterning might raise for social psychological analyses of racism based on the concept of attitude. We turn next to discuss the theoretical implications of these patterns for recent work of this type.

Ambivalent individuals or ambivalent discourse?

As we noted earlier, one can see many parallels, superficially at least, between the patterns we identify and the phenomenon identified by many American experimental social psychologists, described variously as 'modern racism' (McConahay, 1986), 'symbolic racism' (Sears, 1988), 'aversive racism' (Gaertner and Dovidio, 1986; Kovel, 1970) and 'racial ambivalence' (Katz *et al.*, 1986).

In both forms of analysis there is concern with the changing manifestations of racism and an attempt to understand how racism might combine with 'liberal' principles. Both types of research note how the discursive currency of a democracy – freedom, rights, equality – can become applied to oppose, in the New Zealand case, particular reforms, attempts to compensate, and affirmative action programmes and, in the American case, civil-rights policies, attempts to remedy housing discrimination, school desegregation and black political candidates.

Despite these similarities, however, the premises and assumptions underlying the two types of analysis differ fundamentally. We will first outline in more detail the main features of the American approach, which we will call here 'modern racism' for convenience, before noting the points of difference.

A distinction between types of people is common to all the perspectives we have grouped under the label of modern racism. McConahay (1986), for example, identifies three groups: there are the 'tolerant', who experience 'low negative affect' towards blacks and hold strong values of equality and consequently have positive anti-racist reactions; there are those who fall into the ambivalent class, covered by the label modern racism, who experience conflict because they have moderately negative feelings towards blacks but also value equality; and, finally, there are those who experience no conflict because their strongly negative feelings towards blacks 'overpower their values' (p. 99).

The argument is that the middle group, the ambivalent, have become the norm in American society. Modern racism is the outcome of a conflict between anti-black sentiments and liberal values and has, McConahay suggests, become *the* contemporary manifestation of racism. As evidence for this, it is noted that classic measures of racism no longer pick up expressions of prejudice, they have ceased to be sensitive; yet, clearly, American society has not eliminated racism. Racism is the continuing 'tragic flaw in American democracy' (Sears, 1988, p. 51), and attitudes structured by ambivalence are the glaring new symptom of this flaw. Presumably, exactly the same claim could be made about New Zealand society.

In another typical classification of racist individuals Gaertner and Dovidio (1986) distinguish the 'dominative racist' from the 'aversive racist'. The former are the old-fashioned bigots, who express prejudice explicitly and openly, while aversive racists:

> sympathize with the victims of past injustice; support public policies that, in principle, promote racial equality and ameliorate the consequences of racism; identify more generally with a liberal political agenda; regard themselves as non-prejudiced and non-discriminatory; but, almost unavoidably, possess negative feelings and beliefs about blacks. Because of the importance of the egalitarian value system to aversive racists' self-concept, these negative feelings and associated beliefs are typically excluded from awareness. When a situation or event threatens to make the negative portion of their attitude salient, aversive racists are motivated to repudiate or dissociate these feelings from their self-image, and they vigorously try to avoid acting wrongly on the basis of these feelings. (Gaertner and Dovidio, 1986, p. 62)

We are beginning to get a clearer picture of the type of racism involved. Like our Pākehā New Zealand sample, modern American racists tend to disclaim any individual prejudice, claiming that their views merely reflect rational judgement (McConahay, 1986). Modern racists argue for discriminatory policies using egalitarian principles. They believe, for instance, that blacks are equal and deserve a better deal but that they are 'too pushy' in making their claims, and are not prepared to work hard enough for themselves (Sears, 1988). As Gaertner and Dovidio note in the extract above, modern racists may not even be aware that they are racist and believe in their own disclaimers that they act from other motives.

Gaertner and Dovidio's classification paints an almost clinical and even psychiatric portrait of the modern racist. Indeed, they also talk of 'etiology'.

Katz *et al.* (1986) draw explicit parallels between modern racism and psychoanalytic descriptions of ambivalent reactions, such as simultaneously loving and hating the same person. The prediction, following Freud, is that 'racial' ambivalence will generate unstable behaviour and exaggerated reactions.

The modern racism approach thus revives in a novel form old themes in the social psychology of racial prejudice. It takes up the motivational and psychopathological strand evident in studies of the authoritarian personality and also the socialization and social learning themes in the socio-cultural strand of explanation (Ashmore and Del Boca, 1976; Dovidio and Gaertner, 1986). Conflicts are seen as acquired from one's culture, through socialization, but they become built into the character structure of the individual and are thought to function in such a way that the white American might effectively be able to block her/his real emotions about black Americans from consciousness.

A strong distinction tends to be made between emotions (or affect) and cognitions (although see Sears, 1988), such that emotion provides the charge, the impetus, the dynamism and the motive system, while cognitions, and presumably discourse, mediate and express these emotions in a more reasonable and rationalized form. The relevant emotions which conflict with values and cognitions are presumed to be 'fear, avoidance . . . a desire for distance, anger, distaste, disgust, contempt, apprehension, unease, or simple dislike', of black Americans (Sears, 1988, p. 70).

Emotions, however, are not seen as natural reactions but theorized as the product of immersion and development in a 'historically racist culture' (Gaertner and Dovidio, 1986, p. 63). They are perhaps acquired non-verbally without necessarily any contact between black and white (Sears, 1988, p. 70) and perhaps also sustained by the kind of information-processing biases recorded by social cognition researchers. The entire package of affect, cognition and dispositions to behaviour is summarized as a set of attitudes hypothesized to underlie words and deeds and which can be measured by the technology of attitude scales.

Because of this model or theory of the well-springs of racism, it becomes possible to argue that racism can go 'under-ground' in 'times of tolerance'. However, the argument is not that white Americans are essentially and fundamentally racist at heart and have learnt to disguise their prejudice, merely paying 'lip service' to equality and fair play in order to fake social desirability; rather, it is suggested that there is a genuine ambivalence here, a genuine conflict of emotions, values and reason (Katz *et al.*, 1986).

Towards a critique of the modern racism approach

There are several points where discourse analysis disagrees with the modern racism type of analysis. Some of this disagreement reflects points made in Part I of this book and elsewhere (Potter and Wetherell, 1987) – such as the debate over the value of the concept of attitude, for example, doubts about the goals of measurement, and whether the individual is the most suitable unit for socio-psychological analysis. However, the principal point of dispute concerns the origins of the empirical patterns displayed in modern discourse. In essence, it is a dispute about the relation between the social and the psychological.

As Bobo (1983; 1988) has pointed out, the modern racism approach remains locked into the prejudice model of racism. It is assumed that psychological factors – negative affect, conflicted values and irrational reactions to minority groups (individual antipathies, in other words) – are the primary proximal cause. Modern racism theorists do note that social factors are mediated through psychological factors; they point to the process of socialization, for instance, but the thrust of their argument concerns the potent mix of conflicting values and feelings supposedly found within modern individuals. Antagonism to anti-racist causes is brought about by the attitudinal and behavioural effects of this mix.

The modern racism type of approach thus locates conflict and ambivalence, along with the conundrums and dilemmas characterizing contemporary racism, within the emotional and cognitive apparatus of the individual. Moreover, the crucial impetus towards racism is thought to be, not the traditional liberal political values of white America, but the rump of anti-black emotions – distaste, dislike and fear – remaining within white Americans. Liberal values are seen as attenuating anti-black emotions and related cognitions to produce the conflicted phenomenon of modern racism. The strong impression, therefore, is that modern racism theorists tend to perceive contemporary attitudes, if not as an unambiguous improvement on old attitudes, as perhaps more of a step in the right direction.

In contrast to this perspective, discourse analysis locates the conflicts and dilemmas within the argumentative and rhetorical resources available in a 'liberal' and 'egalitarian' society such as New Zealand. The conflict is not between a feeling and a value, between psychological drives and socially acceptable expressions or between emotions and politics, but between competing frameworks for articulating social, political and ethical questions. These conflicts and dilemmas could be said to be realized in a 'psychological' form when the members of society begin to discuss, debate, explain, justify and develop accounts in the course of social interaction and everyday life.

To put it in a nutshell, we agree with Gramsci's point: 'the thesis which asserts that men [*sic*] become conscious of fundamental conflicts on the level of ideology is not psychological or moralistic in character, but structural and epistemological' (cited in Larrain, 1979, p. 81). Conflict may rage in the hearts and minds of ordinary women and men but, in this case, it does not originate there.

The definition of racism is central to this dispute between approaches. As we noted, the tendency within the modern racism approach is to understand ambivalence as a conflict between a negative and a positive: between anti-black sentiment and 'the finest and proudest of traditional American values' (Sears, 1988, p. 52). Racism, therefore, becomes conceptualized narrowly as the negative feelings and cognitions, the reactions defined as prejudiced, which mingle in the final attitudinal expression with more general political values and their associated feelings and cognitions.

This orientation leads to difficulty explaining the main findings from the discourse analysis reported in this chapter. We have seen that political ideologies or political values are not static or constant in meaning – always fine and proud, always positive, for instance. Equality, compulsion, injustice, rights, freedom – the central values – carry different connotations depending on the argumentative context. They can be put to work within many different semantic fields. Liberal principles can be mobilized with discourse about practical considerations to argue either for or against land compensation, for example.

There is no need, therefore, to posit a set of prejudiced feelings and cognitions which conflict with political values to explain modern racism. There are sufficient dilemmas, and there is sufficient flexibility within political discourse to argue for any kind of outcome. Egalitarianism does not seem to require an injection of 'anti-black affect' to make it work for racism. Indeed, we suspect that talk about feelings and sentiments concerning black groups, the discursive small-change recognized as prejudice, will prove just as flexible and inconstant in practice as the discourse of practical politics. What counts as negative, constituting the 'real' source of racism, and what counts as positive, modifying individual prejudice, is extremely difficult to specify in advance of analysis. The enormous advantage of discourse analysis, of course, is that it provides a means of tracking the twists and turns of argument and the Janus face of liberalism as contradictions are fully utilized in practice.

There is a further empirical problem which discourse analysis identifies. Conflict, ambivalence, inconsistency and contradiction seem to be endemic. They do not, that is, seem to be associated with just one group of individuals or one type of person. Everybody is a dilemmatician – anti-racists to the same extent as racists. The appeal to conflicting principles and practical consider-ations as a useful rhetorical ploy which can be used by anyone; it is not a state of mind which uniquely distinguishes one group of white Americans.

We argued in Part I that racism should not be narrowly equated with a particular psychological complex of feelings, thoughts and motives. We see it instead as the symbolic and cultural expression of a society which is systematically organized around the oppression of one group and the dominance of another group. The forms of modern discourse about 'race relations' indicate the requirement now, as in the past, persuasively to justify and legitimate that oppression through whatever means possible.

Bobo (1988) has developed a similar critique of the modern racism approach from the stance of realistic group-conflict theory. He makes the point that modern racism approaches have real difficulty explaining why attitudes have changed. If the crucial motivator underlying racism remains 'anti-black affect', that is, individual prejudice, then why do the forms of expressing 'irrational hostility' towards blacks change? If the primary cause is seen as psychological then there will always be problems accounting for the particular form racism adopts at any given period in history. Bobo documents in detail some of the shifts in the ideological field which have legitimated racism in America and the close connections between these shifts and changes in material, political and social conditions.

A final difficulty with the modern racism type of approach concerns the claim that the conflictual expression of racism is 'new' and, indeed, actually distinguishes present racism from the past. As a contrasting hypothesis, we suggest that the interpretative resources used to argue for racism may have always been varied and contradictory, and mobilized in a flexible and dilemmatic manner, as suits the character of natural discourse, and the ideological demands of the moment. It is simply that the technology of attitude measurement has never been sufficiently supple to note this variation. Inconsistency *was* noted, however, when the results of classic attitude scales seemed to suggest that most white Americans had ceased to be racist although, patently, racism continued. It was only at this point, when some scale results became absurd, that theories of ambivalent attitudes began to come to the fore.

In 1944, in his famous account of the 'American dilemma', Myrdal argued that there was a deep fracture in American political opinion between reactionary principles conducive to racism and liberal principles of egalitarianism. Yet, although McConahay and his colleagues refer to Myrdal's work, they seem to be suggesting that it is only in 'modern' times that this dilemma emerges in public opinion. It seems strange to claim that egalitarianism is strongly rooted in American society, an important traditional value, and yet the majority of white Americans living in the immediate past were in some way immune to this egalitarianism, expressing instead unadulterated, plain, old-fashioned, non-conflictual, unambivalent bigotry.

As Billig *et al.* (1988) note, even in the early studies of the authoritarian personality (Adorno *et al.*, 1950), it was evident that those identified as bigoted authoritarians both categorized and particularized: they displayed prejudice, yet were aware of the social norm and rhetorical value of not appearing prejudiced, made racist statements and developed disclaimers to avoid being labelled as racist (see also Weigel and Howes, 1985). There have, indeed, been ideological shifts over time and it is now, as we have noted, unfashionable to express crude versions of biological racism. Yet, this is not to say that in the past also, interpretative resources may have been used skilfully, artfully and flexibly with judicious blendings of biological racism and other argumentative moves. It is not conflict and dilemmatic argumentation which necessarily distinguish the present from the past.

To summarize, in this chapter we have tried to do three things. First we wanted to document the way Pākehā New Zealanders argued around particular controversial topics. Second, following Billig *et al.*, we wanted to demonstrate the dilemmatic nature of the resources Pākehā New Zealanders drew upon and the way those dilemmas of principle and practice, progress and justice, resonated through important traditions of European political discourse. Finally, we tried to direct our analysis to develop a critique of an important strand of recent socio-psychological work on racism, and tried also to illustrate an alternative.

What emerges from our examination of modern racism research is an impression of the close relationship, once again, between lay and academic discourse, and the way in which lay justificatory and legitimatory concerns, the meat of practical politics, become reified some time later into social psychological science. Ideological dilemmas become 'discovered' through the technologies of social psychology but become transformed into emotional and motivational dilemmas.

This chapter has also reinforced, in a different guise, another theme developed in Chapter 6. We have tried to stress the analytic value of the notion of ideological practice and ideological effects. As the study of ideology moves from the study of the content of 'ruling ideas' to the study of discursive practice, it becomes clearer, paradoxically, what social psychology could contribute to studies of ideology, and the value of investigations of rhetoric and the contextualized mobilization of arguments.

8

The prejudice problematic

> It required years of labour and billions of dollars to gain the secret of the atom. It will take a still greater investment to gain the secrets of man's irrational nature.
>
> (G. W. Allport, 1954, p. xvii)

This chapter identifies and explores a discursive ordering which we shall call the 'problematic of prejudice'. We intend to study this problematic in two of its guises: as a theoretical and analytic practice within social psychology and as a form of accounting within the discourse of Pākehā New Zealanders. We shall argue that the prejudice problematic, contrary to some of the avowed intentions of its advocates within the social sciences, fulfils some important ideological roles for Pākehā New Zealanders. Accounting in terms of prejudice can draw attention away from immediate social reform towards utopian visions; it can provide a logic and method for justifying individual conduct; and it can establish a positive identity and a benevolent 'vocabulary of motives' *vis-à-vis* other, supposedly less enlightened, individuals.

We chose to use the term 'problematic' in this context because it suggests we are dealing with a relatively integrated framework of distinctive assumptions, intellectual strategies, questions and problems. The most integrated form of prejudice talk appears, of course, within the texts of social psychology. The 'lived ideology' is, as usual, much more fragmented, piecemeal and contradictory, caught up as it is in the kaleidescope of common sense. In this chapter we use the intellectuals' version to help chart a coherent path through the lay discourse.

At several points in the interviews our sample were asked about forms of racism, discrimination and disadvantage in New Zealand. When we looked at how this topic was handled, the responses seemed immediately familiar. Here was the social psychology of irrational attitudes and beliefs, the social psychology of 'racial prejudice', transposed from the lecture room to the kitchen table. This diffusion of science into common sense, or equally of common sense into science, is interesting. Why does this particular set of argumentative resources form the basis of everyday stories of motives, injustice and contact between groups as well as populating the papers and monographs of professional social scientists?

It is easy to be scathing about the problematics of the past in the attempt to demonstrate that one's own distinctive set of assumptions, strategies and questions represent a superior and advanced mode of analysis. Rereading some of the classic texts of prejudice from the 1950s and then again from the 1970s (Adorno *et al.*, 1950; G. W. Allport, 1954; Ehrlich, 1973; Jones, 1972), what is most apparent is the moral and political frame in which the concept of prejudice was proposed and investigated in social psychology.

G. W. Allport's belief in the power of science to produce technical solutions to the problems of human relations is evident in his words which introduce this chapter. Allport's texts display obvious respect for the values of 'civilized men' (*sic*), for the potential of the 'human family' and the democratic ideals of America – to a degree which seems naive and quaint when viewed through the lens of the post-modern 1990s. Yet moral fervour and a passion to remedy racism also shine through his text.

This chapter, therefore, is concerned with what is becoming a familiar paradox or pattern – argumentative resources are varied and fragmented, drawn upon in an *ad hoc* and promiscuous manner. The flexibility of argumentative and discursive resources was again evident to us as we compared the social psychology of prejudice, sometimes radical and typically reformist in its stance, with the justificatory and legitimating talk of Pākehā New Zealanders, which seemed, on the whole, to bolster their position of privilege.

The first few sections of this chapter try to clarify the characteristic tensions in the prejudice problematic to show its ideological potential; we then look at some of the typical discursive moves found in prejudice talk. Our aim in both cases is to indicate how prejudice discourse escapes the confines of academic textbooks and itself becomes part of ideological practice. Finally, towards the end of the chapter we will attempt to pull out the implications for anti-racist strategies, focusing on attempts by psychologists and others to develop educational programmes based on prejudice theory and research.

Prejudice in social psychological and lay discourse

Unlike the concept of 'race', the intellectual history of the concept of prejudice has not, as far as we are aware, been traced to the same extent. But, as with other elements of Pākehā New Zealanders' discourse, its roots seem to lie in the classic traditions of the Enlightenment. Billig (1988) points out, following the analysis of Gadamer (1979), that it was as a result of the shifts in thought associated with the Enlightenment that the term 'prejudice' began to acquire a negative connotation. Prejudice became firmly associated with the mischief of irrationality which all decent post-Enlightenment citizens would wish to avoid. The contrast established between prejudice and rationality then became specified more narrowly during the twentieth century, appearing as a contrast between prejudice and tolerance as the term gradually became a convenient shorthand for 'racial prejudice' and 'racial stereotypes'.

The particular ethical flavour of the prejudice problematic and its characteristic modes of explanation thus reflect some dilemmas, fractures and blind alleys within Enlightenment traditions of thought more broadly. The impression is often given in social psychology that concepts spring newly minted from rigorous empirical research. In contrast, we shall assume, as in previous chapters, that the conceptual apparatus of social psychology closely reflects the discursive history of Western culture.

This section focuses on the main themes in accounts of prejudice within both social psychology and lay discourse. We will move back and forth between the academic texts and our interviews to highlight the nodes around which the prejudice problematic revolves. We begin with some anecdotes: one set comes from G. W. Allport, while the other story was told by one of our interviewees.

> In Rhodesia, a white truck driver passed a group of idle natives and muttered, 'They're lazy brutes.' A few hours later he saw natives heaving two-hundred pound sacks of grain onto a truck, singing in rhythm to their work. 'Savages', he grumbled. 'What do you expect?'
> . . . In Boston a dignitary of the Roman Catholic Church was driving along a lonesome road on the outskirts of the city. Seeing a small Negro boy trudging along, the dignitary told his chaffeur to stop and give the boy a lift. Seated together in the back of the limousine, the cleric, to make conversation, asked, 'Little Boy, are you a Catholic?' Wide-eyed with alarm, the boy replied, 'No sir, it's bad enough being coloured without being one of those things.'
> (G. W. Allport, 1954, p. 3)

> Mills: Yes, although there was um, this is diverging a bit, there was a guy at the shows today, er last week, helping with the my husband's firm's stall they had there, and he was a salesman with the firm, he was what I thought was a typical salesman, he was raving on about how there's no way he was going to be turned into a Māori against his will, he came from Britain you know, and he was only my age or younger, would have been about thirty (yeah). I couldn't believe it, I just looked at him in horror (yeah). You know, got all on his high horse with all these Polynesians that were going to make him go back to the grass skirts ha. Oh it was really weird.

Allport's carefully constructed anecdotes appear on the first page of his text and serve an exemplificatory purpose. He uses them to delineate the nature of the problem which will be the subject of his book. The story from Mills is part of an argument about how intergroup relations in New Zealand are changing for the worse.

Our purpose in introducing these anecdotes is also illustrative and to make a point. Both extracts work by turning a spotlight on the character and motives of particular individuals. Further, they identify weak points in that character – emotionality, lack of moderation and extremity in the salesman, inconsistency, stupidity and disingenuous naivety in the case of Allport's various narrative characters. This stress on the failings of individuals is probably the most crucial distinguishing feature of what we wish to identify as the prejudice problematic.

Prejudice accounts are psychological accounts. Allport and his colleagues do not neglect the importance of socio-cultural factors in racism and may even see the social domain as the principal cause of prejudice (e.g. Ehrlich, 1973); but, argues Allport, 'it is only within the nexus of personality that we find the effective operation of historical, cultural and economic factors' (1954, p. xviii). For this reason it is possible to put together a string of anecdotes from different parts of the globe – Boston, Rhodesia, India, London, Auckland and so on. The local manifestations of prejudice might vary but it can be analyzed as a universal human failing. Explanations within the problematic thus tend to focus on this root cause – the deformation of human feelings – before turning outwards to look at how particular social conditions channel its expression.

Social psychologists and Pākehā New Zealanders agree that the difficulty concerns particular sorts of people who suffer from a 'problem'. Strangely, these people are usually always someone else, although there is also scope within this discourse for particular kinds of confessions and self-accusations. One of the typical tensions in prejudice discourse emerges when we try to specify this moral judgement further. Are the prejudiced a special, notably blameworthy, group or can we all be prejudiced from time to time? Lay discourse and socio-psychological theory swing backwards and forwards between these two options.

Individual bigotry and collective guilt

The psychodynamic strand in the socio-psychological analysis of prejudice emphasizes the distinctive character weaknesses of the prejudiced – their rigidity, emotional needs, reluctance to respond to new information, and pattern of vindictive gratification. As Jones (1972) notes, for many theorists, 'race' prejudice becomes seen as a symptom of a basic adaptive inferiority, the sign of a person who is low down in the homo sapiens hierarchy (p. 66). In comparison, the social cognition strand of prejudice work suggests a much more inclusive picture. The prejudiced are not necessarily different from other individuals. We can all be guilty of pre-judgement, this perspective argues, and we cannot help it because life is short and our minds are limited. People are built this way for perfectly sensible reasons, the social cognition researcher might suggest, and so constantly judge in advance of the facts.

These two possibilities – the particular and the universal – provide, in lay discourse, for a range of rhetorical options: magnanimity and victimization, self-distancing and limited apology.

Stones:
I think there's prejudice both ways (yes? uhum). Um (.) I think prejudice is something that uh everybody has. I don't think anybody can honestly sit back and say you don't have some prejudice. Uh in fact uh I I used to think I had very little prejudice, I think, I think colour prejudice, I'm colour blind and I suppose that helps hahaahaha uh 'cos I don't, colour doesn't mean as much to me (yeah, right). So if I see somebody that's dark I I don't even think of colour because I'm colour blind and I switch off colours, because of that, but I found that uh you know this the Canadian election was fought on and uh um you know I started to find that really I'm quite anti-French, without really realizing. And um I suppose I find at times I'm anti-American, having lived next door to them and seen, so you know we all have these prejudices. Irrespective of whether they're colour, or even . . . uh religion or creed or anything.

Wetherell:
Right. What do you think about, what do you think most Pākehās' attitudes are to Māoris? Positive or negative?

Bradman:
Gee I don't know. I I um when you first said that I thought, yeah um it's hard to say I I I guess um a lot of it must be negative, yeah (mmhm) um uh like I know a guy who is quite quite bigoted, irrationally bigoted you know (mmhm) and um that sort of point of view to a lesser degree perhaps than this guy, to a greater or lesser degree perhaps yes overall, um I guess there is a lot of um a sort of stereotyping (mm) I mean they think of the Māori as being um thick and and lethargic (mmhm) and um no-hoper and poor and so forth, whereas this is not necessarily the case (case, mmhm).

Boardman:
Yes. (mm) We've got both, we've got both sort of mental prejudice and verbal prejudice. Um, and both fairly heavily represented (yeah). There is a colossal amount of prejudice some of it, I was almost going to say justified but the word prejudice excludes that (yes). Um, one can understand the basis in some instances but not in others (yes). Uh but one thing that always amuses me 'cos I happen to have an interest in people and their appearance and their mannerisms and their way of speech, is the number of people who are apparently anti-Māori who quite clearly have Māori blood! (Yes) And

they seem to consider, well I say quite clearly, no not quite clearly but you could be (mm) fairly sure that what they're doing in fact is reacting against part of their own character (Mmhm). They're not at war with the rest of the community, they're at war with themselves (yes). Um, they haven't come to terms with both parts of their make-up (mmhm) and as a result they try to banish one part by um denigrating it. I think you will find that's very common amongst people of mixed blood, whether it be coloured to white or um two different European races, two different African races or whatever (yes). Anyone who has two cultural backgrounds, one part usually stronger than the other uh has difficulty balancing themselves (yes). And often it comes out in the form of a racial intolerance against what actually is part of themselves (yes).

Stones, a Canadian now living in New Zealand, argues that he personally has no racial prejudice because he is 'colour blind' but that prejudice of this kind is understandable because everybody has prejudices, and he gives the example of his own attitude to French Canadians. In the other extracts, the prejudiced are displayed as more separated from oneself – they are the irrationally bigoted or, in Boardman's case, some of the prejudiced are seen, albeit in rather an unusual manner, as suffering from a psychological disturbance generated by self-hate at their own part-Māori ancestry. But whether understood as particular or as universal, prejudice discourse locates the problem within the psychological make-up of the individual.

Irrationality and pre-judgement

The 'cognitive' theme in the prejudice problematic, which stresses misjudgement and problems of information processing rather than character structure and psychopathology, creates another form of tension. It highlights the classic dilemma of positivism: facts versus values. The difficulty is this: what counts as a rational judgement? When is a description merely factual and when is it an interested account? If prejudice is 'thinking ill of others without sufficient warrant' (Allport, 1954, p. 6), then what is an adequate warrant? Here, of course, the issues of authenticity and facticity arise once again as in the accounts of social influence described in Chapter 6.

Jones (1972) suggests three criteria for prejudice: prejudice, as opposed to 'justified denigration', involves prior judgement; secondly, prejudice is indicated when an individual continues to hold an opinion despite being confronted with contradictory information; finally, a prejudiced individual will be someone who promulgates their view even when aware, before they judge, of those contradictory facts. However, Jones then becomes tangled in the fact/value dilemma when he notes that good judgement is also often a normative assessment.

Allport similarly stresses the importance of being able to reverse one's judgement in the face of inconsistent information. The failure to do so indicates some 'emotional resistance'. However, in the end he, too, is unable to resolve the fact/value dilemma, arguing that prejudice is also a moral evaluation placed by a culture on some of its own practices and is usually a probabilistic decision. Allport concludes that social psychology needs to draw a distinction between prejudice and realistic group conflict. Prejudice is where there is a low probability that the judgement is rational, whereas in realistic group conflicts, there is a high probability that a negative reaction to another group is warranted. The distinction is vital for Allport, because he wants to maintain grounds for justifying some collective group actions, such as the Allied response to Hitler, while castigating other responses. In other words, he wants to keep open the move of 'you are prejudiced, while I am simply responding to the real negative features of my opponent.'

It is easy to see how this fact/value dilemma of Enlightenment thought could lead social psychologists straight into all the absurdities of the 'kernel of truth' investigations in stereotyping research. The logic of the dilemma is such that it becomes sensible to try and discover whether white Americans' image of the 'Negro', for example, might be based on the 'real characteristics' of 'Negros'.

Again, this fact/value dilemma is not merely academic, and we shall show shortly how 'factual accounting' is a useful rhetorical device for mitigating the 'offence' of prejudice. Many of those we interviewed implied that their hostility was not in fact prejudice but a realistic description of the actual characteristics of Māori people. One interviewee's response was uncannily reminiscent of Allport's insight that group conflict over scarce resources provides a more normatively acceptable justification of negative actions than appeals to prejudiced motives. Sedge, in the next extract, argues, in order to justify white actions in South Africa, that defence of one's group's interests is perfectly legitimate.

Sedge: um and er if they want to, you know they say they're doing, they're getting sport just to to keep apartheid going (mmhmm). I don't think it is, they're keeping apartheid going because as they see it over there, it's the only way that they're going to keep the good way of life (yes). I mean, you know, if somebody came round to me and said, 'look we're going to move a whole pile of these Māoris off Bastion Point and they're going to take over this part of Remuera, just this corner here, going round this block of houses here', I'd say, 'no they're not' (yes). And, you know, no matter what happens they're not going to do it. I shall take such steps as are necessary to avoid it (yes). Now if somebody says, 'oh yes, but this is how it's going to be' (mm), I'd go flat out, I mean I don't care whether it's apartheid or whatever you call it. Build the barricades up there and you know and put machine guns

> on the top (mmhmm) and that is what I see that they're just preserving (mmhmm) um what they've got. Okay maybe it isn't the best but it's far from being the worst.

Because prejudice is usually conceived as an individual or personal reaction primarily concerning private moral standards and rationality, it can be separated from collective group reactions caused by competition for scarce resources, for instance. Prejudice can be distinguished from responses brought about by social processes wider than the individual such as economic recession. Prejudice remains a personal pathology, a failure of inner-directed empathy and intellect, rather than a social pathology, shaped by power relations and the conflicting vested interests of groups.

The manifest and the latent

So far, we have identified two sources of tension within the prejudice problematic: between the particular and the universal and between facts and values. The problematic also supplies a third tension: between appearances and reality or between the surface and the underneath. Unlike the first two tensions, which provide for contrasting forms of analysis, this tension is spotted within the object of study and can be located either within individuals or within societies.

Andrews: I think er the um it's like the racist it's like the class problem again. There are things like race problems, class problems all bubbling away under the surface and to a far greater degree than what than would be sort of officially acknowledged by a lot of people, but you only have to go to a Rotary Club meeting or somewhere and hear the sort of pet prejudices that are trotted out week after week and everybody gets them out, gives them a little polish, 'hey mates isn't that nice' and puts them back in their pocket (haha yes).

Reed: . . . I'm trying to think of that with the racist thing so there's a tremendous amount um, you know, when you boil the kettle and the water gets very hot? (yes) But it's not until it's boiling that it breaks the surface (yes), the smoothness of the top of the water? (yes) And I think that's what's happening here.

The prevailing metaphor, therefore, is almost geological in character – of forces under the surface of society which from time to time break through into normal social intercourse, revealing the true state of affairs. Relations between the conscious and the unconscious of the prejudiced person may be seen as operating in similar ways with prejudice as the repressed or latent force and rationality and reasonableness as the superficial ego traits.

Tolerance and harmony

The ideal identity which contrasts with prejudice is very clearly expressed both in social psychology and in the discourse of Pākehā New Zealanders. 'Racial harmony' comes from the considerate and unbiased treatment of all fellow human beings. All should be treated without pre-judgement – treated equally, on the basis of individual merits, regardless of race. If the prejudiced person is the fallen angel, speaking with bias and lack of sympathy and acting out an insensitive and perverse irrationality, the tolerant individual

> is on friendly terms with all sorts of people. . . . He [*sic*] makes no distinction of race, colour, or creed. He not only endures but, in general, approves his fellow men. . . . Tolerant children . . . come from homes with a permissive atmosphere. They feel welcomed, accepted and loved, no matter what they do. . . . The greater mental flexibility of the tolerant person (even in childhood) is shown by his rejection of two-valued logic. He seldom agrees that 'there are only two kinds of people: the weak and the strong'; or that 'there is only one right way to do anything'. He does not bifurcate his environment into the wholly proper and the wholly improper. For him there are shades of gray.
> (G. W. Allport, 1954, pp. 425–6)

The prejudice problematic feeds into and reinforces a utopian vision of society as well as of the individual personality. The tolerant society is based around rationality, justice and caring feelings for others. We have noted in previous chapters the various manifestations of equivalent ideals in the discourse of Pākehā New Zealanders – in talk of 'one nation', for example; in the trope of 'two cultures, one people'; in the formulation of tolerant understanding and respect for differences found in the discourse of culture; in the functionalist emphasis on a coherent and integrated society working as a productive machine, with all parts in harmony; and in the discourse which imagines history progressing towards a more just and better world.

This vision is both part of the rhetoric of public figures and the private dream of ordinary New Zealanders. In the public domain it has been most evident in the views expressed by church authorities over the years. For there is a common focus in both Christianity and the prejudice problematic on self-examination, individual weakness and moral reform.

> suspicion, fear and hostility have tended to characterize relationships between different human groupings. Human sinfulness is a divisive power encouraging notions of prejudice, disrespect and superiority.
> However, Christians believe that the grace of God can overcome human divisions and sinful attitudes, and make unity and harmony possible. This is illustrated at Pentecost by the 'reversal of Babel'. People of different races were able to understand each other.

> Racial prejudice is an individual problem that makes it impossible for a person of one race to meet a person of another with openness and love.

The Christian church . . . overcomes the alienation between races. As a community of faith its members are meant to enjoy a unity that transcends racial differences. However, because it is a community of fallible and sinful people, the Church can distort the Gospel and fail to be the sign of reconciliation God intends it to be. (Extracts from Te Kaupapa Tikanga Rua: Bicultural development: Report of the Anglican Church on the Treaty of Waitangi, 1984, p. 36)

As Charlie Husband (1986) has argued, taking a critical perspective on this ideal, one of the problems with tolerance is that it represents what Husband describes as a largesse of the powerful. It is a form of talk which hazily suggests unity of interests, charitable beneficience and a positive atmosphere without any detailed examination of ends and means or questioning of the exact nature of the compromises which might be required between opposed vested interests.

This failure to engage with social structural change is encouraged by the focus within the prejudice problematic on changing people's attitudes rather than modes of social organization. A great deal of emphasis is placed on the importance of contact between individuals, 'black and white together, united, but not in struggle'. This is often articulated as a feeling that if only we could get at children young enough, before they are 'contaminated' by prejudice, then the world would be a better place. The innocent and naive reactions of children, in fact, serve within the prejudice problematic as a model for us all.

Ben Couch (Former Minister of Māori Affairs): Well at one stage he er he I was often wondering why do we need a Race Relations Conciliator? And er but we are er made up of a hotch potch, of course, er a mixture of many races in this country and er someone thought of the idea of the Race Relations and mainly because of in the last twenty years, as I've said, everything's become words and trying to make people er aware who you are (yes). Reminds me of a story of young Jimmy going to school and er coming home and telling his Mummy, 'oh I made a friend today', and er they said, 'oh well what's his name', he said 'oh it's Johnny', Jimmy and Johnny, and the Mother said to him, 'oh is he a Māori or is he a Pākehā?' (yes) (0.2) The kid didn't know (hahaha). You see what I mean? (yes) He said 'Eh?' (Wetherell: He had no idea.)

Similarly the benefits of proper information and education are frequently stressed. In social psychology this optimistic face of the prejudice problematic has led to a great deal of research on the benefits of intergroup contact. The theoretical paucity of the contact tradition in social psychology and its reliance on individualistic analyses of racism has been well documented (Hewstone and Brown, 1986; Reicher, 1986).

As in other aspects of the prejudice problematic, there is a tension and possible contradiction in these visions of various remedies for racism. Optimism about the reform of deviant individuals can be contrasted with conservative pessimism. Prejudice can be seen as a conscious choice for a harsh view on another 'race' and thus as morally accountable and alterable; but, if prejudice is framed as a natural and unavoidable human reaction, an unconscious and even instinctive aversion to differences which reflects an inbuilt preference for one's own kind, then the only possible response is scepticism about reforming fallible human nature.

The moral identity of tolerance, as we have seen, tends to be portrayed as the proper state while prejudice becomes the deviant or fallen state: blameworthy and accountable. A tolerant identity does not usually have to be explained. Its moral value provides sufficient accountability and a rationale for the motivation. The whole thrust of the prejudice problematic, therefore, encourages a discourse characterized by circumambulation and avoidance. Everybody wants to be tolerant and nobody wants to be prejudiced.

Across our interviews argumentative and rhetorical work was orientated towards dodging the identity and imputation of prejudice. If possible, prejudice was recharacterized as something less noxious and this description was most definitely not accepted without negotiation and justification. We shall examine some of the patterns of these very common discursive moves in the next section and we will continue our attempt to describe how the prejudice problematic actually turns back on itself, empowering Pākehā New Zealanders, becoming a part of arguments for the status quo.

It is worth noting, first, that the tensions within the prejudice problematic and the ambivalence it produces entirely weaken this discourse as a crusading force for anti-racism. Blaming individuals has been a weapon with mixed effects. It is one of the ironies of the social psychology of racism that perhaps the most earnest and sustained attempt in the history of the discipline to mount a critique of racism should have this paradoxical edge.

Dodging the identity of prejudice: how to deal with accusations

Talk of prejudice and tolerance is always talk to some purpose. We turn now to look at how Pākehā New Zealanders have used the problematic of prejudice strategically in their everyday accounts, as the dominant majority group acting in relation to the minority group.

The pattern of careful negotiation and identity construction around the topic of prejudice has been documented many times (Billig, 1985; 1988; Cochrane and Billig, 1984; Potter and Wetherell, 1987; 1988a; van Dijk, 1984; 1987). Van Dijk describes in detail the pragmatic and semantic moves which structure this discourse, and how lay people simultaneously speak 'prejudice' while attempting to avoid being described as prejudiced. This phenomenon has been described as an example of the rhetorical strategy of prolepsis (Billig *et al.*, 1988). It is an 'on the one hand, on the other hand' discursive move which acknowledges but deflects potential criticism. The pattern of credentialling or disclaiming involved is also evident in the formulations which begin 'I'm not prejudiced but . . .' (Hewitt and Stokes, 1975; Potter and Wetherell, 1987, Ch. 2; van Dijk, 1991).

During the course of the interview, most of our sample were asked the following question or some variant of it: do you think Pākehā New Zealanders are prejudiced? Is there much discrimination against Māori people? Our introduction of the topic and typical question format presented an accounting problem for our respondents. Given the negative identity attributed to prejudice, it sets up a certain kind of accusation, or was interpreted in this way. We could thus treat responses to this question as a set which orientated to a commonly occurring discursive situation: dealing with an unwelcome evaluation.

What are the standard discursive moves for coping with a negative evaluation? Crudely, one can (a) admit the offence but offer mitigations or excuses, or (b) deny the offence and claim that one is wrongly accused, or (c) accept the blaming in its entirety and perhaps intensify or expand on it by giving other examples (ask for other offences to be taken into account, if you like). One could also (d) undermine the accusation itself by renegotiating the nature of the offence, recategorizing it as something less negative and more excusable, or (e) redirect the accusation to another group of people, carefully separating or distancing oneself from the accusation.

In our sample, very few took up option (c). A small number did argue that Pākehā New Zealanders were prejudiced but the form of their argument followed the academic pattern: prejudice was identified as a virulent character fault in other people not in oneself. The majority of those we interviewed thus tried to rebut or renegotiate the accusation. They usually combined several of the possible moves described above, frequently in a dense form, as can be seen below:

Wetherell: Um, yes, we were talking about Māori culture and so on. What er (.) do you think there's any racial prejudice in New Zealand, that people aren't (.) are prejudiced against Māoris (.) or not really?

A. Bickerstaff: I don't really think so, I think that we have grown up with the knowledge that the Māoris are our neighbours and our friends and er I feel that this (.) we've never been at a point where we have had to accept them so to speak. They've been part of us, yes, and ride in the buses, in the cinemas, er, you don't think of them as Māoris, it's just until there's some nasty (.) aggressive types that you feel you must avoid (yes) that the question even arises. Er I feel er in the last few years it's been blown out of proportion.

Wetherell: Do you think there's much sort of racial discrimination in New

Zealand, say by the European majority against particular
Māoris, or for employment, or you know?

Ackland: Um, I don't think it's so much a bias against them, it may be
more a behaviour bar in a way (mm), and unfortunately some
Māoris tend to give their whole people a bad name. But I
don't really think there's uh, a bias, the same with the renting
you know the properties and that (yes), if you've had a tenant,
if you've been a Māori tenanter and mistreated or neglected a
place, you'd think twice before letting it to another one (yes). I
say I'm totally neutral, a lot of Europeans live like that (yes),
they have poor standards.

Ackland's discourse combines several of the strategies identified above (b, d,
a, e). He disagrees with the suggestion that Pākehā New Zealanders might
show racial discrimination (e.g. 'I don't really think there's a bias'), but also
recategorizes any possible offence as a 'behaviour bar' distinguished from
what he describes in another part of the interview as a 'colour bar'. Thus the
offence becomes not racial prejudice *per se* but a reaction to the behaviour of
the minority group. He then mitigates this 'weaker' offence by explaining why
this bias is a justifiable reaction to unacceptable actions. Finally, Ackland
distances himself from the accusation of bias by noting that he himself is
totally neutral.

Similarly, Mrs Bickerstaff denies the imputation of prejudice, but also
provides a truncated mitigation by the categorization 'nasty, aggressive types'
which suggests that any prejudice against such people would be a 'reasonable'
response, and ends by undermining or trivializing the possible offence,
claiming the issue is 'blown out of proportion'. This extract could also be read
as implying that Pākehā New Zealanders might be magnanimous in not
thinking of Māoris as 'Māoris' and thus overlooking their status as members
of what she seems to assume is an inevitably inferior group. Alternatively, she
could be read as suggesting that she and others do not think in 'racial' terms,
but think instead along 'people are just people, not races' lines.

Both Mrs Bickerstaff and Ackland can also be read as orientating to the
issues discussed by Jones (1972), and similar specifications of what counts as
pre-judgement, and what counts as justified comment. Both Ackland and Mrs
Bickerstaff break up the category 'Māori', are careful to particularize ('some
Māoris', some nasty aggressive types), avoiding the impression of sweeping
generalization, and both give a factual version, leaving safeguards against
critique. There is considerable scope for back-tracking introduced into these
accounts.

In general, our sample seemed to regard it as effective rhetoric to weave
different strategies together, denying an offence, while also accounting for or
explaining a version of that offence and, perhaps too, separating oneself from
those being accused. The point we wish to make here is that these
conversational gambits do not occur in a vacuum. There is a complex

interaction between the nature of the interpretative resources within the prejudice problematic, their ideological thrust, and the practical conversational moves of those we interviewed.

Some forms of conversation analysis seem to lack a vital dimension to the extent that they ignore aspects of this interaction, especially cases where conversational moves remain the focus rather than the broader ideological dimensions of argumentative resources. Similarly, attention to the interpretative resource alone misses the flexible application of that resource in practice. When we look at practice it becomes clear how prejudice discourse begins to double back on itself so that what was once an accusation or critique of racism becomes mobilized as an important part of the rhetorical work which maintains a racist status quo. We can see in these extracts how the ideological potential evident in individualistic, positivistic and utopian framings of the 'problem' becomes realized in practice as the members of a society struggle to justify the conduct of the group with which they have become aligned.

We can see how skilful and inventive ripostes to prejudice accusations could become a familiar part of the discursive habits of Pākehā New Zealanders. The social psychologist and the lay person become like two sides of the same coin. The social psychologist accuses and the Pākehā New Zealander defends, but both draw on the same resources to mount their arguments. The forms of both accusation and defence are structured by the tensions within the prejudice problematic.

So, what are the ideological advantages of prejudice discourse in its lay formulation? How does prejudice talk help in the task of legitimation? Some of these advantages have been discussed already – talk of prejudice pathologizes the issue and postpones investigation of concrete grievances, substituting high-minded waffle about the joys of living in harmony. However, the principal benefit lies in the positive/negative contrast in the prejudice problematic which allows for 'splitting'. A bestial other can be constructed who is different from self. The other is presented as driven by 'id-type' forces of irrational emotion and illogical dislike. While the self, in contrast, becomes all ego – a rational, thoughtful and reflective subject who speaks with the authority of facts. Sometimes the split can be placed within oneself ('we are all prejudiced'), but more commonly the splitting is externalized, creating a dramatis personae of malevolent and benevolent actors.

In other words, Pākehā New Zealanders become empowered by this difference. They acquire a voice and subject position of authority partly through projecting the problem elsewhere but also because the association between prejudice and values allows those who rebut the accusation to construct more easily their own descriptions as merely factual. Value, interested motivation and the grinding of axes lie elsewhere with the prejudiced other, removed from oneself. The prejudice problematic effectively pushes the debate from values to the 'kernel of truth'.

The prejudice problematic within social psychology depends on being able to categorize individuals as prejudiced or tolerant types. However, in practice, people are adept at upsetting the dichotomy and muddying the categorizations and, when all of us become skilled at exploiting the rhetorical possibilities of the prejudice problematic, who is to say just which of us are the tolerant sheep and which the prejudiced goats?

Reforming the prejudiced

In the last part of this chapter we wish to examine some of the substantial suggestions for anti-racist practice which have emerged from the prejudice problematic, to consider, that is, some concrete suggestions for the reform of the prejudiced. We will focus on one instantiation – Judy Katz's (1978) *Handbook for Anti-Racism Training* – as an exemplar of a broader movement. Katz's work is particularly apposite as it has been applied extensively within New Zealand (Spoonley, 1988), as well as elsewhere. This critical examination also gives us an opportunity to lay out an alternative framework for anti-racism.

Katz combines the social psychology of prejudice with humanistic psychology, a common move in some forms of anti-racist training. In effect, she argues that racism is a health hazard for white and black alike. Blacks may suffer more but whites are also 'ill' with racism. It can be seen, from this perspective, as a form of white schizophrenia. The remedy is seen as lying in the administration of a good dose of painful self-probing and hard work on oneself, systematically identifying and eradicating stereotypes, guilt and delusions of white superiority.

Katz outlines a series of exercises for group workshops which will allow whites to confront the reality of their racism, deal with their feelings and come to terms with their own ethnicity. The workshops seek to encourage the psychological and intellectual development of the people who take part and, since these participants are also members of institutions, since they talk to friends and neighbours and are capable of translating their attitudes into behaviours, Katz hopes that society may change also.

The short autobiography with which she prefaces her book indicates the flavour of this approach.

> The issue of racism is one of very deep concern to me. Becoming aware of racism and owning my whiteness has been a long process. It is a process that I have often fought and rejected inside myself. It is a process that has been marked by introspection, confrontation, anger, frustration, confusion, and guilt on the one hand and the joy of discovering another level in me and finding a new sense of personal freedom on the other. (1978, p. v)

Katz's assumptions and her personal conviction demonstrate some of the specific strengths and weaknesses of the prejudice problematic when it becomes applied to anti-racist practice.

One strength of this form of anti-racist practice lies in the moral fervour and passion the prejudice problematic allows. The enemy is clear-cut and s/he is obviously evil – it may be other people or oneself – but the locus is plain and action is relatively straightforward. An armoury of techniques for self-improvement also becomes available, so the focus is immediately practical. There is also a clear and sensible logic to the principle of working with individuals in order to change societies. Individuals are, indeed, members of institutions and, as Katz says, highly motivated and anti-racist individuals take an active part in introducing equal opportunities programmes, examining school curricula, tracking down instances of harrassment and in reforming from within.

But are these strengths undermined by the weaknesses of the prejudice problematic? And what are those weaknesses in this context? In common with many other social psychologists, Katz defines racism narrowly. Racism is seen as a delusion of white superiority. It is a set of mental habits and emotions circulating within individuals. Racism is a creation of white people, not 'white societies'.

Katz's approach assumes a relatively simple model of social process and social structure. Society can be divided into two communities – a white ethnic group and a black ethnic group – each with a distinctive cultural and 'racial' essence. Whites belong together because they share the same history, the same perspectives and the same skin colour. It is assumed that this shared cultural, ethnic and phenotypical heritage gives white people common interests and so it is meaningful to talk of whites *en masse*. Racism is thus conceptualized as a form of group antipathy; the mutual distrust of two contrasting communities. In this way, the prejudice problematic displays a strong tendency to 'naturalize' racism; it becomes a ubiquitous phenomenon deriving inexorably from obvious differences.

We have tried in the course of this book to present a very different analysis of racism. The problem, we would say, is not that one ethnic community has irrational delusions in relation to another ethnic community but lies in the way a society, like New Zealand, has been systematically structured and organized around one particular nexus and concentration of power (see also Spoonley, 1988). Indeed, the problem consists in the way rationality (economic, individual, group and 'good sense') has been constructed in New Zealand society. Racism is a manifestation of the pattern of uneven power relations in New Zealand.

Discourse analysis and anti-racism

During most of New Zealand's short colonial history the people involved in this history have been described as 'races' and as separate 'cultures'; but we have tried to analyze this intergroup description as one method in the social construction of difference, rather than as a reflection of natural category differences. The 'racialization' of groups has been seen as just one 'node' within the ideological pattern which sustains and maintains the pattern of power relations.

In contrast to Katz, therefore, we wish to examine how the construction and categorization of groups and communities, including the assumption of shared culture, might be part of the problem. Moreover, we see racism as rooted in the social and structural rather than in the personal and psychological. Of course, the personal and psychological reflect the shape of the social and structural, and we have tried, through discourse theory, to indicate how that relation works in practice, but human psychological peculiarities do not dictate the ideological atmosphere and its shifting pattern.

As we have tried to demonstrate in these chapters, through several different discourse analyses, the ideological justification of exploitative social relations is not necessarily based on emotions of distaste, on anti-black affect, on ideas of hierarchies of civilization or on white people's concepts of innate superiority and inferiority. This form of racist discourse has proved an extraordinarily effective legitimating tool in the past, and we have documented its uses, but its days may well be numbered. Justification also involves other forms of argument, and, perhaps to an increasing degree, types of discourse and practical politics which seem much less objectionable and much more familiar, such as the rhetoric of equal opportunities itself. Without an analysis of power and shifting ideological forms it is very difficult to tackle this opening of a second front.

It is comforting and sometimes crucial to be able to point to moral weaknesses in other members of society; but we need to ask whether racism (which we have tried to study as a collective discursive practice) is solely the province of the inadequate and poorly developed individual. We found much of the discourse of those we interviewed odious and the feeling would probably have been mutual. That is, no doubt they would have found our views equally offensive, if we had explicated them at length. None the less, in common human terms, many of those we interviewed could be described as decent, likable, well-balanced and well-meaning people. They might not want to return the compliment and find us similarly sane and sound, but the point is that the psychologizing of racism seems to misplace the problem.

Katz's solution side-steps the issue of the 'self-actualized', in the terminology of humanistic psychology, who also happen to be racist. Is it possible that if Pākehā New Zealanders became much less 'neurotic' about Māori issues and generally more fulfilled as human beings, power relations would change overnight? Perhaps there would be some important effects within particular institutions and within some arenas; but in the end we are not convinced that individual psychological change generates economic and social change.

A very similar debate occurs within feminism. Men are clearly guilty, who can deny that? But is it their weakness as human beings, their unendearing traits and unpleasant little habits which cause the oppression of women?

Some would argue these failings are precisely the problem and a little painful self-probing is exactly what is called for, and certainly these traits are constituted through patriarchy. But can men be 'reconstructed' so easily without large-scale changes in the social relations of gender? While self-critique, confession and soul searching are important and make life better for individual women and men, do these therapeutic practices overthrow patriarchy? Will the growth of a cadre of 'new men' or cleansed Pākehā New Zealanders be sufficient in itself to change the lot of substantial groups of women and men or substantial groups of Māori and Pākehā? From a different perspective, it could be argued that, as with the social mobility afforded the working class within the education system, a few can move 'upwards' but mobility is not possible for the working class as a whole without a radical change in social organization.

The discourse analysis presented in this chapter clearly demonstrates this particular weakness in the prejudice approach to anti-racism. How would this approach go about working with the people we interviewed? These people would first need to be convinced that, despite their protestations, they were actually prejudiced or racist. Then, once they had begun to attend workshops, the process of self-confrontation and dealing with feelings could begin. We take the point that workshops may sometimes radically change the discourse of the selected individuals attending. Workshops might well provide participants with a new vocabulary of motives, a new set of identity narratives and so on, and that can be a powerful benefit.

It is clear that this route involves working within the logic and the positive/negative dialectic of prejudice talk we identified in the previous section. It does not question the prejudice problematic and its particular framing of the problem, it reinforces its hold. In particular, it firmly instantiates the distinction between the prejudiced and the enlightened, through the blaming of individuals, and gives prejudice discourse immense credibility as a model of racism. There is a vicious circle at work here. Katz and her colleagues wish us all to acknowledge our prejudice and we agree this is necessary but the form of acknowledging precisely sustains the kinds of discursive moves, disclaimers, mitigations and factual accounting we have witnessed.

We are not trying to argue, as an alternative to the anti-racist practice described above, that people should not be held accountable for their discourse. We also agree with Katz that individuals can make a difference within institutions. This book has developed a sustained critique of the discourse of those we interviewed. We have assumed that Pākehā New Zealanders are accountable for their framing of their situation and, equally, that our account should similarly be open to attack and ridicule. The conscious adoption of the problematic of ideology puts us within the same orbit as those we interviewed; obviously we, also, have been 'political' and taken up a stance.

This emphasis on accountability differs from the claim that white individuals create racism and it leads to different strategies for anti-racist practice. We have argued that Pākehā New Zealanders articulate in their discourse a collectively shared set of resources for legitimating their social position. They are responsible for the articulation but not in the sense that racism always reflects character weakness or illogical thought. A few people we interviewed could draw on counter-ideological discourse, of the kind we adopt in this book, for instance, and were crosscut by socialist and feminist interpellations. People were not consistent, either, across the field of debate. Anti-racist arguments became meshed together with support for racist policies. An argument would be mobilized in one direction only to veer back on itself.

From our perspective, then, an important part of anti-racist practice is identifying the forms legitimation takes, and charting also the fragmented and dilemmatic nature of everyday discourse, because it is at those points of fracture and contradiction that there is scope for change and the redirection of argument.

We are not suggesting, however, that discourse is everything and should be the sole site for action. The conclusions from our analyses could be read as depressing for discourse analysts or, rather, for the thesis of the partial autonomy of ideological discourse and its independent effectivity. The pattern could be interpreted as showing how the fluidity of racist discourse provides resilience. The forms of legitimation are varied, florid and forever changing in remarkable ways, yet material disadvantage continues in much the same old direction. Ideological discourse sometimes seems simultaneously crucial and trivial: crucial to maintaining certain practices and yet trivial as an agent of social change.

This reading is in danger of clumsily re-instating an infrastructure and superstructure distinction. We begin to see, once again, real life chugging along 'underneath' discourse, which dances along, 'on top', changing its shape and forever donning new guises in tune to the tug of the real, but powerless to act back on the repressed base. If nothing else, Foucault's work suggests that the relation between discourse, social structures, practices and processes is more complex than that. The semiotic intrudes into more places than the structuralist can imagine, shaping the habits of institutions, disciplining bodies through social practices, redefining simple distinctions between talk and action and so on. Interventions in the discursive, therefore, as the history of anti-racism itself demonstrates, are never interventions in the ethereal.

One final weakness with the anti-racism proposed within the prejudice problematic is its tendency towards global ambitions. The vision, as we noted earlier, is utopian. It is for harmony on a grand scale. Paul Gilroy (1987) has argued that, in contrast, the appropriate anti-racist strategy is both more extensive and more modest.

More modest because these struggles define themselves by their relationship to the everyday experience of their protagonists and the need to address and ameliorate concrete grievances at this level; more extensive because an elaborate and sophisticated critique of social structure and relations of contemporary capitalism has been a consistent if not a continuous feature of the 'racial' politics and culture from which these struggles have sprung. These two tendencies shape each other and their reciprocity dissolves the old distinction between reformist and revolutionary modes of political action. (1987, p. 116)

These proposals are based on Gilroy's experience of black politics within the United Kingdom. It is easy for us to develop ideas about the aims of anti-racist practice in New Zealand from the safe distance of 12,000 miles, but a similar strategy of critique and local action around specific issues, a strategy which some Māori and Pākehā groups have successfully practised for many years, particularly around opposition to South African rugby tours, seems preferable to Katz's rather solemn self-examination. Anti-racism is not just a white task or, indeed, a matter for Māoris, although our forms of practice may sometimes diverge. As Witi Ihimaera puts it: 'A *Māori* affair? Like heck it is. We're both in this *waka* together.' (1977, p. 10). Debate must continue about the best way to steer the canoe.

Appendix 1
Sample and procedure

Our total sample of eighty-one interviewees (forty women and forty-one men) was mainly obtained through approaching voluntary groups and clubs such as Rotary and Lions which tend to be largely associations of male New Zealanders in professional, managerial, agricultural and administrative occupations, and equivalent women's groups such as Zonta. The bias towards middle-class associations reflected our interest in establishment and majority group discourse. Since this method produced a skew in the age-range of the sample towards people predominantly in their late thirties to sixties, we also included groups of senior students from three secondary schools. One was a state school, and eleven interviews were conducted among those students, while the other two schools were private and fee-paying (N = 5 in each case). Not surprisingly, since students from all three schools were in their final year of study (equivalent to English A levels), the majority of these, too, came from professional and middle-class homes. We also contacted some Members of Parliament or candidates for seats and a former Minister of Māori Affairs. On some occasions interviews with one person led to suggestions for other people to interview and these suggestions were sometimes followed up as an alternative contact procedure.

We are grateful to the voluntary groups and schools for giving us permission to approach individuals in their organizations, and indeed, would like to thank all those who gave up their time to be interviewed. We worked in two geographical regions of New Zealand – half the interviews (N = 40) were conducted in a large metropolitan city in the North Island and half (N = 41) in a more rural province on the east coast of the North Island; in both cases these were areas with a substantial Māori population. All the interviews were conducted by the same person – Margaret Wetherell.

Typically, the interviewer would first explain the study and its purposes (an investigation of Pākehā views on race relations and New Zealand society) to a

221

meeting of the voluntary group or association as a whole; contact numbers and addresses were then taken for those who wished to be interviewed. Interviews were then conducted one to three weeks later usually in people's homes in the evenings and less typically in work-places during the day. The response rate obtained from requests to meetings of voluntary groups was high, sometimes 80 or 90 per cent, and, as a result, a range of people were sometimes randomly selected from those volunteering from a particular group. The students were interviewed in school during free periods.

The occupations, ages, sex and political affiliation (where given) of those interviewed are recorded below. We have presented these case by case so that interested readers can confirm biographical details for any extract from a particular individual presented in the text. The occupational descriptions given are the self-descriptions of the interviewees. Some interviewees preferred to indicate their ages in general terms; for political affiliation, they were asked who they intended to vote for at the next election. Labour and National are the two principal political parties in New Zealand, with Social Credit, the New Zealand Party and the Values Party as the minor parties at that period. The interviewees were spread across the political parties, with National voters slightly dominating – again this is not surprising, given the socio-economic status of our sample.

Each interviewee (and school) has been given a pseudonym which has been used throughout this book to protect the anonymity of those who volunteered. There were only three exceptions to the pseudonym procedure, and these interviews are not recorded in the list below. The former National Minister for Māori Affairs, and former Minister for Police during the 1981 Springbok tour, Ben Couch, agreed to speak on record, as did Mr Morrison, the Social Credit MP for Pakaranga at the time. One of our interviews was conducted with Bruce Morris, Chief Reporter of *The New Zealand Herald*, for the purpose of obtaining further background on the events surrounding the Springbok rugby tour of 1981, this interview was not used in our analyses in Part II. In five cases the tapes were too inaudible or faulty to transcribe, and the interviews with these individuals were not directly included in our study nor included below, although, since notes were taken from the tapes, they are included in our total for the sample.

Most interviews were conducted on a one-to-one basis, with the exception of the ten students from the two private schools, who were interviewed in groups of five individuals. On some occasions a spouse or friend present in the house expressed an interest in being jointly interviewed with the person initially contacted and this resulted in four other joint interviews. The following were the interviews conducted in this way: Mr and Mrs Bickerstaff, James and Benton, Mr and Mrs Kenwood, Mr and Mrs Cramer, Hundsworth Girls and St Paul's Boys.

Name	Sex	Age	Occupation	Political affiliation
Ackland	M	52	Farmer	National
Acton	F	17	Student	Labour
Alcott	F	46	Astrologist	Social Credit
Andrews	M	34	Restaurant owner	Labour
Barr	M	43	Company manager	National/New Zealand Party
Benton	F	24	Farmer/mother	New Zealand Party
Mrs A. Bickerstaff	F	50s	Housewife	National
Mr S. Bickerstaff	M	50s	Doctor	National
Bird	F	38	Housewife	New Zealand Party
Bloor	F	49	Clerical worker	Labour
Border	M	17	Student	National
Boyd	F	31	Teacher	Labour
Bradman	M	17	Student	National/New Zealand Party
Broadman	M	40	Bookshop owner	Labour
Browning	M	46	Real-estate manager	National
Burns	M	56	Marketing manager	National
Collier	M	40s	Teacher	Labour
Cord	M	24	Economist	Anarchist
Mr Cramer	M	40s	Psychologist	Labour
Mrs Cramer	F	40s	Teacher	Labour
Davison	M	45	General manager	National
Dixon	F	53	Newspaper editor	Labour
Field	M	67	Retired land valuer	National
Goodson	F	17	Student	None
Hilton	M	52	Youth worker	Labour
Hundsworth Girls (N = 5)	F	17/18	Students	National
Irvine	M	51	Headmaster	Social Credit
Jack	F	55	Farmer's wife	National
Jackson	M	17	Student	New Zealand Party
James	F	26	Screen printer	Social Credit
Johnston	M	17	Student	Labour
M. Jones	F	58	Real-estate agent	National
S. Jones	M	22	Customs officer	National
Mrs H. Kenwood	F	50s	Secretary	Labour
Mr R. Kenwood	M	60s	Teacher	Labour
Kipling	M	43	Self-employed business	National
Kirk	F	40	Nurse	Labour
Knight	F	18	Student	Labour
Krasner	F	50s	Headmistress	Labour
Marriott	F	60	Local-authority manager	National
Maxwell	F	42	Medical-research assistant	Labour
Mills	F	38	Speech therapist	Labour
Munman	M	40s	Self-employed business	National
Oates	F	17	Student	Undecided
Owen	M	45	Company manager	National
Parry	F	32	Teacher	Labour
Pinter	F	36	Marketing manager	New Zealand Party
Pond	F	32	Sales representative	Labour
Pratt	F	17	Student	Values Party
Reed	F	30s	Peace activist	Labour
Rhodes	F	50s	Teacher	Labour
Rock	F	24	Market researcher	Social Credit
St Pauls Boys (N = 5)	M	17/18	Students	National/New Zealand Party
Sargeant	M	66	Barrister	New Zealand Party

Name	Sex	Age	Occupation	Political affiliation
Scarfe	F	23	Teacher	Labour
Sedge	M	52	Merchant seaman	National
Shell	M	46	Entomologist	National
Simpson	M	48	Self-employed valuer	Labour
Smith	F	30	Housewife	National
Steele	F	60	Legal-aid worker	National
Stones	M	40	Managing director	Labour
Waites	M	45	Clergyman	Labour
White	F	70s	Retired teacher	National
Williamson	M	49	Sickness beneficiary	Labour
Wood	F	37	Farmer's wife	National

Although the interviews were open-ended and conversational, the same general list of topics was followed in each case, albeit often introduced in different ways and in a different order. Interviewees were asked to discuss the controversial 1981 Springbok rugby tour of New Zealand, the associated protests and police actions and the implications for race relations; they were asked for their views on various publicly debated models of race relations such as assimilation, multiculturalism and integration; about the reasons for Māori disadvantage; for their views on the introduction of Māori culture and Māori language in schools and the media; about the events surrounding colonization; for their opinions on the notion of affirmative action; about the causes of Māori protest and the events surrounding various specific examples such as the Land Marches, Waitangi protests and the Bastion Point episode; and, finally, about the existence and causes for Pākehā racism and discrimination against Māori people.

Appendix 2
Transcription conventions

The choice of transcription system is closely related to the type of analysis being attempted. Transcription is already a form of analysis (Ochs, 1979) and it is simply not coherent to talk of the completeness or accuracy of a transcript without some frame for deciding what sorts of features of talk are relevant and what can safely be ignored (Cook, 1990). At the same time, the form of transcription cannot be separated from practical constraints: to transcribe the large number of hours of recorded material we collected using one of the most comprehensive of systems would have been beyond our resources, as well as making our text more difficult to follow for those readers unfamiliar with the system.

Our concern was principally with the content of discourse and with broad argumentative patterns. We were less interested in the moment-by-moment conversational coherence of the interviews. For this reason, we adopted a cut-down version of the well-known set of conventions that have been developed by Gail Jefferson for conversation analysis (for example, Jefferson, 1985). Summaries of the more extended system can be found in Atkinson and Heritage (1984) and Button and Lee (1987).

The following examples illustrate the main conventions that we used. The starts of overlap in talk are marked by a double oblique (//). Pauses were not usually timed, but simply marked with a dot in parentheses – (.). Omitted material is marked by three dots – for example,

Wetherell: Right, so it's just um (.) you wouldn't think it should be taught in primary schools, say as // a core subject?

R. Kenwood: // Oh (.) Oh (.) It, it could be an optional (.) but er, what they're going to do I think . . . they'll appoint more and more bilingual er people and with the ultimate aim of teaching Māori and just where it's going to get them I don't know . . .

Note also that although speech 'errors' and particles (e.g. er, umm) which are not full words are included, we have added commas, full stops and question marks in a manner designed to improve the readability of the extracts while conveying their sense, as heard, as effectively as possible.

Brief comments or simple acknowledgement tokens (e.g. yes, mm) from the interviewer are placed in round brackets. Clarificatory or explanatory material is placed in square brackets. Words or particles said with particular emphasis are underlined.

Irvine: [Discussing the protest over South African rugby tours of New Zealand] Why do I think there was <u>so much</u> violence? I think once again it was tied, er brought on by a small band of people (mm) . . . . Some people I'm talking about, er, who will attend any demonstration because it's a <u>demon</u>stration (yes). Er, even pupils that are, that were at the school or, you know, just left, say third form, fourth form [inaudible] whom I recognized at the protest marches (ha).

References

Abercrombie, N. and Turner, B. S. (1978), 'The dominant ideology thesis', *British Journal of Sociology*, 29, 149–70.

Adorno, T. W. and Horkheimer, M. (1979), *Dialectic of Enlightenment*, London: Verso.

Adorno, T. W., Frenkel-Brunswik, E., Levinson, D. J. and Sanford, R. N. (1950), *The Authoritarian Personality*, New York: Harper and Row.

Allport, F. H. (1924), *Social Psychology*, New York: Houghton Mifflin.

Allport, G. W. (1954), *The Nature of Prejudice*, Reading, Mass.: Addison Wesley.

Althusser, L. (1970), *Reading Capital*, London: New Left Books.

Althusser, L. (1971), *Lenin and Philosophy*, London: New Left Books.

Althusser, L. (1977), *For Marx*, London: New Left Books.

Anderson, B. (1983), *Imagined Communities*, London: Verso.

Ashmore, R. D. and Del Boca, F. K. (1976), 'Psychological approaches to understanding group conflicts', in P. A. Katz (ed.), *Towards the Elimination of Racism*, New York: Pergamon.

Ashmore, R. D. and Del Boca, F. K. (1981), 'Conceptual approaches to stereotypes and stereotyping', in D. Hamilton (ed.), *Cognitive Processes in Stereotyping and Intergroup Behavior*, Hillsdale, N.J.: Erlbaum.

Atkinson, J. M. and Heritage, J. (eds) (1984), *Structures of Social Action: Studies in conversation analysis*, Cambridge: Cambridge University Press.

Atkinson, P. (1989), *The Ethnographic Imagination: Textual constructions of reality*, London: Routledge.

Awatere, D. (1984), *Maori Sovereignty*, Auckland: Broadsheet Publications.

Banton, M. (1977), *The Idea of Race*, London: Tavistock.

Banton, M. (1987), *Racial Theories*, Cambridge: Cambridge University Press.

Barber, K. (1989), 'New Zealand "Race Relations Policy", 1970–1988', *Sites*, no. 18, 5–16.

Barker, M. (1981), *The New Racism*, London: Junction.

Barthes, R. (1975), *S/Z*, London: Jonathan Cape.

Barnes, B. (1977), *Interests and the Growth of Knowledge*, London: Routledge.

Bedggood, D. (1975), 'Conflict and consensus: Political ideology in New Zealand', in S. Levine (ed.), *New Zealand Politics*, Melbourne: Cheshire.

Bedggood, D. (1980), *Rich and Poor in New Zealand*, Auckland: Allen and Unwin.

Beechy, V. and Donald, J. (1985), Introduction to V. Beechy and J. Donald (eds), *Subjectivity and Social Relations*, Milton Keynes: Open University Press.

Belich, J. (1986), *The New Zealand Wars and the Victorian Interpretation of Racial Conflict*, Auckland: Auckland University Press.

Bhaba, H. (1984), 'Of mimicry and man: The ambivalence of colonial discourse', *October*, 28, 125–33.

Bhavnani, K.-K. (1988), 'Empowerment and social research: Some comments', *Text*, 8, 41–50.

Bhavnani, K.-K.. (1991), *Talking Politics: A psychological framing for views from youth in Britain*, Cambridge: Cambridge University Press.

Biddiss, M. (1979), *Images of Race*, Leicester: Leicester University Press.

Biggs, B. (1990), 'In the beginning', in K. Sinclair (ed.), *The Oxford Illustrated History of New Zealand*, Auckland: Oxford University Press.

Billig, M. (1978), *Facists: A social psychological analysis of the National Front*, London: Academic Press.

Billig, M. (1982), *Ideology and Social Psychology*, Oxford: Blackwell.

Billig, M. (1985), 'Prejudice, categorisation and particularisation: From a perceptual to a rhetorical approach', *European Journal of Social Psychology*, 15, 79–103.

Billig, M. (1987), *Arguing and Thinking: A rhetorical approach to social psychology*, Cambridge: Cambridge University Press.

Billig, M. (1988), 'The notion of "prejudice": Some rhetorical and ideological aspects', *Text*, 8, 91–111.

Billig, M. (1991), *Ideology and Opinions*, London: Sage.

Billig, M. (1992), *Talking of the Royal Family*, London: Routledge.

Billig, M., Condor, S., Edwards, D., Gane, M., Middleton, D., and Radley, A. (1988), *Ideological Dilemmas: A social psychology of everyday thinking*, London: Sage.

Bloor, D. (1976), *Knowledge and Social Imagery*, London: Routledge.

Bobo, L. (1983), 'Whites' opposition to busing: Symbolic racism or realistic group conflict?' *Journal of Personality and Social Psychology*, 45, 1196–1210.

Bobo, L. (1988), 'Group conflict, prejudice and the paradox of contemporary attitudes', in P. Katz and D. Taylor (eds), *Eliminating Racism*, New York: Plenum Press.

Boudon, R. (1989), *The Analysis of Ideology*, Cambridge: Polity, and Oxford: Blackwell.

Bowers, J. and Iwi, K. (1991), 'The discursive construction of society', paper presented at the Discourse Analysis and Reflexivity Workshop, University of Exeter.

Brannigan, A. (1981), *The Social Basis of Scientific Discoveries*, Cambridge: Cambridge University Press.

Burgess, R. G. (1984), 'The unstructured interview as a conversation', in R. G. Burgess (ed.) *Field Research*, London: Unwin Hyman.

Button, G. and Lee, J. R. E. (1987), *Talk and Social Organization*. Clevedon: Multilingual Matters.

Callon, M. and Latour, B. (1981), 'Unscrewing the big Leviathan: How actors macro-structure reality and how sociologists help them to do so', in K. D. Knorr-Cetina and A. Cicourel (eds), *Advances in Social Theory*, London: Routledge.

Cantor, N. and Mischel, W. (1979), 'Prototypes in person perception', *Advances in Experimental Social Psychology*, 12, 3–51.

Carter, P. (1987), *The Road to Botany Bay: An essay in spatial history*, London: Faber and Faber.

Cashmore, E. (1987), *The Logic of Racism*, London: Allen and Unwin.

Castles, F. (1985), *The Working Class and Welfare: Reflections on the political development of the Welfare State in Australia and New Zealand, 1890–1980*, Wellington: Allen and Unwin and Port Nicholson Press.

Castles, S., Cope, B., Kalantzis, M. and Morrissey, M., (1988), 'The bicentenary and the failure of Australian nationalism', *Race and Class*, 29, 3, 53–68.

Centre for Contemporary Cultural Studies (1982), *The Empire Strikes Back*, London: Hutchinson.

Clarke, J. (1991), *New Times and Old Enemies: Essays on cultural studies and America*, London: Harper Collins.

Cleave, P. (1989), *The Sovereignty Game: Power, knowledge and reading the treaty*, Wellington: Victoria University Press.

Clegg, S. (1989), *Frameworks of Power*, London: Sage.

Coates, D. (1990), 'Traditions of thought and the rise of social science in the United Kingdom', in J. Anderson and M. Ricci (eds), *Society and Social Science: A reader*, Milton Keynes: Open University.

Cochrane, R. and Billig, M. (1984), 'I'm not National Front but . . .', *New Society*, 68, 255–8.

Cole Catley, C. (1990), 'Adventure, space and expectation', in *New Zealand 1990: Official souvenir publication*, Auckland, Dow Publishing.

Collins, H. M. (1981), 'What is TRASP? The radical programme as a methodological imperative', *Philosophy of the Social Sciences*, 11, 215–24.

Collins, H. M. (1983), 'The meaning of lies: Accounts of action and participatory research', in G. N. Gilbert and P. Abell (eds), *Accounts and Action*, Aldershot: Gower.

Condor, S. (1988), ' "Race stereotypes" and racist discourse', *Text*, 8, 69–91.

Consedine, B. (1989), 'Inequality and the egalitarian myth', in D. Novitz and B. Willmott (eds), *Culture and Identity in New Zealand*, Wellington: GP Books.

Cook, G. (1990), 'Transcribing infinity: Problems of context presentation', *Journal of Pragmatics*, 14, 1–24.

Coulter, J. (1991), 'Logic', in G. Button (ed.), *Ethnomethodology and the Human Sciences*, Cambridge: Cambridge University Press.

Coulthard, M. and Montgomery, M. (eds) (1981), *Studies in Discourse Analysis*, London: Routledge and Kegan Paul.

Coward, R. and Ellis, J. (1977), *Language and Materialism*, London: Routledge.

Cowlishaw, G. (1988), 'Australian Aboriginal studies: The anthropologists' accounts', in M. de Lepervanche and G. Bottomley (eds), *The Cultural Construction of Race*, Sydney: University of Sydney Press.

Crocker, J., Fiske, S. T. and Taylor, S. E. (1984), 'Schematic bases of belief change', in J. R. Eiser (ed.), *Attitudinal Judgement*, New York: Springer.

Cuff, E. C. and Payne, G. C. E., with Francis, D. W., Hustler, D. E. and Sharrock, W. W. (1984), *Perspectives in Sociology*, London: Allen and Unwin.

Davidson, J. M. (1981), 'The Polynesian Foundation', in W. H. Oliver with B. R. Williams (eds), *The Oxford History of New Zealand*, Auckland: Oxford University Press.

Der Derian, J. and Shapiro, M. (1989), *International/Intertextual Relations: Post-modern readings of world politics*, Lexington, Mass.: Lexington Books.

Deutsch, M. and Gerard, H. B. (1955), 'A study of normative and informational social influences upon individual judgement', *Journal of Abnormal and Social Psychology*, 51, 629–36.

Donald, J. (1986), 'Beliefs and ideologies: Concepts and questions', Course Introduction to *DE354 Beliefs and Ideologies*, Milton Keynes: Open University Press.

Dovidio, J. F. and Gaertner, S. L. (1986), 'Prejudice, discrimination and racism:

Historical trends and contemporary approaches', in J. F. Dovidio and S. L. Gaertner (eds), *Prejudice, Discrimination, and Racism*, Orlando, Fla.: Academic Press.

Dreyfus, H. L. and Rabinow, P. (1982), *Michel Foucault: Beyond structuralism and hermeneutics*, Hemel Hempstead: Harvester Wheatsheaf.

Eagleton, T. (1983), *Literary Theory*, Oxford: Blackwell.

Earp, G. B. (1853), *New Zealand, Its Emigration and Goldfields*, quoted in H. Orsman and J. Moore (eds) (1988), *Heinemann Dictionary of New Zealand Quotations*, Auckland: Heinemann, p. 242.

Edwards, D. (1991), 'Categories are for talking: On the cognitive and discursive bases of categorization', *Theory and Psychology*, 1, 515–42.

Edwards, D. and Potter, J. (1992), *Discursive Psychology*, London: Sage.

Ehrlich, H. J. (1973), *The Social Psychology of Prejudice*, New York: John Wiley.

Essed, P. (1991a), 'Knowledge and resistance: Black women talk about racism in the Netherlands and the USA', *Feminism and Psychology*, 1, 201–21.

Essed, P. (1991b), *Understanding Everyday Racism*, Newbury Park, Calif.: Sage.

Eysenck, H. J. (1954), *The Psychology of Politics*, London: Routledge and Kegan Paul.

Eysenck, H. J. and Wilson, G. (1978), *The Psychological Basis of Ideology*, Lancaster: MTP Press.

Fairburn, A. R. D. (1966), 'One Race, One Flag', quoted in H. Orsman and J. Moore (eds) (1988), *Heinemann Dictionary of New Zealand Quotations*, Auckland: Heinemann.

Fanon, F. (1967), *The Wretched of the Earth*, Harmondsworth: Penguin.

Festinger, L. (1950), 'Informal social communication', *Psychological Review*, 57, 271–82.

Festinger, L. (1954), 'A theory of social comparison processes', *Human Relations*, 7, 117–40.

Foster, L. and Stockley, D. (1984), *Multiculturalism: The changing Australian paradigm*, Clevedon: Multilingual Matters.

Foucault, M. (1980), *Power/Knowledge: Selected interviews and other writings 1972–77* trans. C. Gordon, Hemel Hempstead: Harvester Wheatsheaf.

Gadamer, H. (1979), *Truth and Method*, London: Sheed and Ward.

Gaertner, S. L. and Dovidio, J. F. (1986), 'The aversive form of racism', in J. F. Dovidio and S. L. Gaertner (eds), *Prejudice, Discrimination, and Racism*, Orlando, Fla.: Academic Press.

Gane, M. (1991), *Baudrillard: Critical and fatal theory*, London: Routledge.

Geertz, C. (1984), ' "From the native's point of view": On the nature of anthropological understanding', in R. Shweder and R. A. LeVine (eds), *Culture Theory: Essays on mind, self, emotion*, Cambridge: Cambridge University Press.

Gergen, K. J. (1989), 'Warranting voice and the elaboration', in J. Shotter and K. J. Gergen (eds), *Texts of Identity*, London: Sage.

Gibbons, P. J. (1981), 'The climate of opinion', in W. H. Oliver and B. R. Williams (eds), *The Oxford History of New Zealand*, Oxford and Auckland: Clarendon Press and Oxford University Press.

Giddens, A. (1979), *Central Problems in Social Theory*, London: Macmillan.

Giddens, A. (1989), *Sociology*, Cambridge: Polity.

Gilbert, G. N. and Mulkay, M. (1984), *Opening Pandora's Box: A sociological analysis of scientists' discourse*, Cambridge: Cambridge University Press.

Gilroy, P. (1982), 'Steppin' out of Babylon – race, class and autonomy', in Centre for Contemporary Cultural Studies, *The Empire Strikes Back*, London: Hutchinson.

Gilroy, P. (1987), *There Ain't No Black in the Union Jack*, London: Hutchinson.

Gleason, P. (1983), 'Identifying identity: A semantic history', *The Journal of American History*, 69, 910–31.

Goffman, E. (1981), *Forms of Talk*, Oxford: Blackwell.

Gould, J. D. (1990), 'The narrowing gap', *Metro*, November, 142–9.

Grace, G. W. (1987), *The Linguistic Construction of Reality*, London: Croom Helm.

Gramsci, A. (1971), *Selections from the Prison Notebooks*, London: Lawrence and Wishart.

Greenland, H. (1984), 'Ethnicity as ideology: The critique of Pakeha society', in P. Spoonley, C. MacPherson, D. Pearson and C. Sedgewick (eds), *Tauiwi: Racism and ethnicity in New Zealand*, Palmerston North: Dunmore Press.

Hall, S. (1978), 'The hinterland of science: Ideology and the "sociology of knowledge" ', in Centre for Contemporary Cultural Studies (eds), *On Ideology*, London: Hutchinson.

Hall, S. (1980), 'Race, articulation and societies structured in dominance', in UNESCO, *Sociological Theories: Race and colonialism*, Paris: UNESCO.

Hall, S. (1981), 'Cultural studies: Two paradigms', in T. Bennett, G. Martin, C. Mercer and J. Woollacott (eds), *Culture, Ideology and Social Process: A reader*, Milton Keynes: Open University Press, and London: Batsford.

Hall, S. (1985), 'The rediscovery of "ideology": Return of the repressed in media studies', in V. Beechey and J. Donald (eds), *Subjectivity and Social Relations*, Milton Keynes: Open University Press.

Hall, S. (1986), 'Variants of liberalism', in J. Donald and S. Hall (eds), *Politics and Ideology*, Milton Keynes, Open University Press.

Hall, S. (1988a), 'The toad in the garden: Thatcherism among the theorists', in C. Nelson and L. Grossberg (eds), *Marxism and the Interpretation of Culture*, Urbana: University of Illinois Press.

Hall, S. (1988b), *The Hard Road to Renewal: Thatcherism and the crisis of the left*, London: Verso.

Hall, S. (1988c), 'Minimal selves', in ICA Documents No. 6, *Identity: The real me*, London: Institute of the Contemporary Arts.

Hall, S. (1988d), 'New ethnicities', in ICA Documents No. 7, *Black Film, British Cinema*, London: British Film Institute and Institute of the Contemporary Arts.

Hamilton, D. (ed.), (1981a), *Cognitive Processes in Stereotyping and Intergroup Behaviour*, Hillsdale, N.J.: Erlbaum.

Hamilton, D. (1981b), 'Illusory correlation as a basis for stereotyping', in D. Hamilton (ed.), *Cognitive Processes in Stereotyping and Intergroup Behaviour*, Hillsdale, N.J.: Erlbaum.

Hamilton, D. and Gifford, R. K. (1976), 'Illusory correlation in interpersonal perception: A cognitive basis for stereotypic judgements', *Journal of Experimental Social Psychology*, 12, 392–407.

Hamilton, D. and Trolier, T. (1986), 'Stereotypes and stereotyping: An overview of the cognitive approach', in J. F. Dovidio and S. L. Gaertner (eds), *Prejudice, Discrimination, and Racism*, Orlando, Fla.: Academic Press.

Haraway, D. (1989), *Private Visions: Gender, race and nature in the world of modern science*, London: Routledge.

Harré, R. (1983), *Personal Being*, Oxford: Blackwell.

Harvey, D. (1989), *The Condition of Postmodernity*, Oxford: Blackwell.

Haslam, S. A. (1990), 'Social comparative context, self-categorisation and stereotyping', unpublished PhD thesis, University of Macquarie, Sydney, Australia.

Heelas, P. (1981), 'Introduction: Indigenous psychologies', in P. Heelas and A. Lock (eds), *Indigenous Psychologies*, London: Academic Press.

Henriques, J. (1984), 'Social psychology and the politics of racism', in J. Henriques,

W. Hollway, C. Urwin, C. Venn and V. Walkerdine, *Changing the Subject: Psychology, social regulation and subjectivity*, London: Methuen.

Henriques, J., Hollway, W., Urwin, C., Venn, C. and Walkerdine, V. (1984), *Changing the Subject: Psychology, social regulation and subjectivity*, London: Methuen.

Heritage, J. (1984), *Garfinkel and Ethnomethodology*, Cambridge: Polity.

Hewitt, J. P. and Stokes, R. (1975), 'Disclaimers', *American Sociological Review*, 92, 110–57.

Hewitt, R. (1986), *White Talk Black Talk: Inter-racial friendship and communication among adolescents*, Cambridge: Cambridge University Press.

Hewstone, M. and Brown, R. (1986), 'Contact is not enough: An intergroup perspective on the "contact hypothesis" ', in M. Hewstone and R. Brown (eds), *Contact and Conflict in Intergroup Encounters*, Oxford: Blackwell.

Hirst, P. and Woolley, P. (1982), *Social Relations and Human Attributes*, London: Tavistock.

Hogg, M. and Abrams, D. (1988), *Social Identifications*, London: Routledge.

Hopper, R. (ed.) (1990–91), 'Ethnography and conversation analysis after talking culture', special issue of *Research on Language and Social Interaction*, 24, 159–237.

Horney, K. (1946), *Our Inner Conflicts: A constructive theory of neurosis*, London: Routledge.

Hunn, J. K. (1960), 'Report on the Department of Maori Affairs', Wellington: Government Printer.

Husband, C. (1986), 'The concepts of attitude and prejudice in the mystification of "race" and "racism" ', paper presented at the B. P. S. Social Psychology Section Annual Conference, University of Sussex.

Ihimaera, W. (1977), 'The Maori Affairs Syndrome', *The New Zealand Listener*, 27 August, pp. 10–11.

Jackson, S. (1990), 'Te karanga o te iwi: Why I don't support Mana Motuhake', *Metro*, December, 182–3.

Jakubowicz, A. (1981), 'State and ethnicity: Multiculturalism as ideology', *Australian and New Zealand Journal of Sociology*, 17, 4–13.

James, C. (1990), 'People and power', in *New Zealand 1990: Official souvenir publication*, Auckland: Dow Publishing.

James, H. (1986), *The Figure in the Carpet and Other Stories*, Harmondsworth: Penguin.

Jefferson, G. (1985), 'An exercise in the transcription and analysis of laughter', in T. van Dijk (ed.), *Handbook of Discourse Analysis*, vol. 3., London: Academic Press.

Jesson, B., Ryan, A. and Spoonley, P. (1988), *Revival of the Right: New Zealand politics in the 1980s*, Auckland: Heinemann Reed.

Jones, E. E. and Gerard, H. B. (1967), *Foundations of Social Psychology*, New York: Wiley.

Jones, J. M. (1972), *Prejudice and Racism*. Reading, Mass.: Addison-Wesley.

Jordan, W. (1974), *The White Man's Burden*, New York: Oxford University Press.

Kalantzis, M. (1988), 'The cultural deconstruction of racism: Education and multiculturalism', in M. de Lepervanche and G. Bottomley (eds), *The Cultural Construction of Race*, Sydney: University of Sydney Press.

Kamin, L. (1977), *The Science and Politics of IQ*, Harmondsworth: Penguin

Katz, I., Wackenhut, J. and Hauss, G. (1986), 'Racial ambivalence, value duality, and behavior', in J. F. Dovidio and S. L. Gaertner (eds), *Prejudice, Discrimination, and Racism*, Orlando, Fla.: Academic Press.

Katz, J. (1978), *White Awareness: Handbook for anti-racism training*, Norman: University of Oklahoma Press.

Kelley, H. H. (1952), 'The two functions of reference groups', in G. E. Swanson, T. M.

Newcomb and E. L. Hartley (eds), *Readings in Social Psychology*, New York: Holt.

Kelsey, J. (1990), *A Question of Honour? Labour and the treaty 1984–1989*, Wellington: Allen and Unwin.

Kia Mohio Kia Marama Trust (1990), 'Devolution and the shadow of the land', *Race, Gender, Class*, nos 9/10, 57–74.

Kovel, J. (1970), *White Racism: A psychohistory*, New York: Pantheon.

Laclau, E. (1983), 'The impossibility of society', *Canadian Journal of Political and Social Theory*, 7, 21–4.

Laclau, E. and Mouffe, C. (1985), *Hegemony and the Socialist Strategy*, London: Vero.

Laclau, E. and Mouffe, C. (1987), 'Post-Marxism without apologies', *New Left Review*, 166, 77–106.

Lakoff, G. (1987), *Women, Fire and Dangerous Things: What categories reveal about the mind*, Chicago: University of Chicago Press.

Larrain, J. (1979), *The Concept of Ideology*, London: Hutchinson.

Latour, B. (1987), *Science in Action*, Milton Keynes: Open University Press.

Latour, B. and Strum, S. C. (1986), 'Human social origins: Please tell us another story', *Journal of Social and Biological Structures*, 9, 167–87.

LeBon, G. (1895), *The Crowd: A study of the popular mind*, London: Ernest Benn.

Leonard, P. (1984), *Personality and Ideology*, London: Macmillan.

Levinson, S. C. (1983), *Pragmatics*, Cambridge: Cambridge University Press.

Lewis, R. (1988), *Anti-Racism: A mania exposed*, London: Quartet.

Litton, I. and Potter, J. (1985), 'Social representations in the ordinary explanation of a "riot" ', *European Journal of Social Psychology*, 15, 371–88.

McLellan, D. (1986), *Ideology*, Milton Keynes: Open University Press.

McLennan, G. (1991), 'The power of ideology', Unit 17 of *D103 Society and the Social Sciences*, Milton Keynes: Open University Press.

McLennan, G., Molina, V., and Peters, R. (1978), 'Althusser's theory of ideology', in Centre for Contemporary Cultural Studies, *On Ideology*, London: Hutchinson.

McCloskey, D. (1985), *The Rhetoric of Economics*, Hemel Hempstead: Harvester Wheatsheaf.

McConahay, J. B. (1986), 'Modern racism, ambivalence, and the modern racism scale', in J. F. Dovidio and S. L. Gaertner (eds), *Prejudice, Discrimination, and Racism*, Orlando, Fla.: Academic Press.

McCreanor, T. (1989a), 'The Treaty of Waitangi: Responses and responsibilities', in H. Yensen, K. Hague and T. McCreanor (eds), *Honouring the Treaty*, Auckland: Penguin.

McCreanor, T. (1989b), 'Talking about race', in H. Yensen, K. Hague and T. McCreanor (eds), *Honouring the Treaty*, Auckland: Penguin.

McCreanor, T. (1991), 'Pākehā ideology and Māori education: A discourse analytic approach to the construction of educational failure'. Paper presented at the International Conference on Language and Social Psychology, University of California at Santa Barbara.

McCreanor, T. (1992) 'Mimiwhangata: Media reliance on Pakeha commonsense in interpretation of Maori actions'. Unpublished paper, Psychology Department, University of Auckland.

MacDonald, R. (1989), *The Fifth Wind: New Zealand and the legacy of a turbulent past*, Auckland: Hodder and Stoughton.

McKinlay, A. and Potter, J. (1987). 'Model discourse: Interpretative repertoires in scientist's conference talk', *Social Studies of Science*, 17, 443–63.

McKinnon, M. (1990), 'New Zealand in the world (1914–1951)', in K. Sinclair (ed.), *The Oxford Illustrated History of New Zealand*, Auckland: Oxford University Press.

Marshall, H. and Wetherell, M. (1989), 'Talking about career and gender identities: A discourse analysis perspective', in S. Skevington and D. Baker (eds), *The Social Identity of Women*, London: Sage.

Miles, R. (1982), *Racism and Migrant Labour*, London: Routledge.

Miles, R. (1984a), 'Marxism versus the "Sociology of Race Relations" ', *Ethnic and Racial Studies*, 7, 217–37.

Miles, R. (1984b), 'Summoned by capital', in P. Spoonley, C. MacPherson, D. Pearson and C. Sedgwick (eds), *Tauiwi: Racism and ethnicity in New Zealand*, Palmerston North: Dunmore Press.

Miles, R. (1987), 'Recent Marxist theories of nationalism and the issue of racism', *British Journal of Sociology*, 38, 24–43.

Miles, R. (1988), 'Beyond the "race" concept: The reproduction of racism in England', in M. de Lepervanche and G. Bottomley (eds), *The Cultural Construction of Race*, Sydney: Sydney Association for Studies in Society and Culture.

Miles, R. (1989), *Racism*, London: Routledge.

Miles, R. and Phizacklea, A. (1984), *White Man's Country: Racism in British politics*, London: Pluto.

Miles, R. and Spoonley, P. (1985), 'The political economy of labour migration: An alternative to the sociology of "race" and "ethnic relations" in New Zealand', *Australian and New Zealand Journal of Sociology*, 21, 3–26.

Milner, D. (1981), 'Racial prejudice', in J. Turner and H. Giles (eds), *Intergroup Behaviour*, Oxford: Blackwell.

Minard, R. D. (1952), 'Race relationships in the Pocahontas coal fields', *Journal of Social Issues*, 25, 29–44.

Minson, J. (1986), 'Strategies for Socialists? Foucault's conception of power', in M. Gane (ed.), *Towards a Critique of Foucault*, London: Routledge.

Mischler, E. G. (1986), *Research Interviewing: Context and narrative*, Cambridge, Mass.; Harvard University Press.

Moerman, M. (1988), *Talking Culture: Ethnography and conversation analysis*. Philadelphia: Philadelphia University Press.

Molina, V. (1978), 'Notes on Marx and the problem of individuality', in Centre for Contemporary Cultural Studies, *On Ideology*, London: Hutchinson.

Moscovici, S. (1972), 'Society and theory in social psychology', in J. Israel and H. Tajfel (eds), *The Context of Social Psychology: A critical assessment*, London: Academic Press.

Moscovici, S. (1974), 'Social influence, I: Conformity and social control', in C. Nemeth (ed.), *Social Psychology: Classic and contemporary integrations*, Chicago, Ill.: Rand McNally.

Moscovici, S. (1976a), *Social Influence and Social Change*, London: Academic Press.

Moscovici, S. (1976b), *La Psychoanalyse: son image et son public*, rev. edn, Paris: Presses Universitaires de France.

Mulkay, M. (1984), 'The ultimate compliment: A sociological analysis of ceremonial discourse', *Sociology*, 18, 531–49.

Mulkay, M. (1985), *The Word and the World: Explorations in the form of sociological analysis*, London: Allen and Unwin.

Myrdal, G. (1944), *An American Dilemma*, New York: Harper and Row.

Nairn, R. (1991), 'Actively maintaining a racist system: Pākehā talk and action'. Paper presented at the International Conference on Language and Social Psychology, University of California at Santa Barbara.

Nairn, R. and McCreanor, T. (1990), 'Insensitivity and hypersensitivity: An imbalance in Pākehā accounts of racial conflict', *Journal of Language and Social Psychology*, 9, 293–308.

Nairn, R. and McCreanor, T. (1991), 'Race talk and common sense: Patterns in Pākehā discourse on Māori/Pākehā relations in New Zealand', *Journal of Language and Social Psychology*, 10.

Nash, R. (1982), 'Measuring up and falling into line: The discourse of Māori education', Paper presented to the NZARE Conference.

New Zealand 1990: Official souvenir publication, Auckland: Dow.

New Zealand Race Relations Office, (1986), 'Investigation into allegations of discrimination in the application of immigration laws in New Zealand', Auckland, Race Relations Office.

New Zealand Race Relations Office, (1987), 'Survey of School suspensions and expulsions in the Northern region for 1987', Auckland, Race Relations Office.

New Zealand Race Relations Office, (1991), 'No longer available: A study of racial discrimination and private rental accommodation', Auckland, Race Relations Office.

Oakes, P. J. (1987), 'The salience of social categories', in J. Turner, M. Hogg, P. Oakes, S. Reicher and M. Wetherell, *Rediscovering the Social Group: A self-categorisation theory*, Oxford: Blackwell.

Ochs, E. (1979), 'Transcription as theory', in E. Ochs and B. Schieffelin (eds), *Developmental Pragmatics*, New York: Academic Press.

Oliver, W. H. with Williams, B. R. (eds) (1981), *The Oxford History of New Zealand*, Auckland: Oxford University Press.

Orange, C. (1987), *The Treaty of Waitangi*, Wellington: Allen and Unwin and Port Nicholson Press.

Orange, C. (1990), 'The Māori people and the British Crown (1769–1840)', in K. Sinclair (ed.), *The Oxford Illustrated History of New Zealand*, Auckland: Oxford University Press.

Orsman, H. and Moore, J. (eds) (1988), *Heinemann Dictionary of New Zealand Quotations*, Auckland: Heinemann.

Parker, I. (1989), *The Crisis in Modern Social Psychology – and How to End It*, London: Routledge.

Parker, I. (1990), 'Discourse: Definitions and contradictions', *Philosophical Psychology*, 3, 189–204.

Parker, I. (1992), *Discourse Dynamics: Critical analysis for social and individual psychology*, London: Routledge.

Pearson, D. (1984), 'Two paths of colonialism', in P. Spoonley, C. MacPherson, D. Pearson and C. Sedgewick (eds), *Tauiwi: Racism and ethnicity in New Zealand*, Palmerston North: Dunmore Press.

Pearson, D. (1989), 'Pakeha ethnicity: Concept or conundrum', *Sites*, No. 18, 61–73.

Pettigrew, T. (1958), 'Personality and socio-cultural factors in inter-group attitudes: A cross-national comparison', *Journal of Conflict Resolution*, 2, 29–42.

Phillips, J. (1989), 'War and national identity', in D. Novitz and B. Willmott (eds), *Culture and Identity in New Zealand*, Wellington: GP Books.

Pomerantz, A. (1984), 'Giving a source or basis: The practice in conversation of telling "how I know" ', *Journal of Pragmatics*, 8, 607–25.

Poster, M. (1984), *Foucault, Marxism and History*, Cambridge: Polity.

Potter, J. (1984), 'Testability, flexibility: Kuhnian values in psychologists' discourse concerning theory choice', *Philosophy of the Social Sciences*, 14, 303–30.

Potter, J. (1988), 'What is reflexive about discourse analysis? The case of reading readings', in S. Woolgar (ed.), *Knowledge and Reflexivity: New frontiers in the sociology of knowledge*, London: Sage.

Potter, J. and Edwards, D. (1990), 'Nigel Lawson's tent: Discourse analysis, attribution theory and the social psychology of fact', *European Journal of Social Psychology*, 20, 24–40.

Potter, J. and Mulkay, M. (1985), 'Scientists' interview talk: Interviews as a technique for revealing participants' interpretative practices', in M. Brenner, J. Brown and

D. Canter (eds), *The Research Interview: Uses and approaches*, London: Academic Press.

Potter, J. and Reicher, S. (1987), 'Discourses of community and conflict: The organization of social categories in accounts of a "riot" ', *British Journal of Social Psychology*, 26, 25–40.

Potter, J. and Wetherell, M. (1987), *Discourse and Social Psychology: Beyond attitudes and behaviour*, London: Sage.

Potter, J. and Wetherell, M. (1988a), 'Accomplishing attitudes: Fact and evaluation in racist discourse', *Text*, 8, 51–68.

Potter, J. and Wetherell, M. (1988b), 'The politics of hypocrisy: Notes on the discrediting of apartheid's opponents', *British Psychological Society Social Psychology Section Newsletter*, 19, 30–42.

Potter, J. and Wetherell, M. (1989), 'Fragmented ideologies: Accounts of educational failure and positive discrimination', *Text*, 9, 175–90.

Potter, J. and Wetherell, M. (forthcoming), 'Analyzing discourse', in A. Bryman and B. Burgess (eds), *Analyzing Qualitative Data*, London: Routledge.

Potter, J., Edwards, D. and Wetherell, M. (forthcoming), 'A model of discourse in action', *American Behavioural Scientist*.

Potter, J., Wetherell, M., Gill, R. and Edwards, D. (1990), 'Discourse: Noun, verb or social practice?', *Philosophical Psychology*, 3, 205–17.

Reed, A. H. (1946), *The Story of New Zealand*, Wellington: A. H. and A. W. Reed.

Reeves, F. (1983), *British Racial Discourse*, Cambridge: Cambridge University Press.

Reicher, S. (1982), 'The determination of collective behaviour', in H. Tajfel (ed.), *Social Identity and Intergroup Relations*, Cambridge: Cambridge University Press; and Paris: Editions de la Maison des Sciences de l'Homme.

Reicher, S. (1986), 'Contact, action and racialization: Some British evidence', in M. Hewstone and R. Brown (eds), *Contact and Conflict in Intergroup Encounters*, Oxford: Blackwell.

Reicher, S. (1987), 'Crowd behaviour as social action', in J. Turner, M. Hogg, P. Oakes, S. Reicher and M. Wetherell, *Rediscovering the Social Group: A self-categorisation theory*, Oxford: Blackwell.

Rex, J. (1970), *Race Relations in Sociological Theory*, London: Weidenfield and Nicolson.

Rex, J. (1973), *Race, Colonialism and the City*, London: Routledge and Kegan Paul.

Rokeach, M. (1960), *The Open and Closed Society*, New York: Basic Books.

Rorty, A. O. (1976), 'A literary postscript: Characters, persons, selves, individuals', in A. O. Rorty (ed.), *The Identities of Persons*, Berkeley: University of California Press.

Rose, N. (1985), *The Psychological Complex: Psychology, politics and society in England 1869–1939*, London: Routledge.

Rothbart, M. (1981), 'Memory processes and social beliefs', in D. Hamilton (ed.), *Cognitive Processes in Stereotyping and Intergroup Behaviour*, Hillsdale, N.J.: Erlbaum.

Royal Commission on Social Policy (1988), *The April Report*, Vol. 1–4, Wellington.

Ryskamp (1963), *Boswell: The Ominous Years*, quoted in H. Orsman and J. Moore (eds) (1988), *Heinemann Dictionary of New Zealand Quotations*, Auckland: Heinemann, p. 132.

Said, E. (1978), *Orientalism*, Harmondsworth: Penguin.

Said, E. (1981), *Covering Islam*, London: Routledge.

Said, E. (1984), *The World, the Text and the Critic*, London: Faber and Faber.

Said, E. (1990), *Questions of National Identity*, interview material taken from Open

University programme for D103 Foundation Course *Society and the Social Sciences*, Milton Keynes: BBC/OU Productions.

Sartre, J. P. with Astruc, A. and Contat, M. (1978), *Sartre by Himself*, New York: Urizen Books.

Sayer, D. (1979), *Marx's Method*, Hemel Hempstead: Harvester Wheatsheaf.

Sears, D. O. (1988), 'Symbolic racism', in P. Katz and D. Taylor (eds), *Eliminating Racism*, New York: Plenum Press.

Seidel, G. (1988), 'Verbal strategies of the collaborators: A discursive analysis of the July 1986 European Parliamentary debate on South African sanctions', *Text*, 8, 111–29.

Seton-Watson, H. (1977), *Nations and States*, London: Methuen.

Seve, L. (1975), *Marxism and the Theory of Human Personality*, Hemel Hempstead: Harvester Wheatsheaf.

Shapiro, M. (1988), *The Politics of Representation: Writing practices in biography, photography, and policy analysis*, Wisconsin: University of Wisconsin Press.

Shweder, R. and Bourne, E. J. (1984), 'Does the concept of the person vary cross-culturally?', in R. Shweder and R. A. LeVine (eds), *Culture Theory: Essays on mind, self, emotion*, Cambridge: Cambridge University Press.

Simon, J. (1989), 'Aspirations and ideology: Biculturalism and multiculturalism in New Zealand', *Sites*, no. 18, 23–35.

Sinclair, K. (1986), *A Destiny Apart: New Zealand's search for national identity*, Wellington: Allen and Unwin.

Sinclair, K. (ed.) (1990), *The Oxford Illustrated History of New Zealand*, Auckland: Oxford University Press.

Smart, P. (1983), 'Mill and human nature', in I. Forbes and S. Smith (eds), *Politics and Human Nature*, London: Frances Pinter.

Smith, D. (1990), *Texts, Facts and Femininity: Exploring the relations of ruling*, London: Routledge.

Sorrenson, M. (1977), *Integration or Identity*, Auckland: Heinemann.

Sorrenson, M. (1981), 'Maori and Pakeha', in W. H. Oliver with B. R. Williams (eds), *The Oxford History of New Zealand*, Auckland: Oxford University Press.

Sorrenson, M. (1990), 'Modern Māori', in K. Sinclair (ed.), *The Oxford Illustrated History of New Zealand*, Auckland: Oxford University Press.

Spoonley, P. (1988), *Racism and Ethnicity*, Auckland: Oxford University Press.

Stead, C. K. (1990), 'More than two cultures', in *New Zealand 1990: Official souvenir publication*, Auckland: Dow.

Stephan, N. (1982), *The Idea of Race in Science: Great Britain 1800–1960*, London: Macmillan.

Stephan, W. (1985), 'Intergroup relations', in G. Lindzey and E. Aronson (eds), *The Handbook of Social Psychology*, vol. II, New York: Random House.

Steven, R. (1989), 'Land and white settler colonialism: The case of Aotearoa', in D. Novitz and B. Willmott (eds), *Culture and Identity in New Zealand*, Wellington: GP Books.

Tajfel, H. (1972), 'Experiments in a vacuum', in J. Israel and H. Tajfel (eds), *The Context of Social Psychology: A critical assessment*, London: Academic Press.

Tajfel, H. (1981), *Human Groups and Social Categories*, Cambridge: Cambridge University Press.

Tajfel, H. and Turner, J. (1985), 'The social identity theory of intergroup behaviour', in S. Worchel and W. G. Austin (eds), *Psychology of Intergroup Relations*, Chicago, Ill.: Nelson-Hall.

Taylor, D. M. and Moghaddam, F. M. (1987), *Theories of Intergroup Relations: International social psychological perspectives*, Westport, Conn.: Praeger.

Thibaut, J. W. and Strickland, L. H. (1956), 'Psychological set and social conformity', *Journal of Personality*, 25, 115–29.

Thompson, J. (1984), *Studies in the Theory of Ideology*, Cambridge: Polity.

Turner, J. (1975), 'Social comparison and social identity: Some prospects for intergroup behaviour', *European Journal of Social Psychology*, 5, 5–34.

Turner, J. (1981), 'The experimental social psychology of intergroup behaviour', in J. Turner and H. Giles, *Intergroup Behaviour*, Oxford: Blackwell.

Turner, J. (1985), 'Social categorisation and the self-concept: A social cognitive theory of group behaviour', in J. Lawler (ed.), *Advances in Group Processes*, vol. 2, Greenwich: JAI Press.

Turner, J. (1987a), 'Introducing the problem: The individual and the group', in J. Turner, M. Hogg, P. Oakes, S. Reicher, and M. Wetherell, *Rediscovering the Social Group: A self-categorisation theory*, Oxford: Blackwell.

Turner, J. (1987b), 'A self-categorisation theory', in J. Turner, M. Hogg, P. Oakes, S. Reicher, and M. Wetherell, *Rediscovering the Social Group: A self-categorisation theory*, Oxford: Blackwell.

Turner, J. (1987c), 'The analysis of social influence', in J. Turner, M. Hogg, P. Oakes, S. Reicher, and M. Wetherell, *Rediscovering the Social Group: A self-categorisation theory*, Oxford: Blackwell.

Turner, J. (1991), *Social Influence*, Milton Keynes: Open University Press.

Turner, J. and Giles, H. (1981), *Intergroup Behaviour*, Oxford: Blackwell.

Turner, J., Hogg, M., Oakes, P., Reicher, S. and Wetherell, M. (1987), *Rediscovering the Social Group: A self-categorisation theory*, Oxford: Blackwell.

van Dijk, T. A. (1984), *Prejudice and Discourse*, Amsterdam: Benjamins.

van Dijk, T. A. (1987), *Communicating Racism: Ethnic prejudice in thought and talk*, London: Sage.

van Dijk, T. A. (1991), *Racism and the Press*, London: Routledge.

van Dijk, T. A. and W. Kintsch (1983), *Strategies of Discourse Comprehension*, London: Academic Press.

Waldegrave, C. and Coventry, R. (1987), *Poor New Zealand: An open letter on poverty*, Wellington: Platform.

Walker, R. (1986), *Nga Tau Tohetohe: Years of anger*, Auckland: Penguin.

Walvin, J. (1973), *Black and White: The Negro and English society 1555–1945*, London: Allen Lane.

Ward, A. (1974), *A Show of Justice: Racial amalgamation in nineteenth century New Zealand*, Auckland: Auckland University Press.

Webster, S. (1989), 'Maori Studies and the expert definition of Maori culture', *Sites*, no. 18, 35–57.

Weigel, R. H. and Howes, P. W. (1985), 'Conceptions of racial prejudice: Symbolic racism reconsidered', *Journal of Social Issues*, 41, 117–38.

Wetherell, M. (1982), 'Cross-cultural studies of minimal groups: Implications for the social identity theory of intergroup relations', in H. Tajfel (ed.), *Social Identity and Intergroup Relations*, Cambridge: Cambridge University Press, and Paris: Editions de la Maisons des Sciences de l'Homme.

Wetherell, M. and Potter, J. (1986), 'Discourse analysis and the social psychology of racism', *British Psychological Society Social Psychology Section Newsletter*, 15, 24–9.

Wetherell, M. and Potter, J. (1988), 'Discourse analysis and the identification of interpretative repertoires', in C. Antaki (ed.), *Analysing Everyday Explanation*, London: Sage.

Wetherell, M. and Potter, J. (1989), 'Narrative characters and accounting for violence', in J. Shotter and K. Gergen (eds), *Texts of Identity*, London: Sage.

Wetherell, M., Stiven, H. and J. Potter (1987), 'Unequal egalitarianism: A preliminary study of discourses concerning gender and employment opportunities', *British Journal of Social Psychology*, 26, 59–71.

Widdicombe, S. and Wooffitt, R. (1990) ' "Being" versus "doing" punk (etc.): On achieving authenticity as a member', *Journal of Language and Social Psychology*, 9, 257–77.

Widdicombe, S. and Wooffitt, R. (1992), ' "Well what do you expect looking like that?": A study of the use of "ordinary identity" in the construction of a complaint', mimeo, University of Edinburgh.

Williams, R. (1975), *The Country and the City*, London: Fontana.

Wooffitt, R. (1992), *Telling Tales of the Unexpected: The organization of factual accounts*, Hemel Hempstead: Harvester Wheatsheaf.

Woolgar, S. (1988), *Science: The very idea*, Chichester: Ellis Horwood, and London: Tavistock.

Yensen, H., Hague, K. and McCreanor, T. (eds) (1989), *Honouring the Treaty*, Auckland: Penguin.

Young, R. (1990), *White Mythologies: Writing history and the west*, London: Routledge.

Yuval-Davis, N. (1986), 'Ethnic/racial divisions and the nation in Britain and Australia', *Capital and Class*, 28, 87–103.

Zimbardo, P. G. (1969), 'The human choice: individuation, reason and order versus deindividuation, impulse and chaos', in W. J. Arnold and D. Levine (eds), *Nebraska Symposium on Motivation*, vol. 17, Lincoln: University of Nebraska Press.

Index

(Asterisks mark pseudonyms of interviewees)

242 *Index*